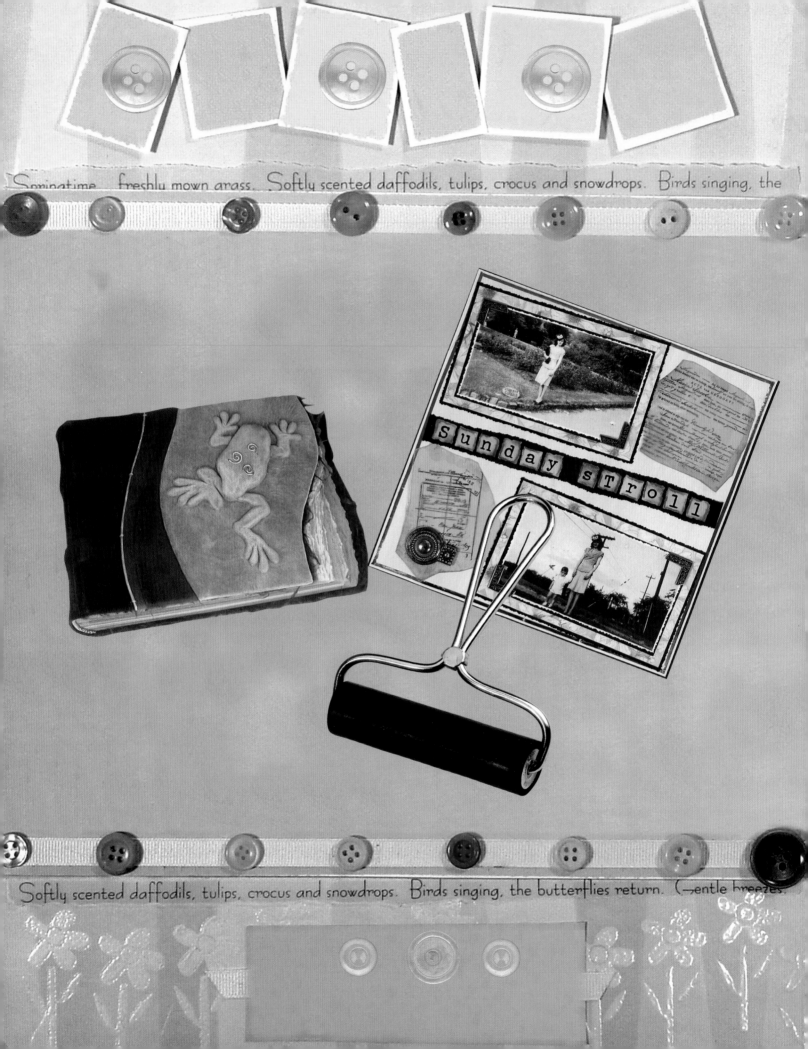

Springtime freshly mown grass. Softly scented daffodils, tulips, crocus and snowdrops. Birds singing, the

Sunday stroll

Softly scented daffodils, tulips, crocus and snowdrops. Birds singing, the butterflies return. Gentle breezes.

The Encyclopedia of Scrapbooking Tools & Techniques

Susan Pickering Rothamel

Sterling Publishing Co., Inc. New York
A Sterling/Chapelle Book

Chapelle, Ltd., Inc., P.O. Box 9252, Ogden, UT 84409
  (801) 621-2777 • (801) 621-2788 Fax
  e-mail: chapelle@chapelletd.com
  Web site: www.chapelletd.com

Library of Congress Cataloging-in-Publication Data

Rothamel, Susan Pickering.
  The encyclopedia of scrapbooking tools and techniques / Susan Pickering Rothamel.
      p. cm.
  Includes index.
  ISBN 1-4027-1031-3
1. Photograph albums--Encyclopedias. 2. Photographs--Conservation and restoration--Encyclopedias. 3. Scrapbooks--Encyclopedias. I. Title.

TR465.R69 2004
745.593--dc22

                                                    2004012512

10 9 8 7 6 5 4 3 2
Published by Sterling Publishing Co., Inc.
387 Park Avenue South, New York, NY 10016
©2005 by Rothamel, Susan Pickering
Distributed in Canada by Sterling Publishing
c/o Canadian Manda Group, 165 Dufferin Street
Toronto, Ontario, Canada M6K 3H6
Distributed in Great Britain by Chrysalis Books Group PLC, The Chrysalis Building,
Bramley Road, London W10 6SP, England
Distributed in Australia by Capricorn Link (Australia) Pty. Ltd.
P. O. Box 704, Windsor, NSW 2756, Australia
Printed and Bound in China
All Rights Reserved

Sterling ISBN 1-4027-1031-3

For information about custom editions, special sales, premium and corporate purchases, please contact Sterling Special Sales Department at 800-805-5489 or specialsales@sterlingpub.com.

Preface

Undoubtedly, writing an encyclopedia is a daunting undertaking. Though daunting, it is most assuredly the fastest way to learn the nuances of any subject. Happily, I can say, the research for this book was no exception. Not only did I learn a great deal about preservation, conservation, materials, and techniques, but also about the myriad ways people embark upon scrapbooking. From simple cut-and-paste to extreme scrapbooking, to stickers, altering, and lumpy scrapbooking, there is a different approach for every idea, concept, and individual.

Interestingly, I came to the realization that scrapbooking is mostly about three things. The first is that scrapbookers want to create a visual story, be it about a person, family, event, or idea. Their style may be to tell it simply, perhaps with just a photo and caption. However, viewing the subsequent albums, I would find pages elaborately illustrated with souvenirs, memorabilia, and extensive journaling. Either way, the album maker tells their story their way, much like any author.

The second realization was enlightening. Coming from a fine-art background, I have always taught archival integrity. I have even allowed myself to dream that someday, after I am long gone, my work would have such value that my great-grandchildren would have Sotheby's begging to auction it off! Little did I know when I began this treatise, that some scrapbookers, while working hard to create their story, are also positively unwavering and uncompromising in their methodology, using only absolutely recommended products and materials; thus assuring themselves that their albums will survive the lifetime of the next fifteen generations and beyond. What is the flipside of that? There are just as many scrapbookers discovering that the materials used are secondary, inconsequential, and irrelevant to the creative process and their particular style of storytelling. Of course, those are both extremes, and I found most scrapbookers to be somewhere in the middle.

The third revelation was that scrapbookers, like collagists and other artists, are collectors engaging in the "rules of acquisition" mindset. Frankly, I too participate in the hunting and gathering process. It just means that we require having a modicum of organizational acumen to house all of our accumulated papers, stickers, ideas, magazines, and photographs.

Scrapbooking manufacturers address this issue with vigor. They have tidiness down to a science, producing nifty carts, folders, and furniture, which provide for us the ultimate in organized living.

While the organization and materials used play an important role in scrapbooking, it is also important to remember that the making of a scrapbook is to tell a story while protecting the contents and photos. The scrapbooker is ultimately like a reporter, writing a column relating the who, what, when, where, and why of it and providing answers for future generations to such questions as Who is that? How old were you? or What were you doing?

This book offers hundreds of those stories, displaying creative techniques and layouts made by both novice scrapbookers and consummate artists. Showcased here is a plethora of examples of those from ultraconservative materials to the most highly artistic works of art ever snapped into an album.

Whether expressing creativity, writing extensively journaled albums, or simply archiving photographs, scrapbooking has taken the nation by storm and is quickly moving into the international marketplace. Researchers say that in 2002, scrapbooking became the fastest growing segment in the stationery industry with over $1.4 billion in consumer sales. The appeal is that it seems to connect families with their past, present, and future, crossing generation boundaries and genres, as well as embracing all age groups. In addition, much like a good book, these albums tell stories that can be read over and again. After all, scrapbooks, journals, diaries, and albums provide a recorded history of people, families, organizations, and events. Some of the best-read albums contain an interesting diversity of materials such as locks of hair, ribbons, badges, pressed flowers, and other three-dimensional objects, each giving us a glimpse into another time and place.

Dedicated to David

Heartfelt thanks for your patience in allowing me to keep long hours without complaint, for learning to cook so we would not starve, for passing the cashews, and for occasionally keeping me company by sitting on the stairs for no good reason other than knowing I missed seeing your face.

Table of Contents

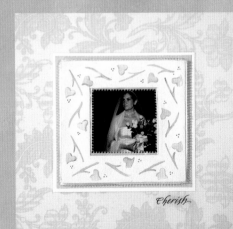

The History of Scrapbooking

Scrapbooking has a long heritage. From the calligraphic exemplars of early Islam to the blogs of the Internet, scrapbooking has been a means of recording personal histories while allowing for a full range of artistic expression.

Commonplace Books

The earliest known reference to scrapbooking, as we know it today, dates back to 1598. At that time, it was common for intellectuals, self-improvement seekers, and aspiring authors to gather and paste poems, quotes, words, and "approved phrases," as well as personal observations and newspaper articles into plain paper books, whether purchased or hand-made. In 1706, John Locke, a philosopher, published *New Method of Making Commonplace Books.*

Despite the fact that commonplace books may sound like the scrapbooks of today, they differed in several ways. While regular books were readily available, they were also cherished possessions, and simply not something one would cut into small pieces and paste into an album. Indeed, commonplace books contained mostly handwritten passages interspersed with pencil drawings and line illustrations. In addition, they were a compilation of disparate fragments of information, unlike scrapbooks, which usually contain a single emphasis such as highlighting an individual person, family, or event.

Nearly simultaneous in time to the commonplace book, were friendship books. Hair weaving being a creative craft in Germany in the seventeenth century, girls would collect hair from their friends and weave it into intricate designs that included ribbons and flowers. These mementos, pressed into "friendship albums," resembled the autograph books of the 1950s and 1960s, including quotes and poems and usually a remembrance about that person.

While Mr. Hubbard dubs his book a "scrapbook," it is more like a printed version of a traditional commonplace book.

Elbert Hubbard's Scrap Book

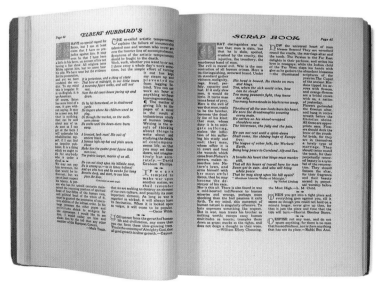

Inside Pages of *Elbert Hubbard's Scrap Book*

Published in 1923 by Roycrofters, I found this treasure in a junkshop about twenty years ago. Note that Mr. Hubbard has included quotes and passages from other books and poems, particularly Keats. Also included in this hand-bound treasure are several pretty watercolor-like prints cut from other books or magazines. Reading this book is somewhat voyeuristic, being nearly as revealing as reading someone's diary. In the foreword, his publishers write, "When Elbert Hubbard was storing in his Scrap Book the fruits of other men's genius, he did not contemplate a volume for publication. He was merely gathering spiritual provisions for his own refreshment and delectation." They go on to say, "Let the reader browse but a moment and—to use Keats' image—he will find the sails of his soul set for one of those high voyages of the spirit which give life its most exalted meaning, and bring back as cargo the thrice-tried gold of ecstasy and vision. What inspired Elbert Hubbard should set other pulses beating. What stimulated and uplifted him should furnish others with strength for the struggle against the eroding sameness of the workaday world."

Unlike Hubbard's miscellaneous collection of prose, Thomas Jefferson gathered newspaper articles of his presidency into leather-bound volumes containing plain paper. Besides the clippings and drawings, they also contained diary entries, dried leaves, and other memorabilia. Jefferson's albums are stored at his former home in Charlottesville, Virginia.

Contrasting the president by profession, a Boston seamstress named Hattie Harlow organized her notes, clippings, and illustrations by topic in separate handmade volumes. Using covers made from cardboard and decorated with wallpaper, her commonplace books even include knitting samples with directions.

pictures, engravings and lithographs; this, due to the fact that Germans were the most highly advanced printers of the day. However, the real craze is due in part to a published book by John Poole. Entitled *Manuscript Gleanings and Literary Scrapbook,* it presented creative ways to display poems, journal writings, and ordinary scraps.

The term "scrapbook" did not appear until the 1830s, and comes from the brightly colored, die-cut, chromolithographic paper scraps that originally filled albums.

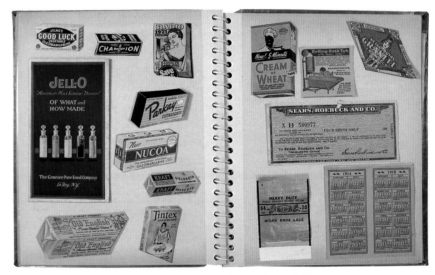

Old Scrapbook Albums Containing Trade Cards and Photos

The Birth of Scrapbooks

It was in the eighteenth century that scrapbooks began to take on their modern form. Scrap collecting started in 1826, in Germany, with albums containing printed

Even Queen Victoria had a scrapbook to display in the royal palace. Thus, by the 1870s, scrapbooks were filled with ephemera collections, such as advertising clippings, greeting cards, diecuts, and

some stamping. The Victorian scrapbooks, generally thematic, orderly, sentimental, and message-laden, turned scrapbooking into a genuine hobby and combined creative journaling with the memorabilia.

Discerning companies began producing images just for album makers, printing sheets of scraps in new styles directed at women and children. Magazines began featuring scrapping articles, touting scrapbooking as an educational tool.

Velvet-embossed Scrapbook with Gilded Clasp

Homemakers clipped labels, product advertisements, and trade cards from new consumer products and included them in their albums; while male and female college students documented their years at school, giving rise to autograph books.

Samuel Langhorne Clemens, aka Mark Twain, was an avid scrapbooker, reserving Sundays to pursue his hobby. In 1872, he patented, then marketed self-pasting scrapbooks, an improvement in scrapbooking because it has water-activated adhesive for adhering paper.

With the invention of the camera in the 1880s, photos appeared on scrapbook pages. By the first half of the nineteenth century, albums had beautifully embossed covers and engraved clasps, hinges, and locks. The photograph became an essential part of a middle-class culture. Small mass-produced photos, known as carte d'visite were exuberantly collected. In the later part of the 1800s, people making "house calls" quite properly left their card at the front door or parlor, even if the person he or she was visiting was at home. Some cards are very elaborate with flowers, doves, and good wishes inscribed. Others are more conservative, engraved with simple gold trim and just the name on the back. Either way, nearly every scrapbook contained the collected calling cards left by visiting friends.

The peak decade for scrapbooking was 1880–1890. Magazines of the times included articles on what to include in scrapbooks. George Eastman and the Kodak camera revolutionized not only the world but also the scrapbook trends.

Carte D'visite and Specially Made Carte D'visite Album

Photography was made available to every man; and with roll-film, the amateur photographer could take dozens of photos at a time. It was quite common to keep, organize, and display photographic prints in scrapbooks.

Like scrapbooking, the idea for the postal card originated in Germany in 1865, although the Austrians actually issued the first one. The United States Post Office issued America's first postcard May 13, 1873, and a new fad began. Scrapbookers collected postcards by the hundreds, some including photographs of the senders themselves. As the trend grew, specially designed postcard albums became popular, and were kept in the parlor for all to view.

Publicized as the twentieth-century pop-artist icon, Andy Warhol was the consummate scrapbooker.

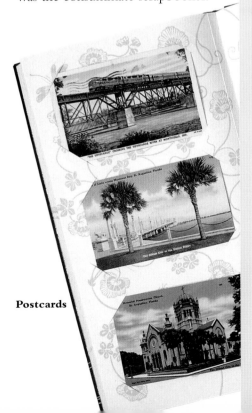

Postcards

Scrapbook Historian: Susan Tucker

Susan Tucker, the Curator of Books and Records at Tulane University's Newcomb College Center for Research on Women, has worked with scrapbooks for almost thirty years. But she can trace her fascination back to her childhood in the 1950s, when she discovered albums an ailing aunt had compiled in the '20s and '30s, clipping, pasting, and precisely documenting to fill the pages with film stars of the day.

Years later, herself a certified archivist, Susan learned how broad the appeal of these memory records could be. "At an annual meeting of the Society of American Archivists," she says, "I heard Katherine Ott speak of the scrapbooks kept by physicians, of their memories being pasted into books. It was then that I thought of how written and visual images were so important and treasured in a variety of ways by all sorts of people."

Educated at Tulane and the University of Denver, Susan used scrapbooks in a number of oral history projects as visual prompts to help people recall their pasts. When she arrived at Newcomb in 1988 and found a vault filled with materials that the college had not transferred to the university archives, she was energized to make collecting, scrapbooking, and archiving a priority. "These were materials either too precious or unwanted," she explains. "I suspected they were not transferred, and in fact almost hidden, for those reasons." Bringing scrapbooks into an academic setting was an innovation: "Women have long valued their albums and, in many cultures, have been the primary guardians of individual and family memories. However, librarians and archivists, who hold these memories in various formats, have long thought of scrapbooks themselves as unwieldy, little-used, overly nostalgic materials. So for me, and for many others, scrapbooks became the perfect documents to offer insight into private life." And for the Newcomb College Archives, they became a major collecting area.

"I created the time line," (shown on pages 12–17) Susan says, "because it seemed to me that the history of scrapbooks showed the history of print and photography. By presenting those dates, I could encourage students, scholars, and scrapbook makers to think about the particular type of memory they used in their own work."

Scrapbook Time Line

Greek and Roman Times The word "album" dates from the days when a prætor's edicts and other public notices were recorded for public information on paper tablets, or tables, that were white.

Medieval and Renaissance Times Scribes sometimes extended their work to produce emblem books, which were bound pages of drawings with accompanying interpretations of allegorical meaning.

1550 Giorgio Vasari (1511–1574) wrote about hundreds of artists in his *Lives of the Most Eminent Italian Architects, Painters, and Sculptors.* Vasari advocated keeping works of art in albums, and his method was to influence the beginnings of museums and libraries all over the world.

1600 Commonplace books are now well established as journals in which "good sayings and notable observations were recorded."

1600–1601 In this year, Shakespeare directs Hamlet to write into his tables or his commonplace book. "Smile and smile and be a villain," Hamlet says as he records notes to himself.

1650 The popularity of the kunstkammer among the wealthy reaches a decided peak. This, the cabinet of curiosities, was a chest where could be kept objects such as stuffed monkeys, botanicals, statuary, jewelry, and diverse exotica. The album found a home, then, within the kunstkammer or was itself the poor man's cabinet of curiosities.

1600–1700 This period also witnessed the development of the use of albums to keep prints and drawings. Following Vasari's advice, "serious amateurs, including Samuel Pepys, preserved most of their prints in this way. Such volumes constituted the backbone of every collection or 'cabinet' formed during that period. These albums are rare in the United States but much more common in Europe where the tradition of making them continued up until the twentieth century. A large proportion of the twenty million prints in the Bibliothèque Nationale are still in such volumes."

1706 The use of a commonplace book becomes even more popular after John Locke publishes his *New Method*

(continued on page 13)

He collected photographs and memorabilia during his entire childhood and until his premature death in 1969 at age fifty-nine.

Warhol labored endlessly over his scrapbooks documenting every aspect of his life, completing forty-two scrapbooks, and more than 600 "Time Capsules" now housed in the Warhol Museum archives. Normally, time capsules commemorate events of special significance. However, these capsules registered his everyday life; documenting the most insignificant detail including not only photographs, newspapers and magazines, fan letters, and business and personal correspondence, but source images for artwork, books, exhibition catalogues, and telephone messages, along with objects and countless examples of ephemera such as announcements for poetry readings and dinner invitations.

Scrapbooking Today

Genealogy, spurred by Alex Haley's made-for-television movie *Roots*, helped scrapbooking gain further popularity when the desire to find our own family roots also necessitated having a place to compile that information.

Scrapbooking today, using acid-free paper, plastic, and adhesive products is documented to have gotten its start in 1976, when the Christensen family of Utah brought to the World Conference on Records, their fifty volumes of memory books.

With the excitement the books generated, the family decided to write the first modern book describing the fine points of scrapbooking. Entitled *Keeping Memories Alive,* they also opened the first retail store using that same name. It appears that Marielen Christensen was first to dub a scrapbook, a "memory book." In 1980, Creative Memories broadened the concept by bringing scrapbooking to the masses. Their concept of home parties, fashioned after other successful home-party businesses, provided scrapbookers with preservation education and readily available acid-free archival materials.

Twenty-plus years later, Creative Memories is still a positive force in the industry, but the competition is greater. There are now dozens of companies, producing thousands of products at good prices, all geared toward archival scrapbooking. Those approaching scrapbooking from the more artistic slant incorporate stamping, calligraphy, and collage techniques. Those artists have found a new
(continued on page 17)

Scrapbook Time Line (cont'd)

of Making Commonplace Books, in which he instructed others on how best to preserve proverbs, maxims, ideas, reference, mediation, self-cultivation, and speeches.

1769 William Granger publishes a history of England, in which he introduces extra prints illustrative of its text. In a later edition, he extends this idea by including blank pages on which could be pasted whatever appropriate illustration a purchaser might choose. Once conceived, a "grangerized" book came to mean one that had been disbound and re-bound with added illustrations, letters, autographs, or other additions. These strange combinations of printed book and scrapbook, also known as extra-illustrated books, reached the zenith of their popularity in the nineteenth century.

1792 The invention of chromolithography, a color-printing process, revolutionizes everyday contact with color on paper.

1799 Scraps (die-cut glossy printed paper images) appear. Developed in Germany, these glandzbilder, chromos, or scraps were the leftovers of a printing job, and were sometimes recycled to the bakers trade for wrapping special breads. Collectors then became interested in preserving them in scrapbooks or as one would say in Danish, glansbillede albums.

1800–1900 The early nineteenth century was the heyday of the friendship album, a book in which people kept the autographs, poetry, prose, and wishes of their friends. Often passed between old and new acquaintances, these books were increasingly considered a feminine form of keeping memories.

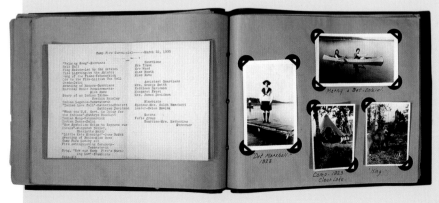

Scrapbook Time Line (cont'd)

1800–1900 Other printing inventions and improvements in engraving, letterpress, and lithography resulted in more collectible paper. Ephemera—throwaway printed-paper artifacts—became a part of everyday life.

1819 The publication of *The Complete Course of Lithography* by Senefelder popularized chromolithography, extending the reach of chromos to England and the Americas.

1820 Publisher John Taylor makes available *A Pocket Common Place with Locke Index,* thus furthering the reach of John Locke and the tradition of the commonplace book.

1832 By this date, the term scrapbook was common enough that a serial called *The Scrapbook* was issued, which defined the hobby as the keeping of a blank book in which pictures, newspaper cuttings, and the like are pasted for preservation. Scrapbooks marketed widely throughout the nineteenth century included *Shipments Common Sense Binder, The Alexander Graham Bell Scrapbook,* and *The Ideal Patented Scrapbook,* among others.

1837 Louis-Jacques Daguerre invents the daguerreotype, the first practical process of pho-

tography. His invention (in which he had been helped by Joseph Nicéphore Niepce and Claude Félix Abel Niepce de Saint-Victor) was quickly followed by improvements from many others. Collectively, these inventors provide a new item to include in scrapbooks: photographs; and forever change the way we remember our own lives.

1839 Daguerreotype and Calotype processes are made public, hence the birth of photography is often given as 1839.

1839 Members of the American Antislavery Society begin clipping from the Southern press, accumulating evidence of the cruelty of slavery in the words of the slaveholders. The antislavery forces amass these clippings in a scrapbook, which they publish as *American Slavery As It Is: Testimony of a Thousand Witnesses.* In the next decade, this book would be as important as Stowe's *Uncle Tom's Cabin* in advocating an end to slavery.

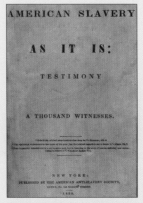

Antislavery Society's Published Clippings

1844 William Henry Fox Talbot publishes the first book with photographs, *The Pencil of Nature.* Talbot is important for many reasons, but especially in terms of scrapbook history. For his invention of a process that includes negatives, and thus multiple prints of photographs, and for his work about producing photographs on paper.

1847 Louis Désiré Blanquard-Evard improves on Talbot's Calotype process and sets up a photographic printing establishment.

1850 Blanquard-Evard introduces albumen printing paper and assembles albums of photographs for customers.

1850 Matthew Brady issues the *Gallery of Illustrious Americans,* an album of twelve lithographic portraits from photographs. Available on a subscription basis, the portraits might be seen as a forerunner to many "false" scrapbooks that will be popular throughout the nineteenth and twentieth centuries. With such publications, the images of politicians and other stars come into the homes of many Americans.

1850–1860 Hippolyte Bayard, Eugene Appert, Henry Peach Robinson, Oscar Rejlander, and others experiment with photomontage. Amateur photographers will use similar techniques as well, to add to albums and scrapbooks.

1852 Talbot patents a prototype of photo-engraving, a precursor to the development in the 1880s of the more successful halftone plates.

1855 Alphonse Poitevin, a French chemist, discovers two methods for printing with potassium bichromate; these methods develop into photolithography and carbon printing.

1857 Carte d'visite photographs arrive in the U.S., producing a craze similar to one begun with their introduction in Europe (1854). Carte d'visite albums contain a pocket for the insertion of photographs.

1860 First advertisement in the national press for photographic albums is printed in *Harper's Weekly* 4., no. 208 (December 22, 1860):815.

1872 Mark Twain markets his patented scrapbook. Twain made $50,000 from these scrapbooks, described as self-pasting and available through Daniel Slote and Company Use but little moisture and only on the gummed lines. Press the scrap on without wetting it. Twain held patents in England, France, and the U.S., and worked hard to improve his self-pasting methods.

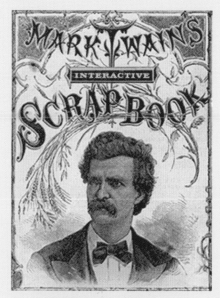

Mark Twain's Self-pasting Scrapbook

1880 Eastman Dry Plate Company is founded.

1880 Stephen Horgan's "A Scene in Shantytown" is printed in halftone in the *New York Daily Graphic.* Thus begins an era where people may clip photographs as well as the written word from the newspaper and other publications.

1880 E. W. Gurley publishes *Scrapbooks and How to Make Them,* a book that notes the foolishness of letting a good article go to waste. Scrapbooks are necessary. The American public now has 8,000 newspapers, as opposed to two in the times of Franklin. "[Too] Gossipy reading can be cured if we read for a purpose, look for something, and keep it when found . . . in the pages of a good scrapbook."

1881 Frederick E. Ives invents the photoengraving process.

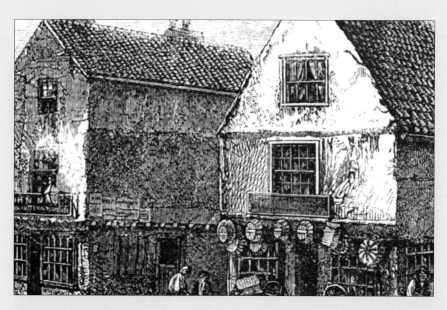

Photoengraved Artwork

Scrapbook Time Line (cont'd)

1886 Frederick E. Ives further develops the halftone engraving process such that it becomes possible to reproduce photographic images in the same operation as printed text.

1888 Eastman markets the Kodak camera and roll film.

**Kodak
Roll-film camera**

1897 The *New Orleans Times Picayune* promotes the scrapbook in a society column, noting that, "a memory book is an interesting tablet for the girl of the present time to keep . . . One New Orleans girl who is famous for her beauty and favoritism in the social world . . . has a record of her social triumphs perpetuated in her memory book, as well as several very charming sketches of herself."

1898 W. E. B. Dubois publishes *The Philadelphia Negro; a Social Study.* In the preface, he acknowledges his debt to William Dorsey and his collection of scrapbooks. In the late nineteenth and early twentieth centuries,

Dorsey created some 300 scrapbooks, cutting from the press to accumulate a vast resource on the lives of African-Americans.

1900 First mass-marketed camera, The Brownie, is created by Frank Brownell for the Eastman Kodak Company.

Brownie Camera

1900–1930 Publishers such as Dodd, Mead, Paul Elder, Lippincott, and others tap into the market for scrapbooks by publishing illustrated and annotated books for school children, high school and college women, and new mothers. Also published are bride books and first communion books. Organizations wishing to commemorate the passing of their members even have bound books for death notices.

1905–1915 The postcard fad adds another dimension to collecting. Some albums and scrapbooks are marketed particularly for these cards.

1906 Panchromatic plates are marketed by Wratten & Wainright. Off-set lithography is invented.

Vintage Photo Albums

1912–1914 Picasso and Braque, followed by many others such as Juan Gris and Joseph Cornell, experiment with collage. Of revolutionary importance in modern art, collage was the "high" art of something many scrapbook makers would recognize as their own technique of cutting and pasting.

Collage Scrapbooking

1930 The photo album, first created in the nineteenth century, becomes the most common form of scrapbook until the very late twentieth century.

1970 T. Harry Williams publishes his biography of *Huey Long*. Like other historians, Williams often relies on the scrapbooks of news clippings, thus offering a Louisiana example of how such albums are cited by scholars.

1987 Creative Memories, a direct sales company, begins marketing scrapbooks, creating a new craze for this form of memory keeping.

(continued from page 13)

canvas to work upon, blending family photographs with highly creative techniques.

Preservation

Until recently, album pages were made of inferior paper with poor lightfastness and high acid content. These papers deteriorated rapidly, becoming stained and brittle with time. In addition, the binding structures of albums were unable to withstand the weight and thickness of the materials contained within. Even our more modern albums, those made as late as the early 1990s, contain unstable plastics, causing further damage to sensitive color photos. Worse yet, the tapes, glues, and waxed albums found even as late as the '60s, '70s, and '80s, have caused irreparable damage to photos and memorabilia.

For scrapbookers, this poses a preservation challenge and means that those photos and scrapbooks must undergo a preservation action. This includes not only preserving the photos, but all the scraps, whether they are newspaper clippings, old report cards, theater programs, postcards, or a combination of these and many other things.

The first consideration is the removal and transference of the items. When the albums' contents have historical value, conservation may be the best option.

Conservation is often an expensive and complex proposition, performed only by experienced conservators. More than likely, it is the average family scrapbook most needing attention, one full of photos of grandparents and old memories. It may be that some parts of an album are neither unique nor intrinsically valuable. If you have the capability, scan these items and print them onto acid-free paper, encapsulating or even discarding the original. Then begins the process of preserving and transferring the valuable mementos such as photos, letters, and drawings, into an archival collection.

Aside from the album itself, consider the photo-safety and permanence of the other products you put into your album, such as adhesives, inks, and embellishments.

Sadly, color photographs are not yet permanent. As film manufacturers learn more about color photography, however, the focus will turn more to the preservation issues. Despite that, scrapbook manufacturers continue to develop products that lengthen their life span significantly. By using them, we may spare future generations from the time-consuming effort of having to preserve the yellowed, faded color photographs most of us now own. Remember to strike a balance between the safety of your photos and the pleasure taken in creating a visually appealing album.

Photo Preservationist: Rhonda Anderson

Rhonda Anderson's Work

At first, Rhonda Anderson preserved family stories in scrapbook albums as a personal tradition. But when she spoke to a women's group about her practice, her presentation generated an astonishing amount of interest in scrapbooking, and the group asked her to help them find appropriate photo albums to use. So Rhonda called Webway, a Minnesota-based album manufacturer. It was after hours, and the vice president of marketing, Cheryl Lightle, answered the phone. The rest, as they say, is history.

Together, the two women founded their own company—Creative Memories—with Cheryl, as president, building momentum at Webway while Rhonda worked at building the field organization, recruiting consultants, and selling albums. Today, their photo preservation tradition is taught throughout the United States and around the world, in Canada, the United Kingdom, Australia, New Zealand,

Events Page

Germany, Japan, and Taiwan. However, Rhonda's passion is not for sales figures or expansion, but for helping each and every family record its history in beautiful, meaningful form. To express her vision, she's coined the term "Faithbooking": a practice that takes

scrapbooking to a deeper level to tell of God's influence at work in our lives, using photographs to illustrate the stories. "I believe scrapbooking as a craft is a fad," Rhonda says. "But Faithbooking will be a lifetime tradition."

Some clients like to get creative in the preparation of their albums, others simply want to preserve their photos safely. Rhonda teaches techniques for organizing, documenting, and preserving photos and memorabilia; even more important, she helps people understand how to create keepsake albums that are both safe and meaningful. "All of us love to have our photos in nice albums," she says. "But it's even more beneficial to write about the miraculous moments of our lives with the photos—those events that influenced our life's direction. When we journal the special story behind the photograph, we are in essence recording history and helping ourselves remember the memorable times in which God has intervened, reached out, and changed our lives. Your stories of miraculous moments are not special secrets to be locked away in your heart. They can be testimonies of God's goodness and faithfulness. To fully experience the power of miraculous moments, tell the stories."

Journaling

The most artistically pleasing album created will lose much of its future meaning without journaling. I have shoe boxes of photos from my parents and I don't know who the people in the photographs are. Even our old black-paged albums, which house dozens of photos per page, are useless without a captioned date, name, or entry. Documenting these things is crucial for future generations.

Scrapbooks are so much more meaningful when they contain a detailed personal history. Even if your handwriting is not perfect, write your stories down. With the myriad fonts available for your computer, personalized journal entries are just a printer away. Families are much more than pictures of birthday parties, Christmases, weddings, and vacations—all wonderful and special events.

However, we should strive to tell a story behind the story. Don't just chronicle the person opening the gift, but whom the gift was from and why, even the story about how the money was saved to buy the gift. Those are the memorable stories your children want to read.

Oftentimes scrapbook makers are doing the photography, leaving themselves out of the history. Be sure to include yourself in the making of each album. Include at the end of each scrapbook the day in which it was completed, by whom, a photo of the person, including items of interest that occurred during its making. Tell your narrative plainly and with directness. Write truthfully, including uplifting or inspiring stories. It is all right to include the sad moments too. Journal entries can include all kinds of topics from songs or movies, to news headlines and how they impact your life.

The future of scrapbooking is now, with the computer altering how everyone views photos, electronic scrapbooking, using digital photos, scanners with the ability to transfer photos to disc, and software that easily manipulates a picture, is producing photographically amazing results. Acid-free computer inks and papers no longer mean faded looking photos of Auntie Anne's last birthday. But no matter how incorporative computers may be, there will still be a need for the physical album. For future generations will still desire to sit next to the fire, with a child by their side and an album in their lap, hoping to capture through those pictures a glimpse of themselves by way of the people from their past.

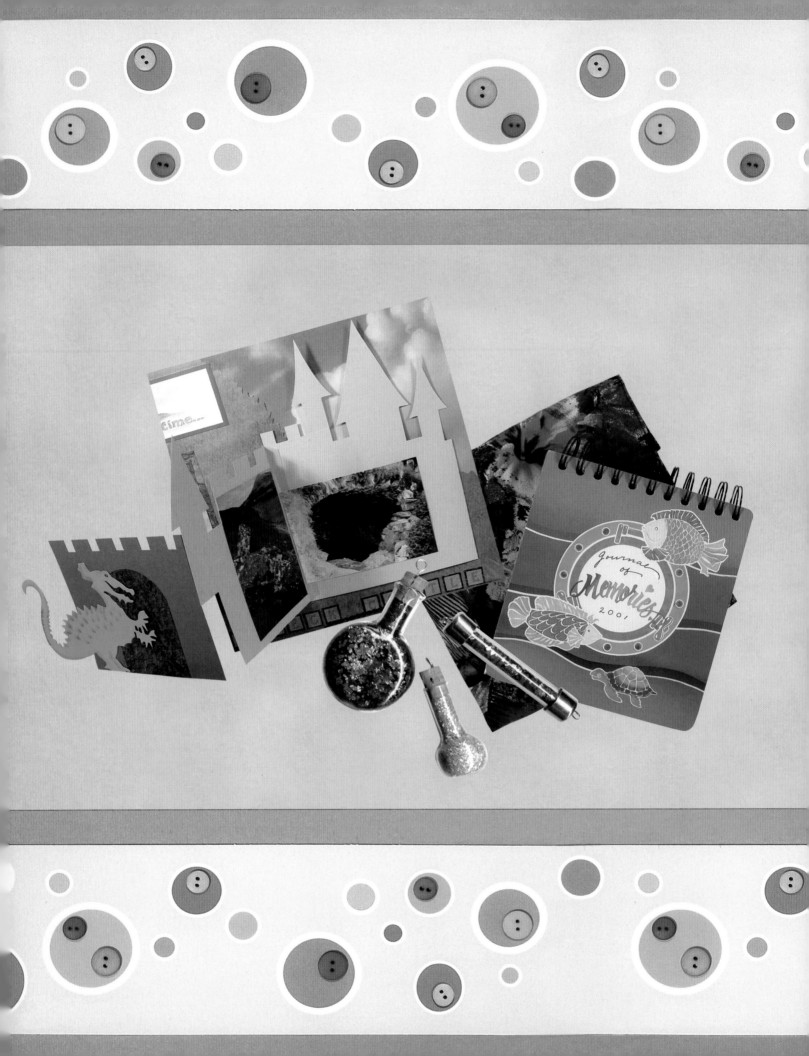

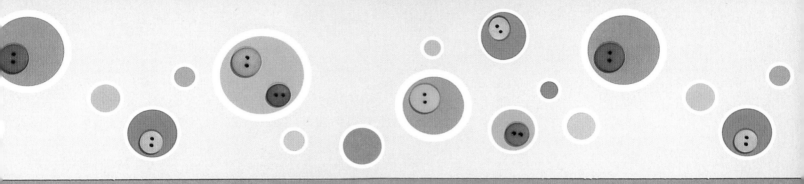

Tools,
Techniques,
Definitions &
Projects

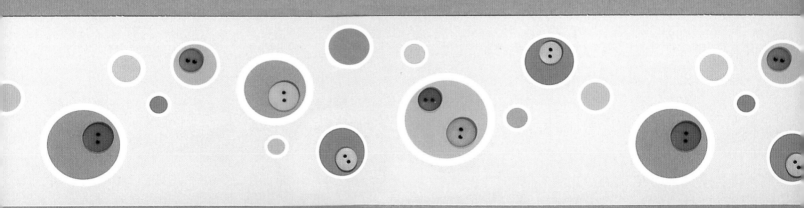

ABC Scrapbook A small scrapbook depicting a singular event or theme and which shows words, phrases, ideas, or concepts in alphabetical order (Fig. 1). These books are usually made for children to teach them the letters of the alphabet, but can be designed so that they are appropriate for any age.

ABC Scrapbook Design Tips

• Add personal messages, dreams and wishes, journal passages, or captions to each page.

• Use familiar names, pets, toys, events, and places.

• Carry a theme throughout the album, such as sports or family.

• ABC Scrapbooks are a terrific way to strengthen the ties between children, relatives, and friends who live far away by having those persons each make a page, then combining the pages to make one book.

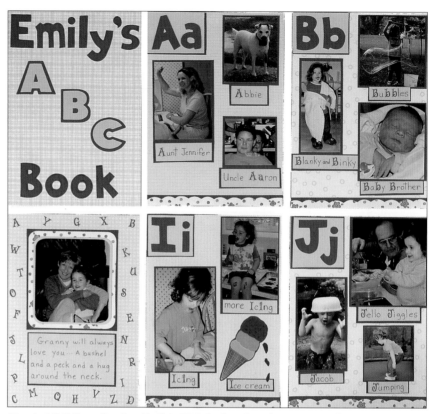

Fig. 1: ABC Scrapbook—*Emily's ABC Book*   People, events, and memories from Emily's life are on the corresponding alphabetical page. Notice how each page letter is highlighted in each title, photo, and caption.

Scrap of History: ABC Scrapbooks

Abecedarian or Abecedary A book containing the letters of the alphabet and basic rules of spelling, used in Europe as a primer before the invention of the printing press. By 1700, some ABC books included children's rhymes.

Hornbook A type of child's primer used in England and America from the fifteenth to the eighteenth centuries, consisting of sheets of parchment or paper with the alphabet, the first ten numerals, the Lord's Prayer, and sometimes a hand-colored illustration protected by a thin transparent sheet of cattle horn.

Accelerated Aging A procedure developed by manufacturers of materials made to simulate long-term product performance by elevating temperatures and humidity, resulting in aging products 10–20 years in six months to one year.

Accordion Book A complexly folded book that resembles an accordion when open and can be tied shut with a ribbon or other closure (Figs. 2A & 2B). These books make interesting miniature scrapbooks.

Fig. 2A: Accordion Book—
Tied closed with a pretty ribbon.

Fig. 2B: Accordion Book—
Open showing the multiple sides
of each page.

Accordion Folding A type of paper folding in which each fold runs in the opposite direction to the previous fold, creating a pleated or accordion effect.

Acetate A transparent or translucent plastic sheet material able to be placed in an inkjet or laser printer

Acetate Overlay A transparent or translucent plastic sheet used as a base for artwork. It is often preprinted with photographs and artwork (Fig. 3).

Fig. 3: Acetate Overlay—*A New Baby*   The preprinted 12"x12" acetate overlay used here clearly shows the background paper, giving it a three-dimensional interest. It is kept in place using small brads.

Acid Any material or substance with a pH of less than 7.0 that weakens cellulose in paper, board, and cloth, leading to discoloring and embrittlement, and shortens paper life span. Acids occur during the manufacture of materials, either unintentionally, or left in by design, such as certain sizings like starch and glue. Acids may also be introduced by migration or by atmospheric pollution.

Acid Migration The natural transfer of acid from an acidic material to a less acidic material or pH neutral material, occuring by direct contact or by acids passing through neutral materials.

Acid Reducer A spray or compound that neutralizes the acid in paper and ephemera. (Figs. 4A & 4B).

Acid Reducing Tips and Facts

- Every item added to a scrapbook should be as archivally safe as possible, with every element producing little or no migration of the chemicals that make up the element itself.

- Traditionally processed photos using the C-41 process on silver halide paper once had more longevity than digitally printed photos. However, the trend toward the use of pigmented inkjet inks and acid-free papers has changed that tradition.

- All photos will eventually fade because of sunlight exposure. Digital prints are more susceptible to deterioration because of ozone air pollution and humidity.

- The gelatin layers used in traditional photo processing aid in forming a protective barrier against air pollutants and humidity.

- Use only buffered photo mats for the prevention of acid migration to surrounding areas.

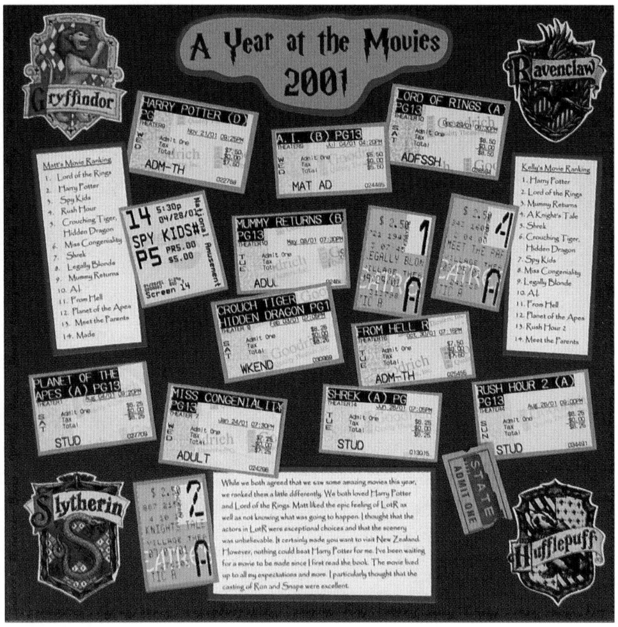

Fig. 4B: Acid Reducers

Fig. 4A: Acid reducer—*A Year at the Movies* **These ticket stubs are made pH neutral by using acid reducers, which give scrapbookers greater freedom when blending acidic ephemera into acid-free albums, thereby preventing acid migration.**

Acid-free A substance having a pH of 7.0–9.5 when tested using a surface probe or cold extraction, indicating it contains no mobile or available acid ions for a chemical reaction. Over time, materials may naturally become acidic by absorption through the atmosphere, or by coming in contact with acidic materials.

Adhesive Any compound that can stick two surfaces together is classified as an adhesive. Adhesives come in many forms including liquids, solids, cements, and pastes. According to archival methods, only acid-free, nonyellowing, flexible adhesives should be used for paper arts and mounting photos. Adhesives may be considered acid-free, but not necessarily archival due to their inflexibility when dry, or their nature to become brittle over time causing photos and memorabilia to detach. Certain adhesives should be limited or avoided entirely in archival scrapbooking due to their tendencies for yellowing, brittleness, lack of durability, ability to absorb moisture, or acidic natures such as simple adhesives made of cellulose, starch, rubber cement, paper cement, high- or low-temperature glue sticks, vegetable glues, stick glues, epoxies, animal glues, and wood glues.

Adhesive Residue The remains of adhesive left by previous application of paste, tape, or glue.

Adhesive Types

ATG A reliable and economical hand- or mechanically-dispensed photo-safe pressure-sensitive roll adhesive, which is evenly distributed from a liner paper. ATG is especially useful for large items and is actually a dry solid adhesive, not technically a tape. Most ATG tapes are immediately repositionable and removable, only becoming permanent over time.

Acrylic A nonflammable, waterproof, white or clear adhesive that holds well under stress. Applied without mixing, acrylic adhesives dry clear and bond most surfaces including slightly oily or porous surfaces. Modern acrylic adhesives are based upon complex polymeric materials. Spread in an unpolymerized form, the adhesive properties increase as polymerization occurs between the two surfaces. Bonds occur in 30–60 seconds, with permanent strength reached in 45 minutes. Acrylic adhesives are not recommended for use on polyethylene or polypropylene.

Cyanoacrylate An extremely fast-curing adhesive. These strong "super" glues are available in various thicknesses and cure times. Bond time ranges from seconds to two or more minutes. Cyanoacrylate adhesives may yellow or become brittle over time and should have limited use in scrapbooking, adhering only the most difficult nonporous surfaces such as polymer clays.

Dimensional Adhesives and Cements Either PVA or acrylic-based adhesives that dry to a raised, clear glass-like finish or a raised opaque finish with varying degrees of hardness.

Dry (Film) Adhesive Generally any photo-safe pressure-sensitive acrylic-based film or tape suitable for mounting photos. Applying firm pressure helps develop adhesive contact, thereby improving bond strength. Properly used, bond strength increases over time.

Epoxy A one- or two-part adhesive used extensively in applications requiring high-strength bonding. Chemically, epoxy is a compound in which an oxygen atom is joined to two carbon

Adhesive Types (cont'd)

atoms in a chain to form a bridge, forming a strong hard adhesive. Bond time ranges from one minute to several minutes. Epoxy-type adhesives may yellow or become brittle over time and should have limited use in scrapbooking.

Glue Stick A round stick of solid paste-like glue used to adhere paper and embellishments to scrapbook pages. Glue sticks are acid-free and slated as archival. However, they have a relatively short adhering life expectancy.

Liquid Adhesive A permanent or reposition-able adhesive available in a bottle, stick, pen, or wand applicator, and packaged with thick or thin applicator tips. Liquid adhesives work best for

collage and assem-blage techniques, attaching small items such as punches or die-cut letters, or for firmly adhering dimen-sional items such as beads and buttons.

Liquid Adhesives

PVA (Polyvinyl Acetate) White glue. As shown by its widespread use in schools, PVA is safe. Bond time is immediate with the tackier versions of PVA, or may take up to several hours to dry thoroughly. Drying time also depends on the thickness of application and the products being adhered. PVAs are water-soluble, which can be a serious issue with moderate to high humidity. Some PVAs may be acid-free or nonyellowing, others may not.

Repositionable Adhesive A pressure-sensitive adhesive that has low ultimate adhesion.

Reversible Adhesive An adhesive that can be undone.

Specialty Adhesives and Tapes The adhesives available for the scrapbooking market are numer-ous and diverse, each having their own qualities and capabilities. It is worth the time to find a few

that work for you and stick with them. It is also time well spent to con-tinually learn about new and different, or even improved adhesives that come into the marketplace.

Specialty Adhesives

Spray Adhesive In either a permanent or repo-sitionable format, spray adhesive is an aerosol used to adhere photos, illustrations, maps, posters, and signs. Generally it is a fast and easy application; just spray, then apply even pressure or burnish to bond. Spray adhesives resist heat and moisture for a strong permanent bond. Not all sprays are acid-free or manufactured specifi-cally for scrapbooking. Read the manufacturer's information, and heed all hazard labels on the can. Always work outdoors as the vapors from spray adhesives are harmful.

Aging and Distressing Paper The act of taking a regular piece of paper and by wrinkling, folding, wetting, sanding, or otherwise damaging the sheet, or by painting, inking and faux-finishing techniques transforming it into a seemingly older version of itself (Figs. 5A & 5B). This technique is used often in heritage album making and vintage scrapbooking.

Figs. 5A & 5B: Aging and Distressing Paper— *Hayes and Ava* and *Cousins*   To re-create the aging technique on the page above, use a bit of fine sandpaper and gently rub the surface of a patterned cardstock. The page at right was sprayed with water to remove some of the color as well as to age the background paper.

Airbrush 1. A hand tool that, when using either canned air under pressure or an air compressor, evenly distributes paint, ink, or dye in a fine mist (Fig. 6). 2. A method of retouching illustrations, black-and-white photos, or color photos, using dye or paint sprayed onto selected areas of the negative or print.

Album A blank book used to store photos, memorabilia, and scrapbook pages. There are a number of different types of bindings available (Figs. 7A–7F). (See also Binding.)

Fig. 6: Airbrush—*Go Confidently*
The airbrush technique shown here uses canned air and solvent-based ink markers. The device, tube and valve, is used to force the air from the can through the brush tip. The skeleton leaf is used like a stencil, leaving a pattern on the background paper.

Figs. 7A & 7B: Album—
The variety of ready-made thematic albums available to the scrapbook is limited only by the shelf space available to the local retailer since there are hundreds of styles. Even a plain album cover can be enhanced by the use of various paper techniques such as collage and decoupage or by rubber-stamping with acrylic paint, creating a theme album as shown in the puppy scrapbook above.

Figs. 7C–7F: Album—Whether ready-made or creatively enhanced, such as Dee Gruenig's *South Africa* and *Journal of Memories* shown here, the album cover sets the stage for the memories hidden inside and ideally reflects the overall theme within. Dee uses lamination techniques as well as stamped, cut, and marker-colored stickers to decorate plain album covers.

Album Selection Tips

- Many album options are available because of the various binding systems and numerous album sizes, colors, and styles.

- Select an album that works, and best displays the photos and memorabilia being showcased.

- Select an archival-quality album, having an acid-free cover and pages.

- For frequently handled albums, select an album with a sturdy binding and rigid cover.

- Select an album with a binding system that fits your needs, such as ease-of-use, page accessibility, flat-lying qualities, etc.

- Avoid magnetic albums. Paper and adhesives in most magnetic albums are very acidic, and cause an acceleration of photographic deterioration.

Album Page A removable paper sheet, usually black or white, used for mounting photographs and memorabilia.

Album Strap Polyethylene strap that holds together the pages in the album.

Alkali (Alkaline) As it pertains to the paper craft industry, an alkali is any material with a pH greater than 7.0. Alkaline materials (buffers), often calcium carbonate, can be added to materials containing acid to neutralize it and causing papers to become more alkaline.

Altered Art, Book, or Scrapbook A contemporary art form of recycling objects originally intended for practical purposes, such as books, furniture, or other objects, and now used to transform any object into a work of art (Figs. 8A–8D).

Figs. 8A & 8B: Altered Scrapbook—*My Dad Remembered* and *The Stygle Family Album* **Fabric-covered altered scrapbook pages make use of family memorabilia, buttons, and found objects as well as journaled entries and photographs. Small twigs creatively frame a woodsy photo on the leaf-embellished page. The entire book is glued and/or sewn and held closed with a pretty ribbon.**

Figs. 8C & 8D: Altered Scrapbook— *My Dad Remembered* (standing) Driftwood and ribbon make an interesting closure for this altered album covered with fabric. *The Stygle Family Album* is beautifully embellished with a mica window and twigs. It is always wise to spray found objects with deacidification sprays prior to inclusion into albums such as those shown here.

Altered-scrapbook Artist Beth Cote

Beth Cote was twelve when she sold her first painting, a summer art-camp project. In high school, she wrote for the school newspaper and the teen page of the *Duluth Herald;* in her junior year, she interned at a Duluth television station, conducting interviews and writing stories. In her twenties, she turned to painting abstract watercolors, then took classes at a fashion design school in Dallas. "I'm what I call a scanner," she laughingly admits. "I like to do many different things. And I'll try anything once!"

With experience in a wide range of three-dimensional work—including clay sculpture, acrylics, jewelry making, printwork, ribbon embroidery, and bookbinding—Beth is the consummate mixed-media artist. But she found it hard to focus on a single medium, until some Internet communities and resources devoted to "altered books" caught her attention,

pushing her talents to new limits and giving her a way to combine her two creative loves: words and art. Today, she is nationally recognized as an altered-book authority.

"An altered book is described as a crossover art-and-craft technique that combines elements of rubber stamping, collage, and scrapbooking," Beth explains. "Altered books struck a chord in me because of the manipulative quality of the art. There are no rules, and I can introduce any medium I want into a piece, including 'found' art, embroidery, pottery, and abstract work."

In her studio, a converted cottage in Winnebago, Illinois, Beth offers a fresh creative approach to art. "Everyone has a creative spirit inside them waiting to be tapped," she says. "As an art instructor, I try to facilitate that experience. As an advocate, I try to ensure everyone has the chance to express his or her natural creative ability. Altered scrapbook making can be a truly creative way to capture memories. From an altered scrapbook incorporating your ancestors—a beautiful alternative to traditional photo albums or scrapbooks—to documenting trips, special occasions, or events, there are as many ways to mix media making them as there are art materials."

In addition to teaching and writing, Beth is the founder of the ISABA (International Society of Altered Book Artists), a nonprofit organiza-

tion. She also works with Design Originals, a craft and hobby manufacturer and publisher, to produce books, videos, DVDs, and scrapbooking paper designs. "At age two, I altered my first book with crayons—and was punished for it," she says with a chuckle. "Today, I travel the country teaching others how to alter books—what a change a few years can make!"

Beth's Tips for Creating an Altered Scrapbook

- Remember there are no rules—the only limit is your imagination.

- Be creative when selecting your medium. Crayons, pastels, stamps, markers, inks, and all types of paints.

- Virtually anything can be incorporated from feathers, pottery shards, embroidery, and metalwork to X-rays. Let your imagination run wild!

- Three-dimensional elements such as pop-ups, envelopes, pockets, pull-tabs, windows, and hidden alcoves give added magnitude to your artwork.

- Select a subject, idea, or emotion that matches the photos.

- Personalize and customize as much as possible.

Beth Cote mounts her photos on laminated vintage oilcloth. The captions are both computer-generated and plastic-embossed strips with adhesive backs.

Beth's vintage vinyl pages and double-spiral-bound books incorporate photos with journaling, colorful found objects, and sheet-music borders. The album on the left incorporates a double-spiral binding, allowing not only the traditional type of opening but also a smaller sidebar flip-out page.

Angel Company A company that allows consumers to use rubber-stamp images or paper to create products for resale. Policies vary widely, so each manufacturer must be contacted individually for information on their copyright policies.

Antistatic Pad A small pillow filled with static-inhibiting powder. Rubbing a paper surface with the pad reduces static electricity, which keeps embossing-powder granules from being heated.

Antistatic pads are used by calligraphers to prevent inks from bleeding into the paper. Antistatic pads are also useful in shaker-box making to reduce the static electricity from the acetate window.

Appliqué A highly detailed, dimensional ornamentation that is tacked or glued onto the paper surface rather than cut from the paper itself (Figs. 9A–9F).

Fig. 9C: Appliqués, Stickers

Fig. 9A: Appliqué—Multiple layers and intricately designed appliqué stickers can be found in nearly any theme, size, or color. Most are found in packages containing several appliqués of exact or complementary designs.

Fig. 9B: Appliqué—
October **These dimensional appliqués add color, texture, and ornamentation emphasizing the flowers held by the bride.**

A

Figs. 9D–9F: Appliqué— *Christmas,* and *Art Day, Barbecue* Whether using charming Christmas trees and bitty descriptive hanging tags or adorable art supplies complete with tiny tubes of paint, there are very few scrapbook pages that will not benefit from dimensional appliqués. These page embellishments add to and help to continue telling the story shown in the photographs.

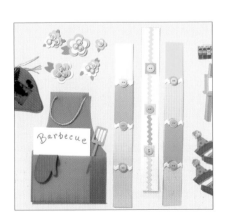

Archival A nontechnical term suggesting a product is chemically stable, durable, and permanent. Archival products are able to withstand environmental conditions and can be safely used for preservation artwork. There are no current standards to quantify the word "archival;" and to-date, artisans must rely on manufacturers to provide materials with archival characteristics.

Archival Processing A procedure designed to protect a print or negative from premature deterioration caused by chemical influence.

Assemblage A modern art term describing objects collected and assembled together to create a harmonious work of art; generally the three-dimensional components are not made by the artist, and not originally intended to be used as an art material (Fig. 10).

Autograph Book A book for collecting small drawings and sketches, quotes, sayings, poems, and signatures from friends, schoolmates, and notable figures (Fig. 11). Acid-free photocopied pages from autograph books make ideal additions to scrapbook pages, often adding bits of historical information about the character and personality of the person being featured.

Fig. 10: Assemblage—*The Old Bag*   Sometimes a scrapbook album is not the ideal way to showcase a page. Here, the photos and ephemera were combined with Auntie's old bag and other memorabilia to create an assemblage worthy of hanging on a wall.

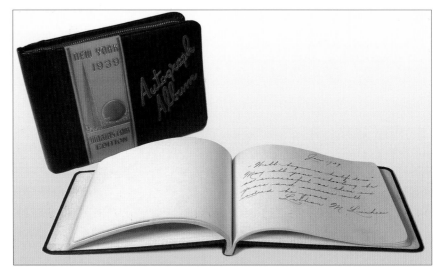

Fig. 11: Autograph Book—Besides the often humorous or sentimental poetry and narrative, autograph books such as these also provide historical time lines and hints of genealogical information.

B

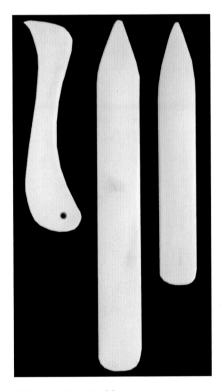

Fig. 12: Binding—*Ixtapa* This spiral-bound book came with the brightly colored paper and individually die-cut edges. The style and colors of the book lent themselves nicely to the theme of vacationing in Ixtapa. The irregular edges on these pages are an idea that can be used with pages in any type of binding and easily reproduced using decorative scissors on colored papers.

Backbone The back of a bound book connecting the two covers. Also called a spine.

Binder's Board A heavyweight layered-paper board used to add stiffness to a book's binding, boxes, photo albums, and scrapbook binders. Most binder's board has a high lignin content.

Binding The archiving and connecting of paper pages or ephemera into a book format either by hand or machine. Such binding methods may include stapling, sewing, gluing, or various other mechanical methods of binding within an album. Album bindings may be covered with cloth, various leathers, paper-covered boards, or other more exotic materials (Fig. 12).

Bitty Book A scrapbook made small enough to fit into a purse or pocket, or made to fit within another scrapbook. Bitty books are generally made with a single theme or subject. (See example on page 77, Fig. 33P.)

Bleed A photo or design element that goes right to the edge of a scrapbook page, such as the on the edge of this book page.

Fig. 13: Bone Folders

BLOG A personal Web site updated frequently with scrapbook-like items such as photos, journaling, links, commentary, and items of personal interest. Blogs can be political journals or personal diaries. The blog may focus on one subject, such as children, college life, a garden, or genealogy, or it may have a broader scope

Bone Folder A smooth hand tool made of bone or a heavy plastic, used for folding, scoring, and creasing papers. Bone folders are also used to press out air bubbles and wrinkles when gluing papers and fabrics onto other surfaces (Fig.13).

Bookbinding The process of fastening the leaves of a book together and enclosing them in a protective cover, formerly done by hand but now largely mechanized.

Comb Binder

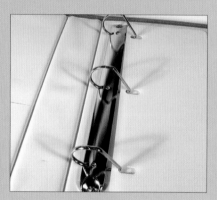

D-Ring Binding

Strap Hinge Binding

Binding Types

Comb Bind To bind pages by inserting teeth of a flexible plastic comb through holes in a stack of paper.

Edge-sewn Pages bound by sewing pages on the side near the backbone.

Pamphlet-stitched Pages bound together by sewing the folded pages onto the backbone.

Perfect Bind To bind pages by stacking and gluing pages onto the backbone, then securing with a wraparound cover.

Post Bind To bind by using sturdy metal posts.

Ring Bind To bind pages together with a series of two or more metal O- or D-rings. Ring binders are easy to use and very versatile. The best thing about using metal-ring binders is that pages are easy to move around. D-rings allow pages to lie flat. O-rings make page turning easier.

Rollabind A patented binding system that punches holes and has discs that connect the papers. Paper can be added and removed easily.

Saddle-stitched Stitching in which wire staples pass through the spine from the outside and are clinched in the center. This method is only used with folded sections of two or more pages.

Side-stitched Pages bound by stapling pages on the side near the backbone.

Spiral Bind To bind pages with a plastic or spiral wire inserted through holes punched along the binding side. Spiral bound books are ideal for a single theme, journaling, or children. Pages lie flat when opened. Without a spiral hole-cutting device, adding pages is difficult.

Strap Hinge or Flex Hinge A plastic strap that runs through the backbone of the album, allowing pages to lie side by side and ease of expansion and page removal.

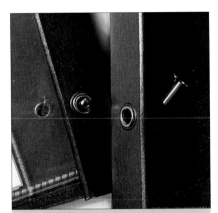

Post Binding

Binding Tip

Occasionally albums are overloaded, causing the posts to tear through the holes predrilled by the manufacturer. Prior to filling an album, or after the tear has occurred, consider using standard paper hole protectors, called reinforcements, to protect the hole and page.

Reinforcements—Acetate and various sized mica reinforcements.

Bookbinder/Album Maker: Marcia Engeltjes

From her first bookbinding experience, during college in Iowa, Marcia Engeltjes was hooked. Initially, she used recycled diesel truck engine parts as design elements in her work. Today, she continues to incorporate truck parts on her book covers; but now she's expanded her repertoire to include components from clocks, stoplights, cameras, motorcycles, telephones, and airplanes, as well as some recent experimentation with stained glass and kinetic features.

Working with various materials she'd carved by hand to focus on specific interests and themes, Marcia taught herself to emboss the highly dimensional carvings under leather; now this method of carving and embossing is her specialty. She also uses many of the skills she honed in college, such as sculpture, woodworking, metalsmithing, painting, drawing, printmaking, glassworking, and composition. Bookbinding has become a synthesis of her many artistic interests, old and new. "Utilizing techniques from classical sixth-century bookbinding," she explains, "I begin with acid-free papers and sheets made by hand and finish them into classically bound books with contemporary cover designs."

Marcia continues to study, taking papermaking and box-construction classes, always striving to find new ways to express herself. She works on custom and one-of-a-kind books, journals, scrapbooks, photo albums, portfolios, boxes, and unique keepsake bindings, as well as restoration, and she has won numerous awards for her work. Proudly she says, "I am the sole creator of each book."

For examples of Marcia Engeltjes's work, see pages 40–41. To learn her bookbinding Technique 1 on pages 42–44.

Marcia Engeltjes feels her album covers are a unique handmade expression of herself. These are just a few examples of her award-winning books.

Elvis Album

Vine Album

Frog Album

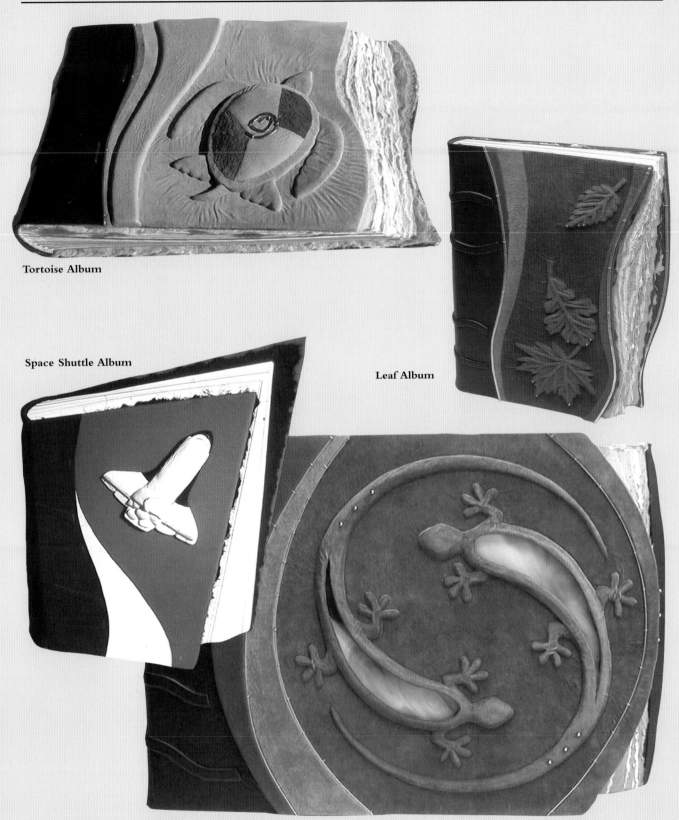

Tortoise Album

Space Shuttle Album

Leaf Album

Lizard with Stained Glass Album

Technique 1: Bookbinding

Begin with a full-sized sheet of acid-free paper, so your memories and photos will be preserved on fine-quality pages.

The papers are folded in half or to a desired page width. Always make certain to calculate the number of pages wanted in the book.

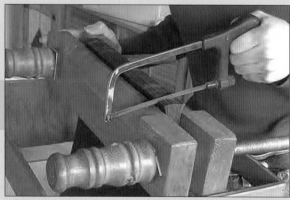

Each folded sheet is cut to desired page height.

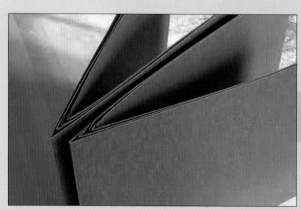

Stack the loose, properly sized pages.

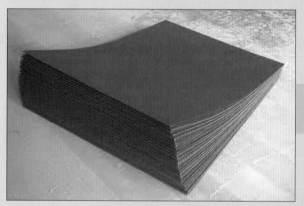

The pages are placed in a clamp. Shallow grooves are cut along the spine, creating a small hole in each page. These holes will line up with the binding cords and act as guides for the sewing needle.

Pages are now stacked inside one another, a few at a time. Each stack is called a signature. If the book is to be a scrapbook or an album, spacers are inserted into each signature at this time.

Stack the signatures for binding.

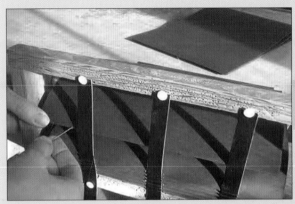

Sew each signature around leather (or sometimes fiber) cords.

Continue this until all signatures are sewn snugly together around the cords and the entire book is bound.

Place the bound book back into the clamp with a slight rounding to the spine.

Brush archival glue onto the spine. It is glue made specifically for bookbinding so the spine will remain flexible and never crack.

Hammer the spine starting at the center and working to the edges. This will tighten and round the spine.

Technique 1: Bookbinding (cont'd)

Stitch headbands onto the spine ends. These will serve to protect the spine edges.

The headbands consist of a leather (or sometimes fiber) cord that is wrapped in colorful thread fibers.

Sew the thread directly into the book for strength.

Finish off the book's paper edge. The traditional method is to shave each page down. Use a straight-edged razor blade while the book is clamped.

To achieve a sculpted deckled edge on some books, hand-rip each page to form a shape complementary to the book's cover composition.

To make the cover, glue two or more layers of cover board together and press beneath white foam condensed under heavy pressure.

Border   A decorative edge, title, line, or design used to surround a scrapbook page (Figs. 14A–14C). Borders may be self-adhesive stickers, diecuts, templates, strips of paper, or the photos themselves. Most ready-made decorative borders are designed to work with 12"x12" scrapbook pages.

Fig. 14A: Border —
Me and My Dad   The border on this page is punched using a decorative hand-punch. Heart-shaped buttons are placed inside each small section, with the sections providing a frame for the page itself.

Fig. 14B: Border—*Summer*   Border stickers were added to this page to add texture and color. They also emphasize the photos. Here, the butterflies and flowers fit the idea of a bright summer day.

Fig. 14C: Border — *Funny Hat Day* Here, borders that would normally surround the page are used to divide the two halves, separating the portrait shots of each child from the group photos. The dark backgrounds of the group photos appear "heavier" and better balance the pages by placing them on the bottom of the page.

Brag Book A small photo or scrap album, usually 4"x6" or smaller, that focuses on a single theme or topic such as a child, grandchild, hobby, or pet (Figs. 15A & 15B).

Figs. 15A & 15B: Brag Book—it*My Grandson Jimmy* The cover, three-dimensional appliqués, embellishments, and photos in the prethemed ready-made brag book work together to portray a baby boy theme that is sure to provide any proud grandmother a unique way to show off her new grandson.

Brayer A small hand tool resembling a paint roller. Brayers are made of numerous materials, each producing a different creative or technical effect by an application technique or by using color. Brayers are used in scrapbooking for making background papers and applying pressure to photographs and embellishments. The most common brayers are made of rubber, hard foam, acrylic, or sponge (Figs. 16A–16C). (See also Technique 2 on page 48.)

Fig. 16A: Various Rubber and Foam Brayers

Fig. 16B: Brayer— *Spring* The brayered areas on this page were overstamped with a flower, using white embossing powder. To make a matching title, the background paper is brayered with corresponding colors before running it through the printer. Each letter is individually cut and mounted onto lighter paper, giving it a highlighted frame.

Technique 2: Brayering

1 Load a brayer, using a rainbow colored dye-based rubber stamp ink pad. Load the brayer by rolling it several times over the pad in one direction only.

2 Roll out the color onto a glossy cardstock, creating a colorful rainbow pattern.

3 Cut the paper to the desired size and affix a photo to the surface. Save the extra brayer-colored paper to use for another project.

Fig. 16C: Brayer—*Sweet Kelly*   While many other patterns would overpower the pretty but busy background paper, the brayered rainbow background perfectly frames "Sweet Kelly," adding color without adding more pattern.

Bristol Board   A stiff heavy paper whose caliper ranges upward from 0.006".

Buffering   A process that neutralizes a paper's acidity over time by adding an alkaline substance, like calcium carbonate, at the pulp stage.

Burnish   The process of rubbing down material using a burnisher, bone folder, the hand, or another device to create a polished finish on paper. Burnishing is usually used on paper folds, in bookbinding, with gilding techniques, and with press-on lettering or stickers.

C

Calendar Scrapping

Placing photos or information onto a calendar page (Figs. 17A–17C) or book format. This technique is used as an alternative to archiving in an album.

Figs. 17A & 17B: Calendar Scrapping— *2003* This special handmade calendar contains photos that symbolize the special dates and events of a whole family, including the extended family— birthdays, anniversaries and holidays. Instead of inserting words, photos of that person (no matter the date of the photo) are placed on that date. Some of them are quite funny, because the person looks far different grown-up, the turkey is yet to be cooked, or a photo with a sour face from a beloved family member stares at you for an entire month. The plants and flowers showcased on each month's page are the original photography of the artist who made the calendar (shown here on her own birthday, April 14th). Calendar scrapbooks can be laminated and make memorable gifts.

Fig. 17C: Calendar Scrapping—*August* This calendar page chronicles the first days of the baby's life. Placing the photo at the bottom of the page allows a standard calendar to fit nicely on the 12"x12" page. A photo taken the first day of every month documents the child's physical growth. The daily journal entries tell of a moment in each day, which tells an ongoing story that will be treasured.

Caliper or Paper Thickness

The average thickness of a single sheet of paper.

Calligraphy Literally meaning "beautiful writing," a style of hand-lettering which features contrasting weights in the horizontal and vertical lettering strokes (Fig. 18). Digital typefaces can only imitate the expressive brush-stroke alphabets and graphic designs of calligraphy. Calligraphy is not a cookie-cutter approach to scrapbooking. There is a creative freedom inherent in not being devoted only to using manufactured titles, captions, and computer-generated fonts. Calligraphy offers scrapbookers methods of combining utility with creative expression that speaks directly to the artisan and viewer alike.

Calligraphic Pen Point Sizes

Italic Nib A sharp straight-cut tip made for a thick line in one direction and a thin line at right angles to that direction, necessary for the italic style of writing.

Nib The point of the pen, which applies the ink to the paper and does the writing. Nib sizes are available in extra fine, fine, medium, broad, broadest broad (bb), etc.

Oblique Nib An obliquely cut nib for extreme angles of lettering.

Standard Nib A round-tipped nib for free-flowing, smooth, and uniform writing. It is suitable for both left-handed and right-handed calligraphers.

Fig. 18: Calligraphy—Traditional Fountain Pens, Nibs, Holders, and Ornamental Pens

Scrap of History: Calligraphy

Antiquity shows us that a split reed was used as a pen to write on papyrus and a frayed reed was used as a brush. In the sixth century, these were replaced with the large flight feather of a goose or other large bird. Special cuts on the nib determined the type of stroke that could be made, be it chisel, flat, or round.

Calligrapher: Suzy Ratto

Lettering is my passion!" says calligrapher Suzy Ratto. "I used to copy paragraphs out of a book just so I could write. Before I found my first calligraphy pen, I would trace the shapes of the letters with a pencil. Then, when my children were older, I joined two local calligraphy guilds and took every class they offered."

A self-taught artist and teacher, Suzy has over fifteen years of experience working with students from preschool to adult. "Depending on the venue," she says, "the skill level in my classes may range from a six-year-old child (taking the class with a parent) to a professional calligrapher. For that reason, I teach to the beginner. I always assume that my students have never picked up a pen before. Moreover, I know that in a group of thirty-five people, two will

be gifted by God to create art. The other thirty-three will be hanging on your every word, hoping that you will give them the basic information and tools they will need to create their own art." And, according to her students, that's just what Suzy does.

"Scrapbooking brings people together," she explains. "It creates an environment of sharing. No matter what they've done, you can't look at a box of your children's baby pictures and stay mad at them." Not that it's always easy: "Working on

12"x12" scrapbook pages can be a little intimidating at times," Suzy admits. "An area that large requires a strong balance of all the elements of design. I like to try out my new scrapbook techniques and color combinations in a card format. It is a much smaller canvas."

Suzy lives in the vineyard area of Livermore, California, with her husband, two college-age daughters, and their cat Boots. "My two daughters watched my business grow," she says. "They have seen me take a passion and turn it to profit. I hope that I

Suzy Ratto's prepackaged calligraphy marker set, palette, and technique sheets

have given them courage to try new things. They know firsthand that it is possible for a woman to raise a family and still have an opportunity to run a successful business doing something she loves to do."

Doug's First Visit with Santa Poinsettias add the traditional Christmas touch to handmade lettering and borders.

Suzy's calligraphic album covers and canvas carriers, pages, and cards are beautifully handmade from her personal collection. Also shown are her signature lines of calligraphic scrapbooking supplies, displaying the variety available, all with colorful lettering and embellishments and ready for scrapbookers to try for themselves.

Camera A photo-taking device usually consisting of a lightproof box, a film holder, a shutter, and a lens to focus the image.

Camera Terminology (See also Film and Photography)

Aperture The circular hole in the front of the camera lens that controls the amount of light allowed to pass onto the film.

Close-up Lens A camera accessory that enables a camera to focus on subjects nearer than the lens normally allows.

Exposure The amount of light needed to render an image on film.

Instant Picture Camera A camera, usually with simple controls, producing a finished photographic print within minutes of the film exposure, such as a Polaroid Camera.

Instant Picture Cameras

Large Format Camera A general term applied to any camera having a picture format of 4"x5" or larger.

Lens A piece or several pieces of optical glass shaped to focus on an image or a subject.

Lens Speed The largest lens opening (smallest f-number) at which a lens can be set. A fast lens transmits more light and has a larger opening than a slow lens.

Lens, Lightbox, and Camera Attachments

Macro Lens A lens specially designed to give accurate resolution of a close subject without the need for other attachments.

SLR (Single Lens Reflex) Camera A camera that uses a mirror to reflect incoming image rays onto a ground-glass screen, providing a system of viewing and focusing.

Wide-angle Lens A lens that has a wider than normal angle of view and usually a short focal length.

Zoom Lens A lens constructed to allow continuously variable focal length. The aperture and focus settings remain unchanged throughout such adjustments.

Caption A word, phrase, sentence, or short paragraph describing the contents of a photo, illustration, or event. A caption is usually placed directly above, below, or to the side of the picture it describes (Fig. 19).

Fig. 19: Caption—*Bee Sting* The caption on this page tells the story of the puppy who was stung by a bee. Ouch! The vellum bee stickers help tell the story graphically.

Card Making Using paper, rubber stamping, scrapbooking, and numerous traditional paper-craft techniques to make handmade cards (Figs. 20A & 20B). Card making is a natural next step for scrapbookers. Using the smaller off-cut scraps that are produced during page making, the myriad embellishments available, and some cardstock, card making is not much more than making a miniature scrapbook page. Rubber stamping expands the creative process by providing an even more exciting way to produce cards. Use stamps for the inside sayings, the focal point instead of a photo, or for making textural backgrounds.

Fig. 20A: Card Making—Card-making Materials and Templates

Fig. 20B: Card Making—*Moe and the Cable Guy* Rubber-stamping and journaling help to carry the card-cover theme inside and tell the story. The plentiful array of scraps left over from page making are ideal for assembling into personal cards, ready to give on any occasion.

Card Maker: Liz Sewald

"I am a true believer in destiny," says Liz Sewald. "In 1995, two months pregnant, I was downsized from a job that I dearly loved in the art supply industry. I ran into a friend and she told me about the rubber-stamping industry and a woman who was looking for a sub-rep to work for her. Reluctantly, I went to see her." Within a month, Liz was "obsessed" with rubber stamping. "My head had so many ideas swirling around that I literally felt dizzy," she says. "I had dreams about rubber stamping for the next six months."

Liz had been immersed in the arts since fourth grade, and when it came time to choose a field, her original choice was printmaking. "While at the University of Kansas, I studied intaglio, lithography, and painting, with a sprinkling of silversmithing and glass blowing," she says. "Ironically, sev-

enteen years later, with a degree in printmaking, I found myself in rubber stamping, which is essentially the same thing."

Today, as a working artist, Liz still radiates infectious curiosity about anything to do with the arts, from the creative side to the business side, from the products she's using to an exciting new technique. Through rubber stamping, she has built a very successful business in sales and marketing, which she credits in part to the "incredible array of wonderful and inspiring people" she meets daily and in part to her background of hands-on experience. "My work in the art supply industry taught me some important lessons about the materials I was using," she says. "Every piece of paper, colored ink, pen, brush, or fiber has a unique working quality to it. You have to be mindful of how these materials will respond in certain situations." Explaining her process, she goes on, "If you put a heavy application of water on a paper that is not designed to accept water, it will be disastrous. If you take the time to experiment with your materials before you actually create something,

you will have a much better result. It is important to know the limits, but also to stretch the products to the limit, seeing how far you can take them without actually destroying them."

Although the availability of countless rubber-stamp and sticker images has eliminated Liz's need to draw, it has also been liberating. "There is a vast library of images right at my fingertips," she says. "The art form, and, yes, it is an art form, is unique in its range of complexity. Anyone, from novice to experienced artist, can latch on to card making and scrapbooking—and be successful!"

Daaahling....you couldn't possibly be more fabulous

And although working has always been fun for Liz, it is most rewarding when she works side by side with her two children. They, too, enjoy dabbling with different products, trying out the same techniques as their inventive and talented mom.

Liz Sewald's cards incorporate stamping and scrapping techniques. Scrapbook-like cards are a highly personal way to update family with memorable events in the form of photos.

Album covers are the ideal place to show-off and have fun, incorporating every conceivable found object, bead, bauble, artifact, and fiber, all of which add creative energy and interest just begging the viewer to come see what's inside.

57

Cardstock Sturdy paper, available in a variety of weights and colors, used for paper crafts and scrapbooking (Fig. 21).

Fig. 21: Cardstock—Retail Store Shelves Well Supplied with Colorful Cardstock

Carte D'visite A calling or visiting card or a card-backed photo (Fig. 22) of a visitor, a celebrity, or a famous place, made popular in the late 1860s.

Fig. 22: Carte D'visite

Cellulose The primary constituent of pulp. Chemically, cellulose is a long-chained carbohydrate consisting of repeating chains of a single simple sugar, glucose.

Chalk Geologically speaking, the chalk used by crafters is actually gypsum, not natural chalk. A sedimentary rock substance, the art material called chalk is ground, pigmented, then formed and held into shapes, using light binders. Chalk is an alkaline substance, versatile and useful for a wide range of scrapbooking projects (Figs. 23A, 23B, & 24B). It can be used to color in stamped imagery, create new background paper, highlight lettering, highlight scrapbook papers, highlight torn paper edges, and shade diecuts.

Chalk Usage Tips

- When working with chalk, use the correct tools (sponges, cotton swabs, or sponge make-up applicators).

- To prevent smearing the finished work, it helps to gently place a piece of computer paper over the majority of the artwork and rest your hand on that, lifting and moving it as necessary.

- It may be necessary to spray finished chalked pages with a fixative to prevent dusting off and the scratching of photos inside page protectors.

Fig. 23A: Chalks and Applicators

Fig. 23B:
Chalk—
Fun in the Sun
Big puffy clouds, made with torn mulberry papers surround and frame the photos on this page. Brushing the edges of the papers with chalk gives them just a hint of color, character, and dimension.

Chalkboard Spray A specialty product that transforms plain paper into a chalkboard. The odor and vapors of chalkboard sprays are harmful, and should be used outdoors only. Projects should stay outdoors until the paint is thoroughly dry. It is available in black and green (Figs. 24A & 24B).

Fig. 24A: Chalkboard Spray

Fig. 24B: Chalkboard Spray—*Tyler's Soccer Picture*   Chalkboard spray was used on this page; soccer balls and titles were hand-drawn with chalk. Once sprayed, dried, chalked, and placed inside a protective sleeve, the chalk will not smudge.

Charm 1. Ancient: an amulet or talisman that has been instilled with energy by an incantation. 2. Modern: a miniature figure, motif, or design usually made of brass-plated base metals, such as silver or pewter. Charms are made to be worn as a decorative piece of jewelry or as an embellishment for scrapbooking. Charms add texture, character, and often meaning to a page (Figs. 25A–25C).

Fig. 25A: Charms

Fig. 25B: Charm—*My Dream for You*   The baby-themed charms embellish the border on this page, complementing the black-and-white photos, adding sparkle and texture.

Fig. 25C: Charm—*Waves*   Beach-themed charms playfully dangle from a beaded bracelet that encircles the title, adding a shimmering curve to a geometric page layout.

Chemical Stability The ability of materials to resist change in their composition when exposed to other materials. In particular chemical stability applies to paper and photographs.

Children's Scrapbooking

Scrapbook pages made with or by children using child-friendly materials: stickers, crayons, tape, etc. (Figs. 26A–26C).

Children's Scrapbook Design Tips

- Use papers, stickers, diecuts, scraps, or old pieces that are no longer suitable for adult scrapbooks.

- Have an adult spray paper with Chalkboard Spray. Give a child some chalk to make a one-of-a-kind background paper.

- Fill a shoebox with envelopes of stickers, diecuts, paper scraps, and found objects taken from your own supplies. Select items that may not be perfect or would not be a personal choice for adult albums.

- Fill a second shoebox with markers, chalk, children's scissors, crayons, and templates.

- Spray several pieces of cardstock with chalkboard spray and cut them into four pieces. Each piece can then be used for, making one-of-a-kind artwork for a specific page.

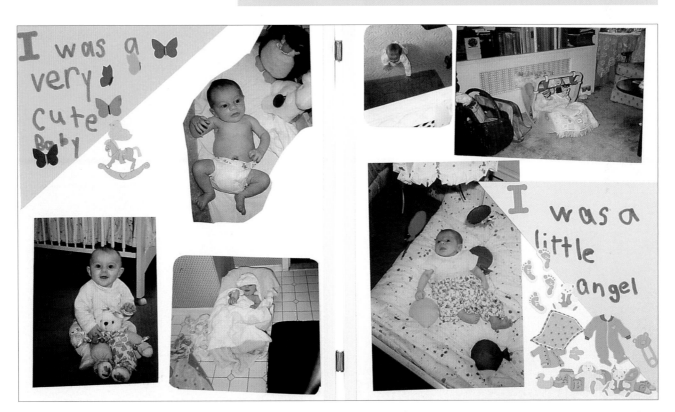

Fig 26A: Children's Scrapbooking—*I Was a Little Angel* The child who crafted this page used scraps of paper and crayons to narrate her story. The sweet little imperfections in the layout make a unique addition to either Mom's or her own scrapbook, making it even more personal than a "more perfect" page.

Fig. 26B: Children's Scrapbooking—*Tell Me a Story*
Using a paper cut-out embellishment that mimics the top photo on this page was a great idea. Other photos on the page keep with the theme and show Hannah reading alone and with her grandma.

C

Fig. 26C: Children's Scrapbooking—*Christmas, 2002*
Creating her own page to document a personal and special Christmas Day, this page demonstrates a colorful energy and child's perspective on page making. The crooked little captions and misspellings add a unique charm, that would have been lost if Mom had helped in the design.

Chromolithography Any lithograph printed in at least three colors (Fig. 27). Victorian ladies saved chromolithograph valentines, birth announcements, calling cards, and calendars, among other colorful paper scraps, because of their beautiful colors, charming embossed patterns, and scenic designs. From use of these chromolithographic scraps came our modern term scrapbook.

Fig. 27: Victorian Chromolithographs

Clay   Any malleable substance able to be molded and fashioned into a dimensional motif. Traditionally, clay consists of tiny mineral particles carried along by rivers in previous years, deposited in the earth, and then excavated. New synthetic clays such as polymer and air-dry are both suitable for scrapbooking and broaden a scrapbooker's repertoire of available creative materials (Figs. 28A–28F and Technique 3).

Fig. 28A: Clay— *Polymer Clay Album Cover* **Rubber-stamped clay squares were used here to frame the photo, adding dimension and a picture-frame-like quality to the album cover.**

Figs. 28B & 28C: Clay—*Art Nouveau* **Even a small embellishment, such as the "Francais" emblem made of clay, adds a dimensional touch to a page.**

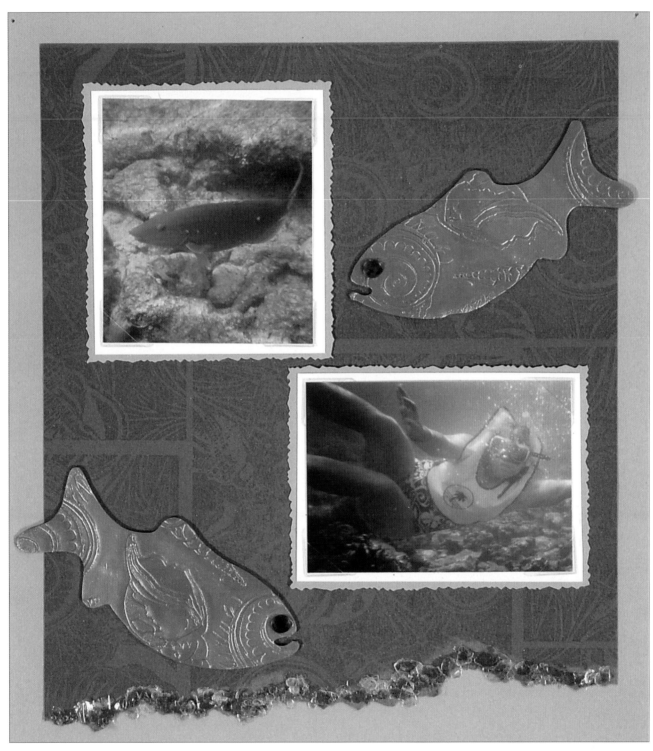

Fig. 28D: **Clay—***One fish, Two Fish*   The polymer clay fish playfully watch underwater photography swimmers watching them back! The blue background paper, stamped with clear ink, using the same rubber plate, gives the page texture without busyness. That same sea-themed printmaker's rubber plate and clay, first run through a pasta machine for pattern, were cut out and bejeweled with a rhinestone eye. Mica Flakes add a look of sea foam and sparkle to the deckled-edged paper.

Fig. 28E: Clay—
Traverse City
To make these clay letters, use a quarter as a stencil to cut the clay. Rubber-stamp or carve letters into the clay and use powdered mica pigments to highlight and enhance them.

Don't follow where the path leads. Rather, go where there is no path and leave a trail.

-Unknown

Riley – age 18 months Summer 2001

Clay Types For Scrapbooking

Air-dry Clay A group of clays that dry without the addition of heat. Always check the manufacturer's packaging to make certain that it is marked acid-free, and suitable for scrapbooking. Overall, air-dry clays are more brittle or fragile than other varieties of clay.

Polymer Clay A modern modeling material composed primarily of resin, plasticizer, and filler material. Polymer clays are colorful modeling compounds. They are permanent and water resistant. Polymer clays remain quite flexible when rolled thin and used for scrapbooking elements.

Technique 3: Polymer Clay

1 Stamp the background paper with a print-maker's plate and block, using an ink pad. Set this aside.

2 Condition pearl and ivory clay by running through a pasta machine several times. Sandwich conditioned clay into a printmaker's plate and run it through the pasta machine again.

3 Using a craft knife and paper frame pattern cut the clay to the desired frame shape. Make enough frames for all of the photos on the page.

4 Carefully lift the frame and bake it according to package directions.

Fig. 28F: Clay—*My Family* The pearl and ivory clay and delicate patterning are perfect for these scrapbook pages, enhancing the photos without overpowering them.

Clipart Ready-made pieces of printed or computerized graphic art such as illustrations, borders, and backgrounds (Fig. 29). Clipart can be copied or scanned and used on scrapbook pages.

Fig. 29: Clipart Books and CDs

Cockle A wrinkled or puckered condition in paper (Fig. 30), book covers, or vellum. Cockling is caused by uneven moisture uptake or uneven tension during drying, or by excessive humidity and wetting. The term also applies to book covers rising, pulling, waving, or curling; or by the use of the wrong type or too much adhesive.

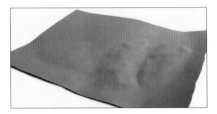

Fig. 30: Cockled Paper

Collage An artistic composition made of various materials such as paper, cloth, or wood glued onto a surface producing a relatively low-relief artwork.

Collagist: Susan Pickering Rothamel

Scrapbooking has changed the way most of us think about organizing, handling, and displaying our precious family photographs. But as Susan Pickering Rothamel points out, it's made us aware of something even more important: the sheer fragility of paper.

As the founder of USArtQuest (a top source for creative mixed-media materials and instruction) and a collage artist for nearly twenty years—starting with papermaking and marbling, then moving on to product development, marketing, and education—Susan learned this lesson early. But she's delighted to see that others, inspired by the popularity of scrapbooking, are starting to pay attention. "For my entire career I have taught about, dare I say even nagged about, archival integrity," she says. "Because of the scrap-

booking phenomenon, in only a few short years, now even a novice will ask about the acid content in an adhesive or whether a colorant is lightfast. This is music to my ears, especially since we are often talking about the difference between the art lasting fifty years or lasting 150 years and more."

It might seem there would be few techniques left untried for someone who makes art every day. But, like most artists, Susan enjoys playing with the latest "toys"—the papers, stickers, diecuts, hardware, and beautiful materials now available to scrapbookers. "It is positively mind-boggling," she says. And it satisfies her curious nature, as well as the requirements of her job, to find and offer interesting new techniques.

Starting USArtQuest ten years ago was a pivotal point in Susan's career. "Not only has the company afforded me the opportunity to meet fascinating people," she says, "it has also allowed me to follow my heart by doing things such as writing, teaching, making art, and doing product development and research.

"I must say, I am still humbled when I see one of my books

or articles on a shelf in someone's home. And I don't think I'll ever stop having those 'golly, gee whiz' moments when a TV appearance of mine has been rerun and I get an e-mail from an excited viewer experiencing it for the first time."

For Susan, there is nothing quite like the feeling of seeing an idea become a product, then seeing that product succeed in the marketplace. She does occasionally dream, she admits, of "spending leisurely art-filled days with people I love"—but she'll have to

live, like her archival pages, to be at least 150. "I'll be needing all that time to complete all of the marvelous projects on my 'yet to do' list!"

Lucille Mefford
1985 - California's Grandmother of the Year
1985 - America's Grandmother of the Year
Every year - my Grandmother of the Year

My Grandmother   The vellum used for this collage allows the floral background papers to play hide and seek, providing an ethereal dimensional quality to this page. The dress's floral pattern is repeated throughout the page, using patterns from art and scrapbook papers.

Mother Oftentimes small collage motifs, created for other work, can be cut down and reused in scrapbook pages. Here, the incorporation of a window, cut out in the middle, then added to an existing collage artwork, makes the perfect frame for a picture.

My Father Paper, painted before and after it was woven, is highlighted with pastels. It makes a beautiful background for photos and journaling. "It is symbolic too, in that it means to me the interweaving of my family's lives and how they weave their way into those life memories, helping shape the person I've become," says Susan.

Color A substance, such as a dye, pigment, or paint, that imparts a hue. As an element of design, color attracts and conveys messages, evokes feelings, and accentuates areas of interest. Color can also enhance clarity, label things, and differentiate concepts and items.

Color Terminology

Color Temperature Cool colors give an impression of coolness. Blue and blue-green are considered cool, such as seen with water and ice. Green might evoke the feeling of walking in a cool dark forest. Warm colors suggest warmth by association. Colors such as red, orange, and yellow are considered warm colors (Figs. 31A & 31B).

Color Wheel A band of colors in the visible spectrum arranged in the shape of a wheel. The colors progress gradually, like the colors of the rainbow, in a regular pattern.

Complementary Colors Colors that are opposite each other on the color wheel. These colors contrast the most and create excitement when placed side by side. Complementary colors are visually appealing. When complements of equal and correct proportions are mixed, they will always form a gray tone (Figs. 32G & 32H).

Monochromatic A color scheme that uses one (mono) color (chroma) in different shades (Fig. 32D & 32E).

Pastel Color The mixture of any color—primary, secondary, or tertiary—with white to achieve a pale, less-saturated color (Fig. 32Q).

Primary Color 1. In light rays, the primary colors are red, green, and blue (Fig. 32F). When mixed in different proportions, these colors produce all others. When mixed together they produce white. 2. In pigments, dyes, and inks, the primary colors are magenta, cyan, and yellow, the basis from which all others can be mixed.

Saturated Any pure color hue, undiluted by other colors. The primary colors, red, yellow, and blue are saturated colors. Secondary colors, such as brilliant orange, bright green, and royal purple, can also be considered saturated colors (Fig. 32F).

Color: Cause and Effect

Color can affect a person in a positive, neutral, or negative way. To bring about a positive effect more often, here are rules to follow:

- Warm primaries are best used sparingly. Allow the strong colors to bring attention to a particular feature or focus.

- Bright or dark colors placed next to each other tend to confuse the viewer.

- A dark background sometimes causes confusion by not allowing adequate contrast with other dark objects. Study nature. It often shows us light and dark colors working well together.

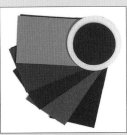

Fig. 31A: Cool Colors

Fig. 31B: Warm Colors

Color Contrast Content consisting of dark blacks and bright whites. High contrast has little or no intermediate gray tones; medium contrast implies a good spread from black to white with shadows and some middle tones; and low contrast implies a small spread of values from black to white most elements are shades of gray (Figs. 32A & B). A scrapbook page featuring pastel pink, pastel blue, and pastel green would be considered a low contrast page. Place on a rose-colored paper and it becomes a medium contrast page. Place a white paper on the top of the rose paper, and that area is higher contrast.

Fig. 32B: Contrast—*The World of Reality* On this page, the contrasting color blocks are used as a background for the photo. The repetition of red and blue match the colors in Hayes's shirt. The solid colors surrounding his more texturally patterned shirt and lighter values in the photograph emphasize the photo and his sweet face.

Fig. 32A: Contrasting Colors

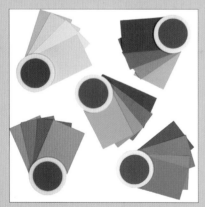

Fig. 32C: Monochromatic Color Families

Fig. 32D: Color Theory—*Father* Monochromatic shades of blue on this page are perfect for framing and using as a background for this baby boy and his proud father.

Color Theory An approach to becoming aware of the relationships that appear to exist between colors in the visible spectrum. The color wheel has made understanding color more comprehensible to the average paper-crafter and scrapbooker. By using the color wheel, almost anyone interested in creating pleasing and harmonious artwork and scrapbook pages can succeed. With even a partial understanding of color theory, artwork and pages produced by using certain color combinations will communicate and emphasize specific areas of interest (Figs. 32D–32V).

Fig. 32E Color Theory—*Ixtapa*
The monochromatic colors used on this page make the viewer feel almost as relaxed as the couple featured in the photo.

Color Theory Rules

- There are three primary colors: red, yellow, and blue (Fig. 32F).

- Mixing a primary color with a secondary color, in equal proportions, forms a tertiary or intermediate color (Fig. 32P).

- Clashing, noncomplementary colors generally convey a sense of aggressiveness because of the mind's inability to resolve them. A vivid orange and bright violet are noncomplementary colors.

- There are three secondary colors orange, green, and violet. Mixing equal proportions of two primary colors together produces a secondary color (Fig. 32F).

- Colors are effected by light, their setting, the viewers vision, and by other colors placed next to or around them.

- Colors forming a triangle on the color wheel are called triads. Triads can be used to attract attention. "Primary" triads consist of red, yellow, and blue. "Secondary" triads are orange, green, and violet (Fig. 32F).

- Analogous harmonies are groups of colors that are next to each other on the color wheel. These are closely related colors. Analogous harmonies are visually pleasing. Blue, blue-violet, and violet are analogous harmonies (Fig. 32N).

**Fig. 32F:
Primary and
Secondary
Triads**

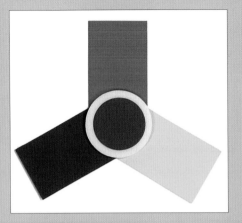

**Figs. 32G & 32H:
Complementary
Colors**

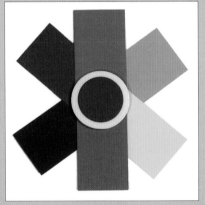
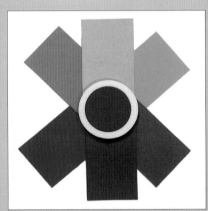

Fig. 32I: Color Theory—*Swim, Pool, Ride, Jeep* The strong use of primary colors can sometimes be overpowering. Here, the solid border along the bottom and blue framing anchor and keep the focus firmly on the photos. Framing the borders with the eyelets and blue fiber also brings in a unifying textural detail.

Fig. 32J: Color Theory— *Holiday* Trees and holiday winter-themed embellishments provide texture on this page, which under less-expert hands can make for a confusing page. The dominant red and green, a complementary color scheme allows the eye to easily sort the patterns of this visually stimulating inspiration scrapbook page.

Fig. 32K: Color Theory—*Key West* Secondary colors fill this page as a background element and contrast the darker colors in the photos nicely. Colorful random shapes soften the static squared family photos displayed here, adding movement and noncompeting color.

Fig. 32L: Color Theory—*Library Flora*   The simple geometric shapes and secondary color scheme balance without competing with the riot of floral patterning.

Fig. 32M: Color Theory—
Pumpkin Carving   The sewn fibers here join the upper and lower portions of this page, featuring a strong secondary color theme, allowing the eye to move up and down without stopping. The composition, divided into thirds, is very effective.

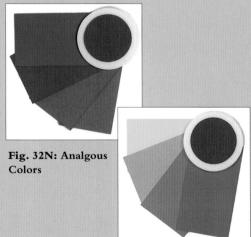

Fig. 32N: Analgous Colors

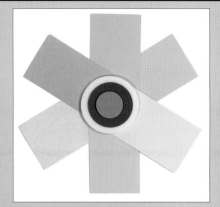

Fig. 32O: Pastel Colors

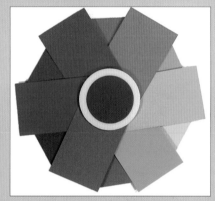

Fig. 32P: Tertiary Colors and their complements

Fig. 32Q: Color Theory—*Wish, Play, Giggle*   The pastel background paper used here was created with chalk. The pale colors of the background and contrasting black framing help the photos stand out.

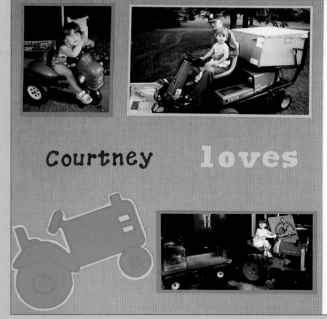

Fig. 32R: Color Theory—*Courtney Loves Tractors*   Playful tractor diecuts contribute a change of shape and movement, repeating the analogous color theme of green and yellow.

Fig. 32S: Color—_Beulah Beach_   Sunshine rays play across both pages, unifying the design and directing the eye to the photos. Even the title, also in bright yellow, plays back the sunrays. The blue background paper complements the yellow, making the page pleasing to the eye.

Fig. 32T: Color—_Mexico_   The shades of red and green on this Mexico page complement each other well. Using a white pen to journal about the trip makes the lettering stand out on the green background.

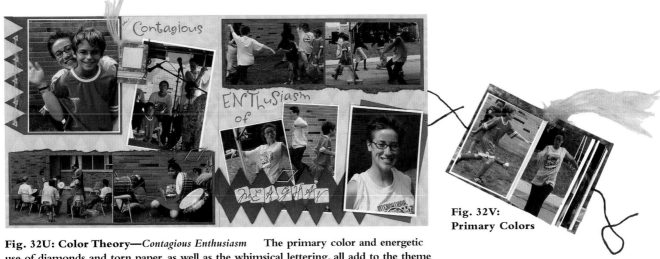

Fig. 32U: Color Theory—*Contagious Enthusiasm*   The primary color and energetic use of diamonds and torn paper, as well as the whimsical lettering, all add to the theme of enthusiasm on these pages. Notice the Bitty Book used to show off all those extra photos that would otherwise clutter a busy page.

Fig. 32V: Primary Colors

Color Blocking A page design technique where album pages are prepared in geometric areas or blocks (Figs. 33A & 33B). Generally rectangles or squares of two or more colors are used. Photos, journaling, or embellishments appear within the blocks to create a larger impact, even when combined with smaller elements (Fig. 32B, 32E, 32M, & 33B).

Fig. 33A: Color Blocking—*Easter*   On this page, the color blocks were hand-made. Each block was cut from pastel cardstock and attached onto the page before the photos were added.

Fig. 33B: Color Blocking—*A Day at the Zoo*   Using the tram's color theme, the color blocking here mimics the bands of color. Tearing the paper edges softens the contrast-ing bold background colors. The laser-cut elephant title adds whimsy and texture, as well as perfectly complementing the color in the photographs.

Color Dye Coupler A special chemical within photographic papers that reacts during photo processing to create the image forming dyes.

Color Transparency A slide of transparent film or glass that contains a positive photographic color image.

Colorant and Substrate System The dye or pigment used in inks, paints, crayons, paper, and other artist materials, such as pens and markers. A substrate system refers to the surface to which the colorant is applied. Responsible manufacturers test both the colorant and the substrate system for harmful interactions and often recommend to their customers which materials, obtain the best results when used together.

Fig. 34A: Composition— *Camel* The torn background papers play hide and seek with the solid color, giving the viewer the sense that the solid-colored paper has worn away. Using small and large photos helps to balance the pages, as do the careful additions of embellishing memorabilia.

Colorfast   An object or paint that resists the harmful UV rays of light, acid, and heat. Also called lightfast.

Composition   The way art or an album's page is put together and how the artist organizes the elements, colors, and shapes into a whole that is satisfying to the viewer. Creative variables such as balance, color, and texture are all subjective considerations, that when combined form an image that is pleasing to view, and can effectively tell a story. Every photograph and element effects how other elements are perceived as a unified whole rather than a collection of parts. The main element of composition is balance and the shape of the unused space, as well as element proportion (Figs. 34A–34D).

Fig. 34B: Composition—*Peace*   Monochromatic pages are often the most difficult to compose, yet are worth the effort because they make striking statements in design. The photographs themselves provided the color scheme for these pages. Keeping the layout simple and using a similar typeface for the title gives these pages a peaceful tranquility and sophistication.

Fig. 34C: Composition—*Shrimp* Sensitive attention to color contrast and the use of complementary colors help the eye travel through this visual story. Photos, lettering, embellishments, and colors add texture. The precise placement of the elements, overlapping edges, corner embellishment "anchors," as well as the color photo mounts, all work to unify the page making for a very pleasing composition.

Composition Terms

Album Consistency Using a similar format, color, type style, and layout throughout the album while still having other variations on each page.

Background The background color or the "ground" in a composition. It is as important as the photos and elements used in the composition. The background gives form to the page. The entire background should be accounted for. This does not mean that it should be completely filled. Rather, it means that when there are areas of white space it should add to the overall compositional balance of the page.

Balance The visual weight of each element. Weight can be calculated by the size of the object, the value (dark objects weigh more than light objects), and the texture. When the contrast between elements is too great, balance is lost. Proportions and size should also be considered when checking for balance.

Balance may be symmetrical or asymmetrical. Symmetry often creates a static page, focusing the eye in one area, rather than having it wander the page, but produces a strong focal point. Asymmetrical balance requires a skillful arrangement of elements with different visual weights, which can be achieved by placing small elements next to a larger one, creating a visually dynamic page.

Focal Point The element on the page that catches the viewer's attention first. If all of the page elements are equal weight, the viewer will be confused as to where to look first.

Positive and Negative Space Page elements and the visible background. Elements are positive and the background is negative. The negative space is important to balance, proportion, color harmony, and framing of the positive shapes.

Fig. 34D: Composition—*Fiesta* The concept of thirds, numerical balance, and the repetition of elements, all work toward the harmony and compositional interest on these pages. Overlapping elements and the occasional angled elements keep pages from appearing static and keep the eye moving around the space.

Composition Tips

While composition rules, like many other artists rules, are made to be broken, below are guidelines to create visually pleasing scrapbook pages:

• Use the "Rule of Thirds." Divide a layout into thirds both vertically and horizontally. Where those lines meet is a good place to put the focal point(s) of a layout.

• Use the same element in odd numbers one, three, or five times on the same page or double-page spread.

• Photographs should show people's eyes pointing inward or looking toward a special element. Otherwise, they appear to be falling out or moving out of the page.

• Repeat certain elements, color, or papers throughout the layout.

• Create contrast in your pages through use of color, size, or texture of the elements

• Place several elements in close proximity to each other, or overlap them. They will appear to become one visual whole, rather than individual elements.

Computer Scrapbooking

Preserving and creating memories, journals, photographs and digitized scrapbooking elements or entire scrapbook pages, by use of a computer, various computer software systems, scanner and/or photocopier.

Confetti

Small pieces or streamers of colored plastic or paper made to be thrown during a celebratory event. It also makes a cheerful addition to shaker boxes and as scrapbooking embellishments

Conservation

The process of repairing paper or scrapbooks.

Contact Print

A print made by exposing a photosensitive surface in direct contact with a photographic negative (Fig. 35). A contact print is the same size as the negative that it was made from.

Fig. 35: Contact Print

Contrast

The difference in darkness or density between one tone of color and another.

Copyright

A legal notice or mark, protecting "original works of authorship" both published and unpublished, that are expressed in a tangible form, but not the ideas themselves.

Corner Punch

A device used to pierce a photograph (Figs. 36A & 36B) or paper corner for decorative purposes. (See also Punches.)

Fig. 36A: Corner Punch— *Christmas 2003* Corner punches can be used to create a filigree pattern on paper. The punched squares give these pages a festive and colorfully decorative look, improving the overall color and compositional balance of the page.

Fig. 36B: Corner Punch— *Rose Marie* Special corner punches can be used on most any type of paper to create custom photo corners, and act as a decorative frame for holding photographs and memorabilia.

Computer Scrapbooker: Maria Given Nerius

"Computer scrapbooking, or what I call digital scrapbooking, has been my style of creative scrapbooking since the beginning of the memories trend," says Maria Given Nerius. "I really enjoy using the software to make digital elements and combine them with traditional scrapbooking techniques." Maria doesn't feel that scrapbookers need to have the "latest and greatest" gadget or tool, sticker or diecut to go beyond current skills and achieve beautiful results. "In some cases all you need is the printer and basic programs," she says. "Moreover, the greatest advantage of going digital is that it is the ultimate in acid-free and family photo preservation."

Maria, the author of *Digital Scrapbooking*, has worked in the craft industry for more than fifteen years writing articles, press releases, and marketing materials for major and small companies, as well as magazine and book publishers. "I write on a regular basis for *Craftrends/ Primedia, Scrapbooks And Beyond/All American Crafts,* and *Paper Works/House of White Birches/DRG.* I use a PC with a scanner and inkjet printer and any of the photo software that's currently available. Since many photo-editing and word-processing programs share the same features, you can apply most of what you already know to digital scrapbooking."

From creating background papers to artistically styled titles, from photo-editing to clipart, Maria finds that the process is not only done faster, but also considerably "neater," using the computer for scrapbooking. "Once you understand that you don't have to abandon all the wonderful traditional scrapbooking skills, supplies, and tools you love, you'll see that the computer is just another way you can preserve your precious family and life memories."

Corner Rounder A punch or scissors used for rounding the corners of photographs and paper. (See also Punch.)

Corrugator or Crimper A hand tool that ripples paper (Fig. 37).

Fig. 37: Corrugators

Cotton Linter Fibers that adhere to cottonseed after ginning. Cotton linter is used as raw material to produce pulp for cotton-fiber paper. Cotton linter is ideal for making paper castings for decorative accents or even making three-dimensional impressions of a baby's footprint. (See also Papermaking and Paper Casting.)

Crackle Medium A medium, liquid, powder or paste made to alter the surface of paper or paint, by creating fissures, crazing and crackling, thus giving it an aged appearance. Crazing refers to the finest of lines that occur in a crackled piece, often enhanced by adding paint or glaze by rubbing it into the crazed areas (Figs. 38A–38C).

Fig. 38A: Crackle Medium—*Summer 1942* Crackle paste adds a crazed and suede-like finish that is suitable for antiquing and coloring and perfect for showing off these old photographs.

Fig. 38B: Crackle Medium—*Baby Shower* Crackling creates interesting background papers. When used and mounted onto solid papers, it can add a textural interest to scrapbook pages without overwhelming the photographs.

Craft Knife A craft knife is a pencil-shaped tool affixed with one of several shaped razor blades, attached to one end. Craft knives are used for lightweight, precise, and intricate cutting (Fig. 39). They are suitable for cutting wood, cardboard, paper, plastic, cloth, and foam-core board. Also called artist's knife, hobby knife, or mat knife.

Fig. 39: Craft Knives

Fig. 38C: Crackle Medium—*Big Catch* This page demonstrates the fine crazing technique. The paste medium was tinted with inks and applied onto the paper with a credit card. This medium leaves a subtle suede-like crackled finish. Overstamping, using permanent light- and dark-colored inks further enhance the effect.

Craft Knife Usage and Safety Tips

- Change knife blades often. It is imperative to maintain a sharp blade. Dull blades not only make rough cuts, but also slip easier. Paper, cutting mats, metal surfaces, and coarse materials (like corrugated cardstock) will dull blades quickly.

- Don't throw stray blades in the trash—purchase refill blades available in a plastic box (there is a slot for disposing the used blades in the side). Alternatively, wrap the blade in a piece of masking tape or tape it to a scrap of rigid cardboard.

- When using a ruler as an edge for cutting, hold it firmly in place, but keep the ruler, held with fingers, well clear of the blade.

- Metal rulers are better than plastic ones—you will not be able to accidentally slice into them.

- Store knives with the blade side down. Safety caps are often unreliable.

- Cut a piece of Styrofoam to fit inside of a coffee cup and store knives, blade side down, inside.

- Protect your furniture, including glass or plastic laminate. Use a specially made self-healing mat for cutting. If this is unavailable, use thick cardboard under your working surface.

- Wrap a rubber band around the handle of the knife so it doesn't roll off of the work surface.

Crop   To trim the edges of an image, often to improve the composition (Figs. 40A–40E).

Fig. 40B: Cropped Photos—*Grape* Notice that the top portion of the bottle and the leaf were cut with a craft knife. These portions were cleverly used as photo holders.

Cropping Tips

- Photocopy treasured photos before cropping (or use duplicate prints).

- Decide what the most important part of the photo is and crop away anything unnecessary.

- Never crop a Polaroid photo—it contains an acid that can seep out when cut.

- Cut photos into shapes using templates as a guide, focusing on the subject and design of the scrapbook page.

- Do not use too many differently shaped photos on one page. Generally selecting one style and varying the size is the most effective layout.

Fig. 40A: Crop—*South* Instead of layering photos on top of the mounting papers, a craft knife was used to cut out the center of the papers, creating unique backgrounds with a "hide and seek" quality. In addition, several of the photos were heavily cropped, directing the viewer's focus to the center of the photo. Notice how much of the background is cut away. Backgrounds often have important features worth remembering, but in this case, however, the focal point was the person, not the background.

Fig. 40C: Uncropped Photo

Fig. 40D: Cropped and Enlarged Photo

Fig. 40E: Crop—*Dow Gardens* The butterflies are the subject of this picture and to help show them clearly, the photos were cropped to the same size, centering the butterfly as the focal point.

Crop Mark A line or marking indicating where the page or photograph will be trimmed.

Crop Night A time set aside, usually in a retail store setting, for scrapbookers to get together and share ideas and work on their own individual pages. Cropping nights are usually times of socializing with acquaintances and friends while enabling retailers to share tips and techniques as well as the newer products in the marketplace.

Cropping Party Formal or informal gatherings of people for the express interest of working independently, while together, on scrapbook pages. In addition to idea gathering and sharing, cropping is often mingling with a social agenda. Cropping parties can be home-based or commercial events (Fig. 41).

Fig. 41: Cropping Party

D

Daguerreotype An early photographic process where the image was made on a light-sensitive silver-coated metallic plate (Figs. 42A–42C).

Fig. 42A: Daguerreotype Leather-tooled Cover

Fig. 42B: Daguerreotype in Case with Velvet Embossing and Embossed Metal Frame

Fig. 42C: Daguerreotype—*Ancestry* Although names and historical data were not found for these photos when they were discovered in an old cigar box, it was obvious that they were family because of their resemblances. The historical value was so amazing that they absolutely had to be mounted and included into the family scrapbook. Some of the tintypes shown here are framed in exquisite gold-flashed copper-embossed frames.

Dark Stability A material's ability to resist degradation when stored in the dark.

Dark Storage A photo or memorabilia storage environment in which the materials are not regularly exposed to light.

Deckle Edge/Decorative-edged Scissors Scissors with a decorative pattern on the blade (Figs. 43A–43E and Technique 4). 1. The naturally rough or feathered edge of untrimmed handmade paper. 2. A type of edge imitated in commercial papers. 3. Hand-cut paper edges created using special scissors or rulers to resemble untrimmed handmade papers.

Fig. 43A: Deckle Edge—*Downtown Orlando* Simple scrapbook pages such as this one are made by using decorative-edged scissors and die-cut lettering. This title works because it echoes the movement of the signage in the photos.

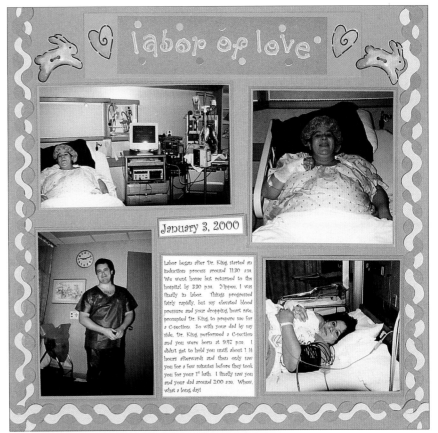

Fig. 43B: Decorative-edged Scissors

Fig. 43C: Deckle Edge—*Labor of Love* This page's border was cut using decorative-edged scissors, then assembled by interweaving two different colored papers.

Technique 4: Deckle Edging

1 Using cardstock, tear down and toward the deckling ruler to achieve a soft deckled edge.

2 Another method is to run a wet brush down the edge of a ruler, onto the paper.

3 When the water has soaked through the paper, tear it down and toward the ruler, creating a fibrous deckled edge.

Fig. 43D: Deckle Edge—*Roadside Sunshine*   The deckled edging on these pages repeats the soft feathery forms of the sunflower petals.

Fig. 43E: Deckle Edge—*Black-faced Sheep*   Decorative-edged scissors created charming elements for this page. The edge resembles grass and the repetition of the photo montage provides consistency.

Decoupage   A decorative paper art technique using figurative paper illustrations cut carefully from a range of sources, including books, magazines, and newspapers, as well as computer-generated material. The cut pieces are then pasted onto nearly any surface, including scrapbooks (Fig. 44). Decoupage was made popular in Victorian times, when young women would decoupage everything from floor screens to furniture, and boxes to album covers.

Fig. 44: Decoupage—*My Heritage* This album cover was made to resemble a traditional decoupage album, that will contain daguerreotypes and old sepia prints. The images were carefully cut from catalogs and magazines. The cutouts were reassembled as a scene.

Decoupage Materials

Adhesive A clear-drying acid-free wet adhesive to glue your pictures down and seal them.

Brayer To roll out and remove wrinkles, remove excess glue, and adhere your photos down better.

Craft Knife Used to cut out detailed pictures, release air bubbles, and pick up small cut paper pieces.

Credit Card Gently used to help smooth out wrinkles and remove excess glue.

Damp Rag To wipe up excess glue and other cleanup.

Soft PaintBrush For smoothing the adhesive and the paper.

Decoupage Tips

- **Bubbling** If after gluing a print down you discover an unattractive bubble, there may be insufficient glue or too much glue. Slice it, making a tiny sideways cut into the lump. Remove the excess glue or use a toothpick to slip some more glue under the print before pressing it down firmly. If it is just a small air bubble, a tiny pinprick will often do the trick.

- **White Edges** While cutting, hold your scissors at an angle away from you, so the edge is cut on the slant rather than straight up and down. This method of cutting will help bevel and hide the white cut edge. When you are using particularly thick paper and the white edge still shows, try using a watercolor marker to match the edge.

Degradation Any product that is initially low in acid but becomes increasingly more acidic over time due to chemical reactions, from aging, or migration. Examples of degradation: Paper yellowing (Fig. 45), brittleness, tape yellowing, and loss of tack.

Fig. 45: 1960s Newspaper Showing Degradation

Depth of Field The focused areas between the nearest and farthest points from the camera lens.

Diary A daily record of events, transactions, or observations; especially a daily record of personal activities, reflections, or feelings.

Die 1. Cut metal shapes of motifs, letters, or shapes, usually imbedded into wood and rubber forms, which are then used for cutting paper into the shape of the metal design. 2. An engraved stamp used for impressing an image or design.

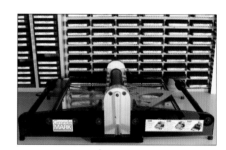

Fig. 46A: Flatbed Roller Die-cutting Machine

Fig. 46B: Pressure Die-cutting Machine

Die Cutting A method of using sharp steel-ruled dies and pressure rollers (Figs. 46A–46B) to cut various shapes, generally called diecuts (Figs. 46E–46J).

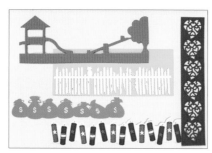

Fig. 46C: Decorative Diecuts

Fig. 46D: Die Cutting—*Speedy Gonzales* Diecuts are cleverly used not only to replicate the cars in the photos with the children, as well as their use as a photo frame.

Fig. 46E: Word Diecuts

Fig. 46F: Die Cutting—*Crab Feast* The photos and titled tags have a repetition of movement that shows the viewer that this crab feast was nothing but fun. The straight line of photos anchors the tags and angled photos, keeping them from dancing off the page. The bright red crab diecut nicely balances the bold orange block of color on the left page.

Fig. 46G: Die Cutting—*Maui*
This colorful scrapbook page tells a great story through not only the journaling but through the use of die-cut sunglasses and sunscreen, and the colorful photos.

Fig. 46H: Die Cutting—*Golf* Using die-cut titles and dimensional die-cut embellishments are an effective way to add additional storytelling to any scrapbook page.

The mini photos running down the facing page add interest, texture, and balance to the overall page composition.

Fig. 46I: Die Cutting—
Karate Kid Cute diecuts and a strong black, white, and red color scheme fit the karate theme of this page. Take note of the single overlapping corner in the center of the page. This design strategy keeps the photos from floating individually and unifies the entire scrapbook page.

Fig. 46J: Die Cutting—*Dog Gone Cute*
There's no doubt the photos take center stage on this page. An effective technique, the white background bordered by the dark torn papers forces the eye to the center. The brown paper against the black die-cut puppy prints and title gives the page lots of texture without overwhelming the photos.

97

Digital Image An image obtained by using digital cameras, camcorders, scanners, etc. Digital imagery captures and stores pictures without film and when printed, the images are still considered color photos (Figs. 47A & 47B).

DPI (Dots Per Inch) The dots per inch measuring the resolution of a digital image, printer, or scanner. Dots are also known as pixels.

Dry Brushing Loading a brush with paint, removing virtually all of it, and then brushing the nearly dry brush across paper to alter and subdue color, pattern, or texture. Dry brushing is used to enhance protrusions, wrinkles, and paper embossed areas.

Dry Mount Pasting with heat-sensitive adhesives.

D-series Paper Paper that is acid-free, lignin-free, buffered, and passes the PAT.

Dummy A preliminary layout showing the position of illustrations and text as they are to appear for final reproduction.

Dye A soluble substance made to color ink, paper, and textiles. Dye colors are less stable over a long period than pigment colors; however, when used and protected properly, they have longevity and allow a greater color variety.

Fig. 47A: Digital Image—*Cody* The quality of a 4"x6" photo from a 35mm camera is equal to a 300 DPI digital image that measures 1200x1800 pixels.

Fig. 47B: Digital Image—*Dog Parade* When printed onto photo paper, digital prints resemble traditional photographic prints. The diecuts and warm colors of this page evoke the feelings of those "Dog Days of Summer."

E

Element As the word pertains to paper crafting: any photograph, embellishment, journal entry, or item used in the creation of a larger design concept or composition.

Embellishment An element that adds decoration to a scrapbook page. Embellishments can include buttons, cabochons, charms, found objects, game pieces, hardware, paper fasteners, rhinestones, ribbons, sequins, silk flowers, twine, watch parts, and wire shapes. (Figs. 48A–48I).

Fig. 48B: Titles

Fig. 48C: Buttons

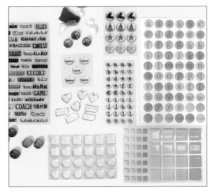

Fig. 48D: Cabochons

Fig. 48E: Beads

Fig. 48A: Embellishment—*With This Ring* Hanging cabochons, resembling wedding bells, make for a clever title.

The large variety of appliqués used on these pages adds color and texture.

Fig. 48F: Embellishment—
I'm Having a Bad Day
Beads embellish this page as
photo corners and borders around
the title and journaling, as well
as provide an element that helps
to balance the composition.

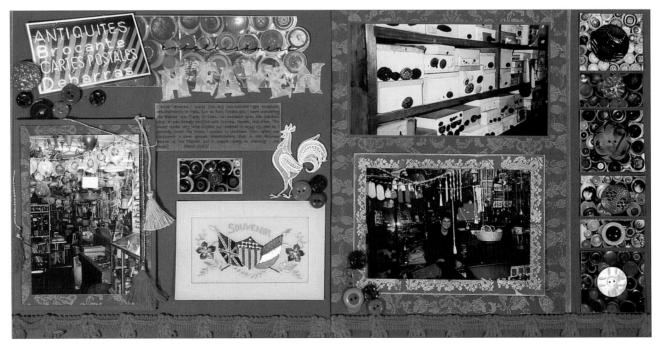

Fig. 48G: Embellishment—*Embellishment Heaven*   This two-page spread really is embellishment heaven. Added buttons, beads, tassels, thread, and paper cutouts along with the wildly textural photography give the feeling of really being in the antique shop.

Fig. 48H: Embellishment—
If I Catch One Can I Then Fly
Natural and store-bought embellishments work to make this page a success. The seashells and seagulls bordering the page were adhered to coordinate with the photos. The vellum title, simply torn and attached with brads, adds a nice contrast to the smoothly cut paper edges.

Fig. 48I: Embellishment—
Froggin Buttons and bows, scattered down the side of this page, perform several functions: as a border and texture, as well as a touch of whimsy and charm.

101

Emboss   To create a raised image or words, by using one of several methods, including pressure, or heat and resins (Figs. 49A–49H).

Fig. 49A: Dimensional Embossing— *My Dream Garden*   A stencil makes beautifully embossed tiles, perfect for any scrapbook page.

Embossing Types

Deboss A technique using two identical stencils or by freehand, using a stylus to create a recessed pattern in paper or metal sheets.

Dimensional Embossing/ Wet Relief Embossing Achieving dimensional results using stencils and relief products such as clay, artist cements, and pastes (Fig. 49G & 49H and Techniques 5 and 8).

Dry Emboss To impress on paper or thin metal an image, creating a subtle raised or relief surface (Figs. 49B–49D & Technique 6).

Heat Embossing Using a stamped image or tool, ink or gilding adhesive, thermal embossing powder, and a heat source together to create a raised image (Also called Thermal Embossing or Thermography). (Figs. 49E & 49F and Technique 7).

Fig. 49B: Stencils, Lightbox, and Dry Embossing Tools

Technique 5: Dimensional Embossing (Clay)

1 Use air-dry clay or condition polymer clay by running it through a pasta machine.

2 Impress a stencil into the clay. Buttons, molds, and anything with an embossed or debossed design might be pressed into clay, creating a unique pattern.

3 If using air-dry clay, allow it to dry. If using polymer clay, bake it according to the package directions. If it is made thin, the clay may be trimmed with scissors after baking or drying.

Fig. 49C: Emboss—*Paper Flowers* Flowers first dry embossed, then cut and assembled together. Overlapping the edges gives the appearance of a bouquet that nearly jumps off the page with color and ornamentation.

Fig. 49D: Emboss—*Cherish* Dry embossing adds a touch of class, texture, and if needed, color to nearly any page. Stencils with every pattern and theme imaginable make dry embossing a desirable way to embellish nearly any page.

Technique 6:
Dry Embossing

1 Tape a stencil onto a window or lightbox.

2 Position paper over the stencil, securing it with removable tape. Dry as directed by the manufacturer.

3 Firmly but gently press the paper into the stencil, moving the stylus only around the edges of the design.

4 Use the larger end for more open areas and the smaller end for the detail areas.

Dry Embossing Tips

- A heavier paper will give a nicer effect. Ninety-pound watercolor paper performs beautifully.

- There is no right or wrong side to a stencil, except with letters and numbers. Simply turn a stencil over to get a mirror image.

- Tape the stencil to the lightbox using a low-tack tape.

- The center is not, nor should necessarily be traced.

Technique 7: Heat Embossing

Apply pigment ink onto rubber stamp, then stamp on paper.

Sprinkle on embossing powder, and tap off any excess.

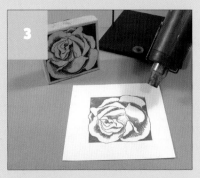

Heat embossing powder until it is smooth and shiny.

Use the image as is, or trim around it with scissors.

Heat Embossing Tips

- Avoid rocking the stamp and creating shadow images.

- Work on a padded surface to obtain a better image with less pressure.

- Different papers and inks have varying drying times. Humidity and the amount of antistatic powder used will effect drying speed.

- Avoid overheating the powder or the paper. This will cause it to curl or burn.

Fig. 49E: Heat Embossing—*Baker* Colorful collage-like heat-embossed stamping frames vintage photos, preserving precious "Baker" family photos.

Fig. 49F: Heat Embossing—*Mom is Wow Upside Down* With a torn-paper overlay, the heat-embossed stamped areas add movement and texture, as well as a unique way to attach photos.

Technique 8: Wet Relief Embossing

1 Position and tape the stencil to the paper. Secure it with tape. Using a palette knife or credit card, smooth the stenciling paste or artist's cement over the openings to the thickness of the stencil.

2 Using great care, lift the stencil to reveal the pattern. Wash the stencil immediately in warm water.

3 Sprinkle on glitter or mica and allow the stencil to dry, or allow to dry without any embellishing (Fig. 49G).

Fig. 49G: Emboss—*My Love, My Friend* The embossed motifs bordering the right side of the page are simple yet effective textural accents for this page. The sparkling mica flakes add emphasis to the sparkle in the couple's eyes.

Fig. 49H: Emboss—*Lizzie* The trimmed dimensionally stenciled flourishes, with added bits of colored mica flakes, add texture and nicely frame the journaling while unifying the left and right columns of photos. The pom-poms are a nice touch, repeating the fluffy costume buttons.

Embroidery A type of ornamental needlework, often on fabric and paper, produced either by hand or by machine sewing (Figs. 50A & 50B).

Fig. 50A: Embroidery—
Zachary and Zazdu's
The interwoven journaled captions blend well with the movement of the machine-made embroidered paper, adding a lyrical quality to the page.

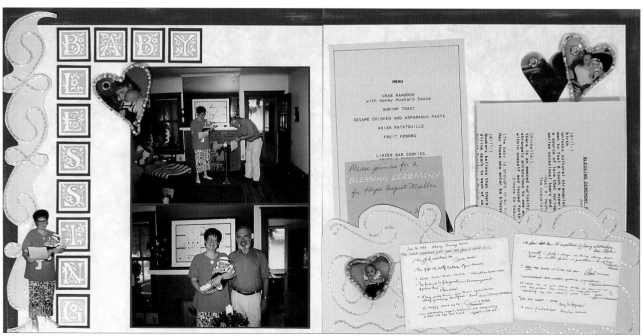

Fig. 50B: Embroidery—*Baby Blessing* Embroidered papers, trimmed along the edge, make lovely borders, photo frames, and as shown here, pockets for baby blessing certificates and other memorabilia.

Encapsulation Placing an element such as paper or other memorabilia in an acid-free envelope (Fig. 51A), between layers of mica or sheets of transparent polyester film, and sealing the sheets together. Encapsulation protects elements from damage caused by handling, moisture, and contact with acidic material (Figs. 51B–51D). Papers should be deacidified before encapsulation.

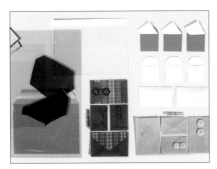

Fig. 51A: Encapsulation Devices

Fig. 51D: Encapsulation—*Official Lunch*   This encapsulation bag protects and holds cards from an important luncheon, while adding a soft sophisticated textural element to this scrapbook page.

Fig. 51C: Encapsulation—*Baby's First Haircut*   Encapsulation envelopes are perfect for saving a baby's first curls. On this page, the artist noted the name of the event as well as the date and name of the hairstylist.

Fig. 51B: Encapsulation—*Dominican Republic*   Encapsulating sand into glass vials brings a little bit of the vacation home, and is far more interesting than gluing the sand directly onto the paper. The vials also keep loose granules from scratching photographs.

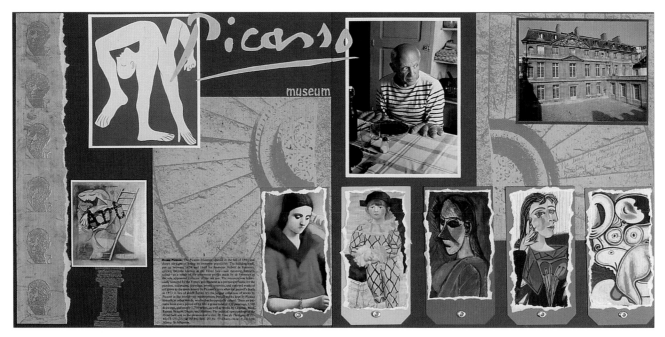

Fig. 52: Environmental Stewardship—*Picasso* This asymmetrically composed scrapbook page incorporates a striking balance of texture, color, and composition. Note that there are no real photos on these pages, just recycled paper ephemera and postcards.

Environmental Stewardship

An inherent respect for the environment by use of recycling or using environmentally friendly products. The best way to ensure that your paper meets the highest environmental standards is to find a PCF or TCF symbol from the not-for-profit CFPA (Chlorine Free Products Association). These products are certified and not made using harmful, chlorine-containing compounds (Fig 52).

Environmental Stewardship Terms

ECF (Elementally Chlorine Free) A paper produced without any "elemental" chlorine; however, other chemicals containing chlorine are used for bleaching. ECF manufacturing only "reduces" the quantity of dioxin and other toxins produced, but is not as environmentally friendly as TCF manufactured paper.

PCF (Process Chlorine Free) A paper produced by using recycled paper processed back into paper without using chlorine or chlorine derivatives.

TCF (Totally Chlorine Free) A paper produced without chlorine or any chlorinated derivatives, using instead oxygen, hydrogen peroxide, or other environmentally friendly bleaching agents.

Ephemera Printed items produced with the intent of being short-lived or transitory. Ephemera includes newspapers, magazines, cigar wrappers, fruit-crate labels, ticket stubs, matchbook covers, invitations, and pages from books nearly anything printed (Figs. 53A & 53B). Considering the unimportant nature of the items, it is amazing that vintage ephemera has survived and was not simply thrown away. In fact, ephemera has become a collecting specialty.

Eyelet A metal ring or gromet, or short metallic tube, the ends of which can be bent outward and over to fasten it in place, used to line an eyelet hole.

Eyelet Punch A machine for punching eyelet holes and fastening eyelets, as in paper or cloth Technique 9.

Fig. 53A: Ephemera

Technique 9: Setting Eyelets

1 To simplify the process, punch a hole in thicker papers prior to setting the eyelet.

2 Place the eyelet in the hole, face down onto a mat and place the setter onto the eyelet shank. Strike the eyelet setter with the hammer until the shank has rolled to a flattened surface.

Fig. 53B: Ephemera—Paper Coasters, Ticker Tape, and Broadway Bills

F

Fade Proof Color that does not fade or resists change when stored away from a direct light source or a variety of other environmental factors. Also called fade resistant.

Fading Partial or complete loss of color due to excessive heating or environmental influences. Common causes include intense sun and improper storage in a nonarchival environment.

Family Tree A chart, or group of photos aligned by date, that shows how members of the family are related to each other (Figs. 54A & 54B).

Fan Fold A paper fold that emulates an accordion or fan, the folds being alternating and parallel. (See also Accordion Folding).

Fiber A textile material that has a high length-to-diameter ratio, meaning the length is much greater than the diameter. Fiber adds dimension and personality to scrapbook papers (Figs. 55A–55C).

Fig. 54A: Preprinted Family Trees

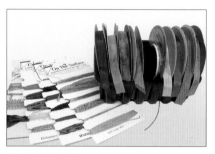

Fig. 55A: Fibers

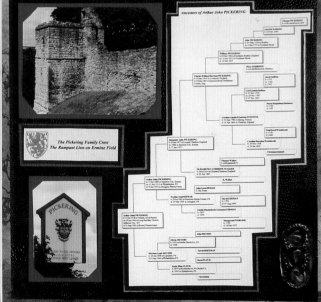

Fig. 54B: Family Tree—*Pickering Family Tree* The photos on these pages are laid out nicely alongside photos from the English town of Pickering. By showcasing the family, the town, and other genealogical background information, any member of the Pickering family can trace their lineage.

Fiber Usage Tip

The next time the perfect color of fiber is not available for a project, use chalks, inks, or paint to recolor the fiber to match the page exactly.

Fiber-based Print A photo printed on a photo paper that does not have a plastic coating. These papers were used predominantly before the 1960s and are typically found in heritage photo making or fine-art photography.

Field Guide Scrapbook A scrapbook featuring a complete record of an outdoor environment including photos, sketches, found objects, observed information, and research regarding flowers, plants, animals, insects, etc.

Fig. 55B: Fiber— *Tea Party* A whispy fiber was strung across the top of this page to hold on the floral appliqués.

Fig. 55C: Fiber— *Memories* A border made from different types of fibers adorns the left side of this page, and ribbons wrap around to the backs of the photos, making unique photo corners. Strategically placed stickers massed under the fibers add color, texture, and balance.

Film Terms

Daylight Film Color film intended for use with daylight or a light source of similar temperature. Daylight film is color-balanced to 5400K.

E6 Kodak's standard chemical process for developing Ektachrome or compatible slide films.

Film Speed The relative light sensitivity of film. When traveling, it is important to note that there are several rating systems: ISO is the most common in the US and Great Britain. DIN is the most common in Europe. Film can be fast (High ISO) or Slow (Low ISO).

Instant A film that contains chemicals needed to automatically develop an image after exposure without additional darkroom development.

Type A Color-balanced film that produces accurate color when the light source illuminating the scene has a color temperature of about 3400K, such as a photoflood light.

Type B (Tungsten) Color-balanced film that produces accurate color when the light source illuminating the scene has a color temperature of about 3200K.

Type C Color-balanced film used to make a positive transparency slide.

Film An emulsion–coated, chemically sensitized, flexible acetate or plastic sheet used in a camera (Fig. 56). When exposed to light and chemical processes, it records a printable image.

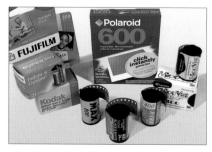

Fig. 56: Various 35mm and Instant Films

Film Processing and Developing

- An opened camera lens exposes the film to the incoming pattern of light that makes up the scene in front of the camera.

- The patterns of light hit the film and a chemical reaction begins.

- Once exposed to a large number of light photons, the silver halide begins to react chemically with imbedded dye couplers.

- Oxidized developer molecules combine with the color-forming couplers to create a silver image and the dye image.

- The reaction is stopped by chemically washing the silver image and any remaining unexposed silver halide, using a solution called BLIX.

- The processing chemicals and silver-halide grains are then carefully washed from the surface gelatin binder, using fresh water so that the colored image contains no residual silver.

- The print is dried.

- For instant-camera developing processes, the developing chemicals are already present in the film.

Film Facts

- Normal film consists of a plastic base coated with particles of silver halide.

- Black-and-white film has one layer of the silver compound. Color film has three layers.

- In color film, the top layer is sensitive to blue light, the next layer is sensitive to green, and the bottom layer is sensitive to red.

Findings   Components used in making jewelry (Fig. 57). This usually refers to the mechanical pieces.

Fig. 57: Findings Used for Scrapbooking Closures and Decorative Features

Finish   The condition of a paper surface. A high finish refers to a smooth hard surface. A low finish refers to a relatively rough, toothy surface.

Flash   A light source that emits a very brief intense burst of light necessary for creating sharp photographic imagery, usually indoors in areas not having enough natural light.

Flip Page   An acetate envelope that attaches to a scrapbook page and allows more photo space (Figs. 58A–58E). The flip addition may duplicate the size of the page, creating a true fold-out or a smaller window, adding a "surprise inside" effect for the viewer. Add flip pages by using any fastening device or tapes.

Fig. 58A: Flip Page—*Mothers, Daughters, Friends*   **Additional precious photos taken of this first birthday party are stored in flip pages to view separately.**

Fig. 58B: Ready-made Flip Pages

Fig. 58C & 58D: Flip Page—*Paris Metro*
A racy French subway advertisement is tucked into a flip page. Notice that the underside of the flip page keeps with the French tourist theme of the rest of the page.

114

Fig. 58E: Flip Page—*Colorado Memories*
Held in place with pretty fibers, this page has two
flips, one on the left and one on the right.

Fig. 59: Flowers—*Flowers, Flowers, Flowers*
Pressed fresh flowers were used on the background of this
page. Before adhering the pressed flowers onto the page, they
were sprayed with an acid reducer. Then flowers were sprayed
on both sides with a UV acrylic adhesive and adhered in place.

Flowers   Any floral accent or
flower used as an embellishment
on the scrapbook page (Fig. 59).
The use of flowers in scrapbooks
has always been a desirable accent
or piece of memorabilia. With
special precautions, most any type
of flower or leaf (dry, pressed, preserved, silk, or plastic) can be used
in a scrapbook album.

Flush   Typeset copy that is either
aligned on the right or on the left
(copy is thus either Flush Right
Justified or Flush Left Justified).

Focal Point   The main area
of visual interest in a photograph
or on a scrapbook page.

Safe Flower Usage Tips

- For plastics and other ques-
  tionable acid-producing
  flowers, use encapsulation
  envelopes and pockets.

- Use deacidfying sprays and
  flexible adhesive coatings
  for dried or pressed flowers and leaves. The sprays
  will give them the longest
  life possible, causing little
  or no damage to scrapbook
  pages.

- Use a nontacky, lightweight
  UV acrylic adhesive, on
  both sides of the pressed
  flowers before using the
  adhesive to paste it onto
  a page. This particular
  type of adhesive will prevent leaves and flowers
  from becoming brittle and
  provide a longer retention
  of color.

F

Focus   The singular position in which rays of light from a lens converge to form a sharp image.

Focusing   The system of moving the lens in relation to the image plane to obtain the required degree of sharpness of the film.

Foil   A metallic plastic-like material applied to album covers and paper, using a heat-set method, hot stamping, or with adhesives using pressure. Foil comes in rolls or sheets, a multitude of colors, and is made up of five layers (Figs. 60A–60C and Technique 10).

Foiling   The art of applying foil onto pages or album covers to form words, lines, patterns, borders, or to enhance imagery (Figs. 60A–60C and Technique 10).

Fig. 60B: Foil—*Halloween 1998*   The foiled Chinese characters and fan add an Asian feel to this themed page.

Fig. 60A: Foils and Foiling— Adhesives and Tapes, Including Diecuts

Foil Layers

Adhesive Coat Bonds the foil to the substrate being stamped.

Color Coat Transparent or translucent layer, carrying the color tint in the form of dyes or pigments.

Metal Coat Most often composed of aluminum, which provides the reflective qualities and opacity desired in metallic foils.

Polyester Film Carrier Used to protect the foil layers.

Release Coat Allows the other layers to release from the film carrier upon application of heat or pressure.

Technique 10: Foiling

1 Apply an adhesive or double-sided tape border to the surface to be foiled.

2 Paint or draw with embellishing adhesive, forming leaves, names, or other designs, either separately or alongside of the border.

3 Apply foil and burnish.

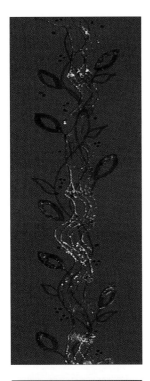

Fig. 60C: Foiling—_Summer Friends_   The border, titles, and dates on this page were foiled. The photos were slipped into paper photo corners to preserve any writing on the back side.

Font   The complete set of characters in a type style including the upper and lowercase letters, numerals, punctuation marks, points, reference marks, etc. (Figs. 61A & 61B).

Fig. 61A: Scrapbook Fonts

Font Terminology

Caps and Lowercase Using a capital letter to begin a word or sentence and lowercase for everything else.

Caps and Small Caps Two sizes of uppercase letters made in one style of type.

Condensed Type A narrow elongated typeface.

Descender The part of a lowercase letter (g, j, p, q, y) that goes below the line upon which the other letters rest.

Display Type Type on a page that is noticeably more prominent from the rest of the type, attracting the attention of the viewer.

Expanded Type Type with width greater than normal.

Italic Type denoting emphasis by slanting forward.

Sans Serif Lettering or typefaces without serifs.

Serif The small tabs on letters, as seen within the fonts Times Roman and Garamond.

Typeface Any full range of type in the same font.

Fig. 61B: Font—*You Are My Sunshine*   The title and journaling fonts chosen for this page are almost as bright and happy as the sunflowers. Yellow was the perfect color scheme for this page because it coordinates with the background pages. Printing the titles, journaling, and even words to a song onto vellum softens the yellow and adds a layer of smooth texture.

Found Object A mass-produced or natural object transformed into a work of art or used on a scrapbook page (Figs. 62A–62C).

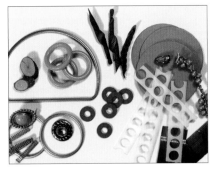

Fig. 62A: Found Objects

Fig. 62C: Found Object—*Don't Fence Me In* The found objects on this page are Western themed. Even the buttons from an old pair of blue jeans were used as embellishments.

Fig. 62B: Found Object—*Fall Guys* These broken sticks and twigs are found objects that look right at home with the hiking photo shown hanging from a twig. Use sharp scissors to cut the twigs and a strong wet adhesive to adhere the pieces onto the paper. The uncut jute strings add a nice natural touch.

Frame The wood, metal, paper, or plastic frame around photos and artwork. Frames for scrapbooks are clever, colorful, and often beautiful paper diecuts or stickers that literally frame the photo or artwork (Figs. 63A–63C).

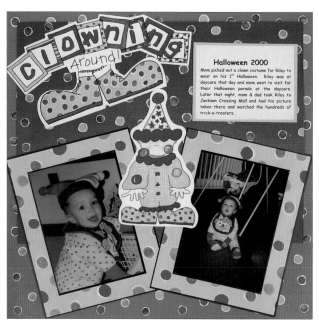

Fig. 63B: Frame—*Clowning Around* The coordinating primary-colored frames and background paper, along with titles and diecuts, were perfectly selected to match the photos and arranged using compostional techniques.

Fig. 63A: Scrapbook Frames

Fig. 63C: Frame—*Do You Know the Muffin Man?* To create the frames on these pages, the photos were mounted on brown cardstock. Punch holes and thread pipe cleaners through them to add dimension.

FTP (File Transfer Protocol)
A system that allows a user on one computer to transfer files to and from another computer.

Fugitive Inks
Colors that lose tone and permanency when exposed to light.

G

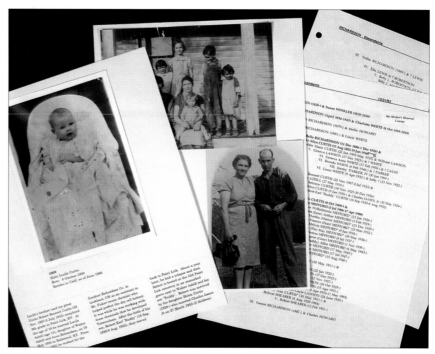

Fig. 64: Genealogy—*Mefford Genealogy*   This genealogist keeps track of the family's lineage and photos. Those pages are then photocopied and sent to all of the family members, each keeping their own scrapbook with second-generation images.

Genealogist   A person who collects and compiles information on the descendants of an individual or the history of a family.

Genealogy   1. The study of the history of a person or family from an ancestor (Fig. 64). 2. The enumeration of ancestors and their children in the natural order of succession; a pedigree.

Generation Imagery   A first generation image is the original; second generation is made from the original and third generation is made from the second generation. In scrapbooking, photocopies of an original photo are second-generation resolution. Clarity and definition are often lost in subsequent generations.

Gift Book   An album with scrapbook pages (Figs. 65A & 65B) and prepared in advance of an event, such as a wedding, shower, or birth, and given as a gift. The recipient fills the pages with photos taken during or after the event.

Fig. 65A: Gift Book—This gift album, made especially for the proud parents to be, makes a perfect shower gift.

Fig. 65B: Gift Album Pages

Gilding A technique that uses adhesives, soft brushes, and ultra-thin sheets or pieces of gilding material, often gold, silver, aluminum, brass, copper, or colored metals to produce a metallized surface (Figs. 66A & 66B and Technique 9).

Fig. 66A: Gilding *Live, Laugh, Love*— In this page, a highly textured sponge was used to apply gilding adhesive. When it turns clear and tacky, the gild is applied, giving the page a sparkling brilliance.

Scrap of History: Gilding

The art of gilding is of ancient origin and was lavishly employed in ancient Egypt, Greece, and Rome during the Renaissance. It has been used continuously in Asia and has seen resurgence in contemporary art due to new technology of adhesives and more user-friendly materials.

Technique 9: Gilding

1 Using gilding adhesive, coat the paper evenly and allow it to air-dry. Note: The adhesive is dry when it turns clear; it is then ready for the gild to adhere properly.

2 Apply the gilding leaf to the surface, covering every area.

3 Gently brush off the excess gilding material, saving every piece for another project.

4 Use the gilded piece as is. If a variegated leaf is used, try overstamping to create an allusion of the image.

Fig. 66B: Gilding—*Autumn Fun* The gilded leaves add beautiful autumnal color, as well as texture to the background paper.

Fig. 67A: Glitter—*Fireworks* Great background papers, diecuts, and lots of glitter add up to great scrapbook pages. The torn-frame edging on some of the photos also adds to the moderately "explosive" feeling of the photos, all in keeping with the theme.

Glassine A translucent paper made into a sleeve or envelope for the storage of photographic negatives. This material is harmful to photographic materials and is not recommended for use by the ISO.

Glitter A colored metallic-plastic material chopped into various-sized particles for use in art or craft projects (Figs. 67A & 67B). Glitter should be adhered using pressure-sensitive tapes and sheets, or by using a gloss adhesive. After applying glitter, place a clean sheet of paper over the surface and brayer it well to firmly adhere the particulates to the surface. Tap the paper from behind to remove the excess glitter.

Grain The predominant alignment of fibers that correspond to the direction in which paper flows on the wire screen during the paper manufacturing process.

Gum Arabic 1. A water-soluble gum obtained from the acacia tree and used in coatings of a number of photographic processes. 2. An acid-free powder or liquid binder used to make watercolors.

Fig. 67B: Glitter, crushed glass bits, Mylar opalescent chips and mica flakes are all different-looking products that produce glittering highlights for scrapbookers.

H

Handmade Paper   Paper that has been formed from pulp using a hand-held mold, matrix, or other device. Handmade papers add a warmth and natural quality to scrapbook pages (Figs. 68A–68C). (See also Paper.)

Fig. 68A: Handmade Papers

Fig. 68B: Handmade Paper—*I Don't Know About This, Uncle Terry*   Handmade papers give this photo interest and texture.

Fig. 68C: Handmade Paper—*My First Boat Ride* The natural colors of the handmade background papers nicely contrast the bright blue waters in the photos. Handmade papers transform machine-made papers, offering multiple textures and an added warmth, even when the colors come from the family of cooler tones.

Hardware Pieces of metal that add texture, whimsy, high style, or vintage charm to a scrapbook page (Figs. 69A–69G). Find hardware in the plumbing and electrical aisles of hardware stores, picture framing departments, bookstores, or a box in the basement. (See also Paper Fasteners.)

Fig. 69A: Miscellaneous Hardware

Fig. 69B: Metal Frames

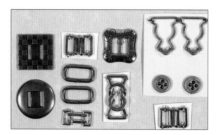

Fig. 69C: Buckles

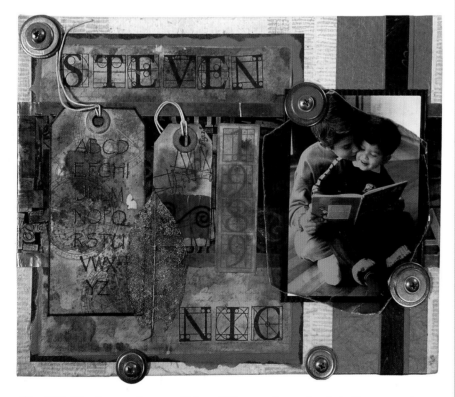

Fig. 69D: Hardware—*Steven and Nic* This complex and artistically arranged page incorporates hardware, found objects, inks, and papers. Notice the circular repetition used, providing a continuity of design.

Hardware Types

Buckle (Ribbon Slides) An open metal shape with a bar in the middle (Fig. 69C). The bar is used to hold paper strips, ribbon, or cord as they slide up, over, and through the buckle. Buckles are usually glued onto pages.

Corner A dimensional, decorative, metal corner piece used to embellish photos and artwork. Generally, an adhesive is used to attach this to a page (Figs. 69E & 69F).

Frame A flat yet dimensional, decorative, metal frame shape (Fig. 69B), used as one would use a standard picture frame. As with corners, these require attachment using adhesive, wire, or sewing methods.

Word Plate A small metal plate containing words and phrases in brass, nickel, antique brass, and copper. Plates are attached with adhesive and eyelet methods (Fig. 69G).

Hardware Usage Tip

Make certain that the metal item used will not corrode or rust. Clean any metal object thoroughly prior to attaching it to a page.

Fig. 69E: Corners

Fig. 69F: Hardware—*Elizabeth* Hardware such as charms, corners, buttons, and other embellishments can really add sparkle. The bold flowers embellished with buttons and charms anchor the page and repeat the flowers in Lizzy's jumper.

Fig. 69G: Hardware—*By the Seashore* Metal plates emphasize the story told on the pages shown here, as well as letters and photo corners.

127

Hardware Designer: Bridgette Server

She'll admit it—she saves everything! From the pink arm cast she wore in fifth grade to her first retainer, to a copy of her first paycheck, Bridgette Server has preserved milestones not just in writing, but in their physical form as well. It's a trait she picked up from her parents and one that fits perfectly with her passion for scrapbooking. "As a child, I was an avid journal keeper," Bridgette says, reflecting on how she got her scrapbooking start. "So I just started adding more dimension to my journaling. It became a living document."

While she was earning a degree in advertising and marketing at Brigham Young University, Bridgette did not consider scrapbooking as a vocation. Instead, when she graduated in 1992, she began working in the marketing field. But "I kept thinking how much I loved genealogy and memorializing family," she says. "I knew that I could do this all day, if I could just turn it into a job." Once she came to that conclusion, it didn't take her long to become an authority on scrapbooking, consulting with some of the most respected figures in the industry.

Bridgette opened her first scrapbooking store in Bountiful, Utah, in 1997. When she discovered how challenging it was to find a variety of quality products at a price that was not laughable, she began teaching herself everything she could about product sourcing, and she learned that many of the businesses from which she purchased goods for her store were secondary or side businesses. Seeing an opportunity to produce the goods other stores needed, she started her own innovative wholesale scrapbooking company, fittingly christened Making Memories.

Because she had run a retail storefront herself, Bridgette fully understood the needs of scrapbooking stores; Making Memories became a success with her at the helm. Today, the company is firmly established in the wholesale industry and Bridgette is still actively involved as vice president of creative development, continuing to identify and create new product innovations as she drives the company's creative vision.

Beautiful Butterfly

Birthday Girl

Daddy's Girl

Precious Angel

Heading   The caption or title that explains the theme of a layout.

Heat Tool   A tool (Fig. 70) designed to heat thermal embossing powder to a temperature where it becomes liquid and smooth. Temperatures range from 140°F–1000°F, with thermal embossing powders melting at approximately 140°F–180°F (60°C–82°C).

Fig. 70: Heat Tools and Holster

Heritage   All the tangible and intangible materials (Figs. 71A–71D), as well as the traditions, passed from generation to generation.

Heritage Photos   Tintypes, daguerreotypes, and vintage sepia-toned photos, printed on heavy stock that are typically irreplaceable. Negatives are even

Heritage Album Usage Tips

- Avoid gluing photos onto the scrapbook page. Use photo corners or encapsulation techniques.

- While it might make design layout more complex, old photos should not be cut. If a negative is available, have extra prints made, or photocopy the original.

- When information about a photo is available, it is often on the back. Photocopy and use this information on the page as journaling.

- Vintage-appearing scrapbook papers, captions, and embellishments are widely available to complement heirloom photos and memorabilia.

- Tea-staining, chalking, and sepia or walnut inks add character and age to papers, stickers, and titles. In addition, the process of producing such papers is satisfying, adding a personal creative touch to a heritage album.

Fig. 71A: Heritage— *Sunday Stroll* **The sepia-toned background papers used behind these photos add to the antique look of this page.**

harder to come by. When they are available, heritage layouts preserve a family's history, bringing life to past generations.

Fig. 71B: Heritage Ephemera and Technique Books

Fig. 71C: Heritage—*Auto Repair* The front and back of the photo on this page was photocopied so that viewers can read the original handwritten note.

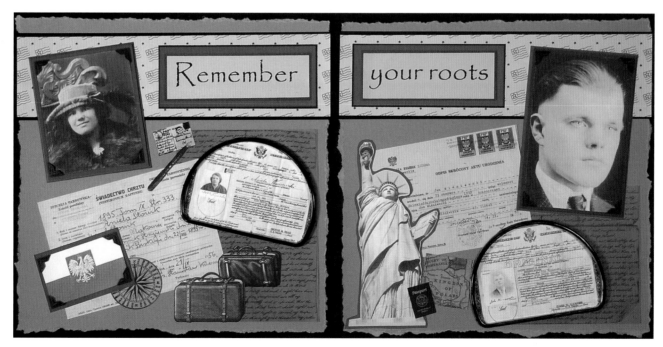

Fig. 71D: Heritage—*Remember Your Roots* Heritage pieces used on these pages include photocopies of immigration papers and visas. Found objects and travel-themed stickers add a modern touch with a distinctive vintage look.

Hobby Scrapbooking

A scrapbook featuring a complete record of a particular hobby, including photos, sketches, found objects, documentation, observed information, and research regarding the hobby or person involved in the hobby.

Hole Punch

A mechanical device (Figs. 72A & 72B) that makes a hole in paper, cardboard, and other materials. Unlike decorative punches, hole punches are used extensively in scrapbooking. It is far easier, and certainly neater looking, to insert a brad through a small hole than tearing it through the paper.

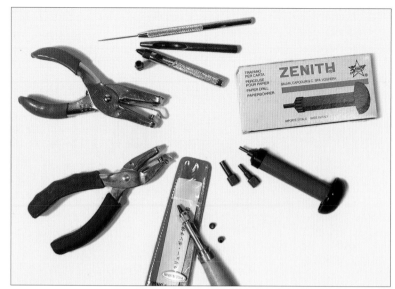

Fig. 72A: Hole Punches

Hole Punch Tip

While there is no perfect hole punch, it is useful to have one that reaches to the inside parts of a page, as well as a standard office-style hole punch.

Fig. 72B: Hole Punch—*Barbara and Merle*   **Hole punches were used here to decorate the photo corners and to create the heart flourishes at the top and bottom of the page.**

Incire   The paper-crafting technique of using a template to cut small V or C shapes into duplex, or duo-colored, paper. The cut shapes are then folded up or down, and are burished with a bone folder to create a unique pattern with alternating colors (Fig. 73). (See also Paper Craft Technique.)

Fig. 73: Incire—*First Christmas*   **Incire makes an effective and decorative frame for most photographs and with a change of paper, the colors used will fit any theme or holiday. In red, green, and white, a colorful Christmas pattern frames this sweet** *First Christmas* **portrait.**

Inert   A material that is stable and does not react with itself, the environment, or any other materials surrounding it; something that is not chemically active.

Ink   A fluid, semifluid, gel, or paste material containing a colorant used in pens, brushes, and pads for drawing, writing, stamping, and printing (Figs. 74A–74D and Technique 10). Each type of ink has its own purpose, composition, and individual physical properties. All inks chosen for an album, whether for decorating or journaling, should be acid-free, fade-proof, and waterproof pigment inks. Use specially designed inks for fabric, wood, papier-mâché, foam, leather, and a variety of other surfaces.

Fig. 74A: Permanent, Pigment, and Dye-based Fluid Inks and Stamp Pads

Fig. 74B: Ink—*Flowers*   **Stamped and colored with dye-based inks, these "Posh" flowers were made on label paper. Once cut out, then adhered to a patterned background paper, they not only form the frame for the portrait, but also hold it in place on the page.**

Ink Types

Dye-based Ink Water- or solvent-based transparent ink that dries quickly on most matte and glossy papers. Solvent inks are usually permanent. Dye inks may fade more easily than pigmented inks, but they also produce brilliantly colored results.

Hybrid Inks Innovative technology has brought a variety of hybrid inks to the scrapbooking market. From fast-drying solvent-based inks, waterproof and not, to gels that glisten and glitter, this area of technology literally is changing by the month. Whether in marker, pen, or pad, look for the highest standard of ink: one that is permanent, acid-free, and has UV protectants.

Hybrid Inkjet Printer Ink Dye-based ink is used with most inkjet printers. They have limited lightfastness. The relatively recent introduction of hybrid dye/pigment-based inks specially formulated for desktop printers has increased the lightfastness dramatically. They have an extremely high degree of UV resistance and are highly water resistant. When used on acid-free papers and stored properly, the estimated archival life of these inks is 200 years for lightfast color prints.

Pigmented Ink Oil-based, generally acid-free, and fade-resistant, pigmented inks are opaque as well as thick, slower drying, and typically color rich. Once dry or embossed, they are permanent and can be safely rewet for watercoloring techniques.

Fig. 74C: Ink—
Katie and Kelly
Solvent-based inks colorfully blend together on glossy cardstock. Free-formed hand-cut daisies act as photo corners with eyelet centers. Stamped with pearlescent inks, the overall daisy pattern balances the composition while keeping with the overall theme.

Technique 10: Inking - Surface Design

1a Stamp a large, relatively open pattern on heavy cardstock. When cut, this will be your stencil.

1b Using a spreader, palette knife, or credit card, spread heavy artist's cement through cutout onto waxed paper.

1c Make several images, taking care not to bump into one that is wet.

2 While still wet, dribble on various colors of dye-based alcohol inks, allowing the colors to bleed and blend together.

3 When the leaves have thoroughly dried, gently lift them off the waxed paper.

4 Overstamping creates even more texture. Use foam to apply acrylic paint to the original stamp.

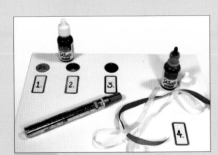

5 Highlight clay-stamped letters with ink and gilding pens. Age or color ribbon with coordinating inks.

Fig. 74D: Ink—*Home* This richly textured scrapbook page incorporates dye-based alcohol inks into the paste-paper background.

Inspirational Scrapbooking: Julia Davenport

"Being inspired to create isn't hard," Julie Davenport says. "It's the getting inspired while thirty other things are going on." The art department is the hub of USArtQuest and everything that happens at the company happens there first. With sales meetings, photo shoots, and booths being built, it's imperative for Julie to stay focused and seize creative opportunities whenever she can. "My scrapbook of ideas and inspiration is continually being built," she explains. "If I see an idea in a magazine, I clip it. When I have a minute or two, I'll try using that idea, interpreting and pushing it to extreme limits, using whatever is at hand. I try to keep good notes on what works and doesn't work. Then I mount it in my scrapbook. When needed, I can go to the book and determine if one of those techniques—maybe something from a year or more ago—will translate into the artwork needed for a project."

Creativity is in Julie's blood. "Both of my grandmas were very creative," she says. "I can remember doing arts-and-crafts projects with them from a very young age. I guess my love of art began there." Like most creative children, Julie took every art class she could in school, then ("with thanks to my parents")

Julia Davenport's Inspirational Pages

attended Siena Heights College in Michigan to pursue art further. In 1998, with her B.A. in art and graphic design, she began working at USArtQuest just two months after graduation.

Working here has opened a whole different creative arena for me," Julie says. "Often Susan [Pickering Rothamel] will come to me with some vague idea for a project using a papier-mâché box, a piece of furniture or fabric, or even a piece of paper she found interesting. She'll say, 'I see something pink'—or blue or purple—'maybe with lots of texture and lots of energy and oh, by the way, we need it for an article due tomorrow.' That's all

the information I'll have to work with. It's my job to translate that into a project that's interesting for the consumer and will sell the project or idea that was originally in her head. Thankfully, we work well as a team. Sometimes I'll be working on a project and Susan will walk by and throw in two cents more of ideas. Suddenly the artwork takes a whole new twist, becoming something entirely different and a lot more exciting. Creating artwork here is always an adventure."

For Julie, organization is essential when creating art on demand. "Besides inspiration scrapbooks, I keep bins of incomplete parts, scrap, and used projects using

various products," she says. "These I work into my scrapbook as soon as I have a spare moment, because I never know when they'll be useful. I don't have much time for experimentation during a regular business day, but I have to say my favorite times are when the shop is quiet. Maybe the staff and Susan will be at a convention and I'll find a few days to work on new ideas of my own. I believe that on those days, I produce some of my best artwork."

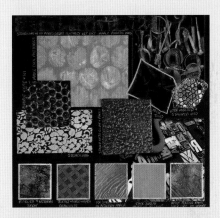

If It's Red, It's Right

These pages showcase different types of texture using various art materials, stencils, plastic wrap, and painting techniques.

Iris Folding The art of folding, then layering paper to form patterns resembling the iris of the human eye (Figs. 75A–75C). Iris-folded frames are easy and make unique patterning for scrapbook pages. Try using any paper, from a sophisticated solid to these colorful checker-patterned papers. Iris-folded frames are great for photos and easy to make.

Technique 11: Iris Folding

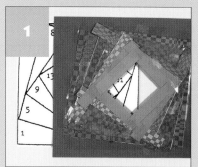 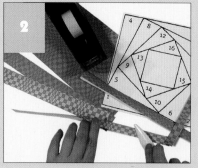

Cut strips of paper approximately 1¼" wide and fold them in half, smoothing them with a bone folder.

Lay them out onto the pattern, taping each piece firmly in place using acid-free tape on the back side.

Fig. 75A: Iris—Folding Books, Papers, and Tools

Figs. 75B & 75C: Iris Folding—_Laurel_ and _Julia_ The iris-folded papers on these pages coordinate with the background papers and serve as a good frame for the photographs.

ISO (International Organization Standardization) An organization that develops manufacturing and performance standards for many industries, including photography, photo albums, and other enclosures. ISO requires that material for photographic enclosures be acid-free, lignin-free, buffered, and bleed-resistant.

J

Journaling The written remembrances of special memories and events in one's life. (Figs. 76A–76H)

Fig. 76A: Ready-made Journals

Figs. 76B–76E: Journaling— *A Year in Review* Capturing a year in pictures, including lists of top movies, songs, and news is a novel way to scrapbook. These special pages will surely come in handy in a future game of Trivial Pursuit.

How to Journal

Journaling is more than just captions and titles or names of people under a photo. Real journaling provides future generations with a more complete story than with just the photographs of a person or event. Like the word journalism implies, it is the who, what, when, where, why, and how that goes along with the photograph, obtaining information derived from the photograph, memorabilia, or from personal experience. In fact, an album without journaling may be charming and even fun to look at now, but it will lose much of its meaning when the families who inherit the albums do not even know the names of the people, much less the places and events they represent.

Journaling may be biographical in nature or simple story-telling. It can also be nothing more than a fleeting memory. But, the best albums include good journaling and the very best are those that include comprehensive ancestral information.

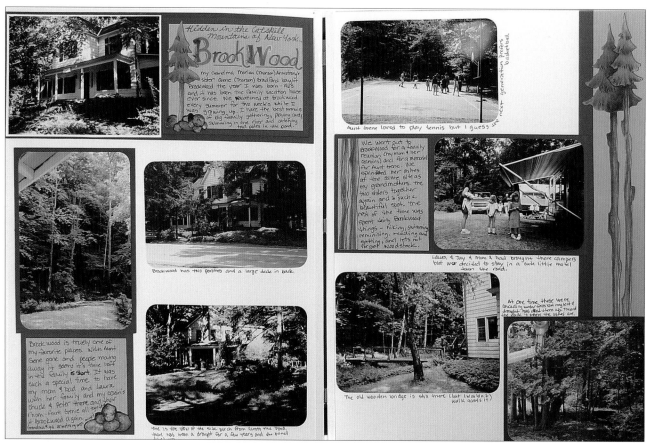

Figs. 76F: Journaling—*Brookwood*   These pages show us basic scrapbook journaling at its best. Telling the story is often as important as the photos. The towering border of trees elongates the oversized scrapbook pages and is nicely repeated onto the journaled squares and the title area.

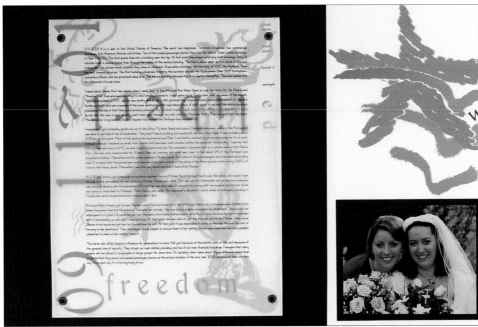

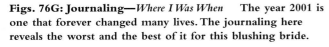

Figs. 76G: Journaling—*Where I Was When* The year 2001 is one that forever changed many lives. The journaling here reveals the worst and the best of it for this blushing bride. No reporter can tell a story better than someone who was actually there and then completely journaled the events.

Journaling: Writing a Family or Personal History Tips

- Tell a story plainly.

- Write truthfully.

- Include the "everyday" events and comments.

- When writing about yourself, include: schools attended and memories of each grade, the teachers, events, activities, friends, achievements, awards, and remembrances of yearly promotions and graduations.

- Include interesting items about dating, first impressions, wedding, marriage (especially how the question was popped), wedding parties, showers, receptions, gifts, honeymoon, and the first meeting of the in-laws.

- Include any hobbies, sports played, travels, summer activities, vacations, and first jobs.

- Include news clippings, popular social customs or words, songs, movies, and events of the time. Remember, journaling these things brings a "groovy" and "totally awesome" experience to scrapbooking.

- Write about the living family and impressions of those you know personally.

- Write about those you did not know through stories and tidbits gleaned from other family members.

- Include items of interest or remembrance about siblings, such as their names, dates, places of birth, accomplishments, occupations, spouse, and children.

- Include family traditions and activities, recipes, and ideas that represent the family values.

Journaling Tips

- Use only photo-safe pens either in black or in colors that coordinate with the album page or photo. According to Daniel Burge, a research scientist at the Image Permanence Institute, the best option for journaling is still a pen containing a resin-coated pigment ink, these are the most stable and last longer than both dye inks and inkjet printer inks. When purchasing pens, it is important that they are pigment-based ink and waterproof.

- Use lined templates, drawing light pencil lines to keep the journaling straight and neat. Legibility is important. Later, erase the lines with a white eraser.

- Journaling need not be in paragraph form.

- Create a border around a photo or group of photos, using words or poems.

- Write in shapes created by templates, die-cuts, laser cuts, or freehand drawings.

- Journal on the computer using interesting fonts, then print it on acid-free paper. Journal on lined paper and mount it onto paper alongside the photos.

- It may sound obvious, but when journaling, make sure to write the subject's full name, even a child, husband, or mother. Future generations viewing the album may not know if the person labeled is your friend, cousin, or a spouse, if the full name is not included.

Journaling Helper A template with space left for writing.

Justify To align lines of type with both left and right margins flush.

Fig. 76H: Journaling—
Snuggle's Vacation Nightmare
The tragic (and humorous) saga of Snuggles the Bear is recounted in digitized journaling, printed onto vellum, then layered over the background, keeping the focus on the terrain yet still integrating the journaling. The photograph shows Snuggles at first, safely perched on the rock. Then suddenly he tossed headlong into the river! The expert use of paper-cutting techniques to imaginatively demonstrate his sudden drenching mishap is not only creative but effective storytelling.

L

Lamination Covering paper with thin, translucent plastic (Fig. 77). Many forms of lamination are considered unacceptable as conservation methods because of the high heat and pressure used during application, or because of the irreversibility of the lamination to the materials being covered.

Fig. 77: Laminating Machines

Laser Cut A decorative paper accent resembling a diecut (Fig. 78A), but generally far more detailed. Laser cut shapes are made using a laser beam to cut the paper, leaving a silhouette of the design (Figs. 78B & 78C).

Fig. 78A: Lasercut Paper Embellishments

Fig. 78B: Laser Cut—*Bruges* A laser-cut border embellishes this page, which is chock-full of terrific imagery and journaling. Overlapping the elements works nicely, unifying the eclectic, well-balanced, yet asymmetrical composition.

Laser Printer A computer printer that uses a laser light to draw an image onto a photosensitive drum, which electrostatically picks up powdered ink and transfers it onto paper, where it is baked hard. Some laser printers print in color, while most only produce black print. A color laser printer produces an excellent digital photo image offering a wide range of resolutions from 300–1200 dpi.

Fig. 78C: Laser Cut—*Daddy's Girls* Laser-cut leaves decorate the border on this page. The leaves add texture and movement and appear to be growing off the fiber vine. Small glass tiles contribute yet another texture as well as adding to the overall color scheme.

Layering 1. Achieving dimension through the use of dimensional tapes or pleated spacers, causing slight shadows, enhancing the uppermost layer or layers. 2. Achieving dimension by layering multiple like items, such as stickers, diecuts, and punched paper shapes (Fig. 79).

Fig. 79: Layering—*Rose Garden* The beautiful border of this two-page spread is made of hand-torn and layered vellums and scrapbook papers, overlaid with a sticker rose border, repeating the overall floral theme of the page. Notice the generous use of embellishments and the balancing of the textural elements, as well as how the shapes help to keep the eye moving over both pages. After enjoying the overall design of both pages, it is then more interesting to stop awhile to peruse each photograph.

Layout A sketch indicating the arrangement of text, headlines, and graphic elements including the location of the geometric patterns, illustrations, photographs, and memorabilia (Figs. 80A–80C). Some scrapbooking layouts fit on a single page, while others are designed to fit two or more pages.

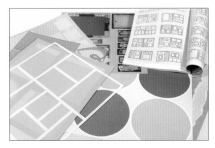

Fig. 80A: Layout Templates

Layout Usage Tips

- Incorporate both large and small objects in a picture to create harmony, movement, and texture.

- The number of photos that fit on a page depend not only on the album page size but also on cropping and overlapping. Over lapping is an acceptable practice as long as nothing of reference is covered.

- Silhouette photos by cutting close to the subject and removing most of the background. This is especially effective with enlargements.

- Use diecut shapes such as hearts or flowers as a charming way to showcase a person's face, pet, or topic.

- For a more casual page, angle one or more photos.

- For large albums, consider making a creative table of contents.

- Crowded photos cause confusion, and usually mean a lack of focal point. Instead, consider putting a single large portrait on one page with the corresponding page showcasing several related photos.

Fig. 80B: Layout—*Riding the Gondola* Templates make quick work for scrapbookers, providing ready-made "holes" to drop in photos, scraps of color, and captions.

Fig. 80C: Layout—*Signs of Spring* Using a template means that one only need crop a photo to fit a particular space, then add journaling, titles, and small embellishments—or not!

Layout Artist: Becky Higgins

Becky Higgins discovered her passion for scrapbooking a decade ago while visiting her family in Utah. Today, after publishing hundreds of layouts and traveling thousands of miles to teach her techniques, she is known as one of North America's premiere scrapbookers. "The hobby encompasses many of my other interests, such as photography and family history, while providing a creative outlet," she says.

In 1996, to share her newfound interest, Becky began teaching scrapbooking and creative lettering classes in local specialty stores; a year later, she started her own scrapbook magazine, Creating Keepsakes. As creative editor, she writes feature articles on topics ranging from techniques for spicing up page layouts to tips on creating themed albums. She also travels to events around the country, sharing her scrapbooking concepts and techniques, and

appears frequently on television to promote America's fastest-growing hobby. In her scrapbook designs, she offers ideas for various page elements, then leaves the details—colors, materials, placement—up to the scrapbooker. She recommends keeping ideas simple so that "with a change of cardstock color or punch design, you can develop an accent, border, or photo mat that will suit your style and requirements."

In addition to her fresh scrapbooking style, Becky is well known for her handmade greeting cards. "Most anyone can make a card," she says, with a few simple guidelines. "No matter what the season or reason for sending a handmade greeting, let it be an expression of you. Remember to send cards just because, and not only on expected occasions. Unexpected surprises often end up in recipients' hands at the moment

they need encouragement. Let loved ones know you're thinking about them, that you care about them, and that they have blessed your life."

A few years ago, Becky came across a quote that had a profound effect on how she looks at scrapbooking: You are the link that ties the past and the future together. Think of how important your role is in giving continuity to your family's traditions and stories. Are you a strong link or a weak one? Becky challenges herself with that question in her own work, and she invites you to do the same.

Creative Sketches and Creating Keepsakes

Johnson Farm Home

Taking cues from her own layouts, Becky's pages are beautifully composed and photographically perfect. Her emphasis on journaling provides memories for many generations.

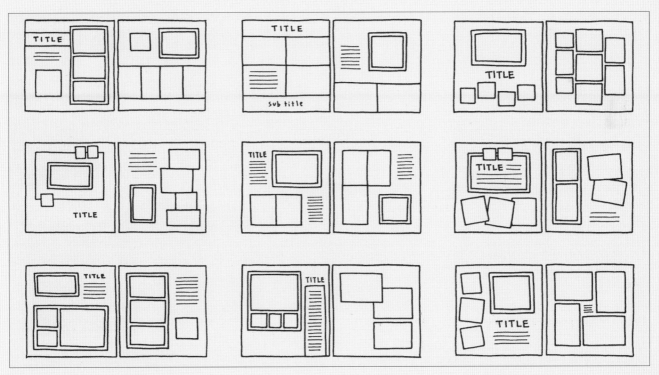

Becky Higgins's Layout Templates

Legacy Album An album that focuses on one's heritage. Its presentation focuses on the preservation of ancestral documents, history, memories, stories, and events. Legacy albums may also include peripheral information that place ancestors on a historical time line. Information on the time line might include facts found during research that include people living or events taking place at that time.

Legacy Album Design Tips

- Use a permanent binding system to help ensure the album's survival from one generation to the next.

- Avoid tapes and adhesives. Use photo sleeves or mounting corners instead.

- Preserve not only the photo but valuable data that may be on the back.

- Use only museum-quality materials for legacy album making.

Fig. 81A: Lettering—*Sam* Creative lettering on this page, the title was spelled out using hot glue. The seal in the corner adds balance to the weight of the title without taking any attention away from the close-up photo of Sam.

Fig. 81B: Lettering—*Bill Knows Soccer* The clever use of "Bill" as the "i" in the title, along with the various fonts and strong journaling, gives this well-balanced colorful page a delightful composition and appealing titling.

Lettering An art form accomplished with any writing implement including crayons, markers, pens, and pencils of any kind (Figs. 81A–81G). Creative lettering for scrapbooking can also include an abundance of ready-to-use fonts, stick-on, rub-on, and cut-out letters, or even fully printed word titles and captions.

Fig. 81C: Lettering Books and Stickers

Lettering Design Tips

Handwritten creative lettering can enhance a scrapbook page and even become the focal point. Alas, some also find it the easiest way to ruin a completed, almost perfect page. Here are a few tips that will make creative lettering easier for the brave of heart:

Fig. 81D: Lettering Guide Stamp

- Straight lines look neater. Keep the lines straight, whether vertical, horizontal, or diagonal.

- Use a ruler to lightly pencil in a top and bottom line. Every uppercase letter should touch both the top and bottom line. When using lowercase lettering, draw a third line in the middle or slightly above the middle. Lowercase letters should touch the middle and bottom lines.

- Pick up the pen between strokes, starting at the top of the letter each time, and pull downward. After each separate line in the letter, pick the pen up and move it into position for the next stroke. For instance, an M or W will take four downward strokes.

- Make the lettering motion come from the shoulder, moving the whole arm, rather than the fingers and wrist. Practice makes perfect.

- To see how a title or sentence will fit, first sketch the letter onto scrap paper, cut it out, then lay it on the page. Check the spacing as well as the size of type.

Fig. 81E: Lettering—*Tigers* This four-page foldout was a unique way to use lots of photos and creative lettering for a fun and memorable page. Scorecards added to the final page remind this family of how this day at the ballpark ended.

Fig. 81F: Lettering— *Hayes—Eighth Wonder of the World* The creative lettering shown here as the page title combines multiple mediums, from diecuts to metal lettering to stickers. The word spacing helps in keeping the reader's eye focus on each element of the title, skillfully laid onto the dark border of the background paper.

Fig. 81G: Lettering— *Jeffrey* Pages need not be complexly designed to be interesting. These bold letters cut from templates add texture, interest, and balance.

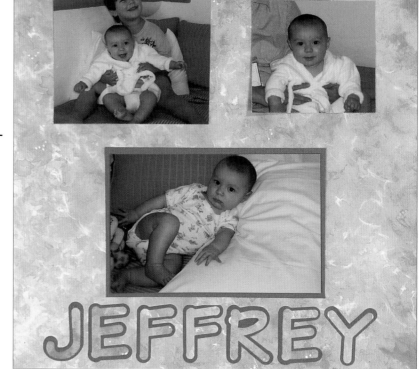

Light Stability A material's ability to resist change when exposed to light. Materials that are not light stable can become brittle, discolored, and react adversely with adjacent materials, such as adhering to each other, becoming sticky, stretchy, pliable, or bleed through and stain another element.

Scrap of History: Illuminated Lettering

Historically, the adornment of books and manuscripts, complete with colored illustrations, decorated text, an embellished page, or just the beginning letter, was left to only the most talented artisans, usually monks working on precious parchment.

Now, through the magic of computers, scrapbookers can add this type of creative lettering to their journaled pages, captions, or titles by downloading fonts resembling illuminated lettering. Mixing the illuminated first letter with a standard typeface will produce the look of medieval parchments. Print them onto real parchment or vellum for an authentic look.

Fig. 82: Lightbox

Lightbox A tabletop box-like device (Fig. 82) equipped to allow an artificial light source to radiate through a glass or plastic top, then through paper. It is also used for tracing, dry embossing, and other paper-craft techniques. It is used for viewing, registering, or correcting film negatives and positives.

Lightfast A colored material that resists fading caused by natural and artificial lighting.

Lignin The naturally occurring binding material found in the cell walls of plants giving them their strength and rigidity. Paper containing lignin, such as newsprint, will turn yellow and brittle fairly quickly when exposed to light, heat, and humidity. Lignin degrades paper, causing discoloration and brittleness. Paper is considered lignin-free when it contains a maximum of one percent lignin. Despite the trend to label any scrapbooking material lignin-free, only paper products can contain lignin.

Lumpy Scrapbooking or Assemblage A form of scrapbooking using three dimensional items, which make a scrapbook page texturally dimensional and the entire album very thick (Fig. 83). (See also Spacer.)

Fig. 83: Post-bound Lumpy Scrapbook with Spacers

L

Magazines A good place to find examples of scrapbook layouts. Some magazines focus on simple scrapbooking, others on high-style and "artsy" styles.

Manipulate or Photo Manipulation To mechanically move the emulsion surface of a Polaroid photo, prior to complete hardening, using a pointed device to influence or control the likeness.

Marbling or Marbleizing 1. Decorating paper (Figs. 84A & 84B) to simulate the grain and appearance of polished marble. 2. A faux-finishing technique.

Fig. 84A: Marbling—*Motorman* Detail

Marker A pen-like instrument (Fig. 85) with a felt point, housing watercolor or inks in a felt-like bladder, which dispenses through capillary action and gravity.

Fig. 85: Various Water, Dye, and Permanent Markers

Mask Covering stamped images, drawings, or album pages to protect them from subsequent applications of color.

Fig. 84B: Marbling—*Motorman* The faux-marbled photo frames and background bring attention to the motorman's photo and artifacts, and add a classic touch to these vintage photos. Marbled paper, whether handmade or machine made, typically adds a touch of sophisticated design to scrapbook pages. This is because, traditionally, marbled papers have been used to mat botanical watercolors, drawings, and photographs.

Marker Types

Artist's A large felt-tipped marker with a chisel shape at one end and a point at the other. The difference between these markers and others is the ink, which is usually solvent-based and has a distinct odor. These come in a large color range.

Brush Point A marker with a flexible paintbrush-style tip, brush markers are suitable for coloring in images and come in a multitude of colors.

Chisel Point A versatile marker with both broad and narrow edges producing a distinctive decorative style of lettering and design.

Dual-tipped Brush A double-ended single-color marker, usually with a different sized tip on each end.

Monoline An all-purpose detail marker. The size of the tip is usually specified in millimeters ranging from very fine to thick. The tapered nibs create smooth lines for lettering techniques, borders, line art, and illustrations.

Scroll Point A notched-tip marker that produces a double line with a single stroke. Use it for calligraphic lettering and straight, double-lined borders.

Mat Board A semirigid board with or without a buffered acid-free core and backing paper (Figs. 86A & 86B). Those with an acid-free decorative paper surface and buffered core are suitable for framing most photography. For vintage photos and fine art, it is preferable to use those mats that are considered acid-free throughout.

Fig. 86A: Mat Boards

M

Fig. 86B: Mat Board—*Making Fun* Corrugated premade mat board was matched with corrugated papers for these scrapbook pages. It adds plenty of texture and character.

Corrugated boards and papers can also be handmade using a handheld corrugator.

Matte A dull finish on coated paper, or any medium applied to dull the finish.

Mechanical Element A handmade, die-cut, or preassembled moving element that adds a decorative component, versatility, and function to a scrapbook page (Figs. 87A–87C).

Fig. 87A: Mechanical Element—*Ardvreck Castle* **with a Closed Foldout**

Figs. 87B & 87C: Mechanical Element—*Ardvreck Castle*
This simple form of mechanical element usage is a foldout, carefully cut to resemble a castle. To protect the elements from use, everything on the page was laminated, or contained within a protective sleeve. Altering protective sleeves only requires a craft knife and a bit of ingenuity.

Mechanical: Protecting Mechanical Elements

- Laminate all pieces before assembling a scrapbook page with mechanical elements to protect them from dust, fingerprints, and use.

- Slide the entire finished page into a page protector.

- With a gel pen or permanent marker, make dots on the surface of the page protector, just around the edges of the moving part.

- Remove the finished page from the page protector.

- Slide a cutting mat into the page protector.

- Using a metal ruler and craft knife, cut between the dots, removing the desired area.

- This method will protect the mechanical element with lamination and the rest of the page will be protected by the standard page protector.

Memento An item of remembrance passed on through a family.

Memorabilia A collection of remembrances, such as fabric scraps, handkerchiefs, pressed corsages, signed photos, tour programs, tickets, T-shirts, historical information, or personal items reminding the user of a special event (Figs. 88A–88E). Incorporating memorabilia into scrapbooks gives them a safer haven than keeping them in an old cigar box and creates a unique visual experience for the viewer.

Fig. 88A: Military Memorabilia

Fig. 88B: Military Memorabilia

Figs. 88C: Memorabilia—
D. H. R. Containing mostly authentic memorabilia, a diecut Marine Corps. emblem and an extra dog tag, combine to balance this composition. Overlapping the cards keeps this double-page spread from becoming too busy. This is a good example of the one-third compositional rule (see Composition Tips) with both a strong vertical and strong horizontal movement.

Figs. 88D: Memorabilia—*Great Lakes Naval Training Station*
This oversized album double-page spread also uses horizontal and vertical compositional guidelines. The large portrait, title, and doc-ument also make use of the 1\3\5 rule, as does the three post-cards. It is hard to go wrong using one-third page compositions, for they work well with a 12"x12" page, or a 12"x15" page.

Fig. 88B: Memorabilia—*Summertime Memories*
Memorabilia, contained within the envelope and poking out from behind it, conveys capricious movement that borders on abstraction. But because it mirrors the size and shape of the photos, it balances the page layout. While it is considered a stronger composition when something as directed as the car photo would point inward on the page, here it structurally balances the dark square of the oversized postage stamp on the bottom right.

Memory Album An album containing personal bits of ephemera that helps remember an important event.

Scrap of History: Memory Albums

A memory album differs from a scrapbook because scrapbooks hold paper and colorful items of interest, including magazine photos, drawings, pressed flowers, and chromolithographs.

Memory albums were especially made to commemorate a special time or event, using photos and other items of nostalgic interest.

Mesh A fabric characterized by its net-like open appearance, and the spaces between the yarns (Figs. 89A–89E). Mesh is available in a variety of constructions including paper, jute-like materials, and soft fabric. Mesh is a popular embellishment choice for scrapbookers because it adds a casual textural appearance to pages.

Figs. 89A & 89B: Mesh— *Snip* and *Ruby* and *Friends* Mesh used on these pages as background embellishment adds texture. Notice the different types used and the effects each has on its corresponding page.

Fig. 89C–89E: Mesh —These pages show mesh adding background texture in a number of ways, whether it covers the entire background or works as a second-level background behind photos.

Fig. 89C: *La Playa Muy Bueno*

Fig. 89D: *Le Jardin*

Fig. 89E: *Snow*

M

Metalwork Scrapbooking metalwork encompasses many kinds of decoration using various metals including tin, pewter, copper, and others (Figs. 90A–90D). Metalwork can be purchased or handmade (Technique 12).

Fig. 90A: Metal Sheets, Rolls, and Metalworking Tools

Technique 12: Metalwork

Lay a plain or adhesive-backed lightweight copper foil face down on top of a brass stencil. With a stylus, gently press with the ball end, imprinting the stencil design into the metal.

When the design is complete, trim the edges with deckle scissors or corner punches. To enhance copper further, use a hot-temp heat gun to "flash" it with color.

Fig. 90B: Metalwork— *Ethel* The handmade embossed copperplate coordinates with the choice of background papers, adding a personal touch and creative element to this page.

Fig. 90C: Metalwork—*Corrieshalloch Gorge* Handmade metalwork was used on this spread to frame the photos and as background for the handmade, hand-torn papers that were used as accents. Notice that the plaid background papers coordinate nicely with the patterned pages used for the layout.

Fig. 90D: Metalwork—*Weekend Pass* Handmade metalwork stars accent this page. Metal rivets, polymer clay, and stamped letters also adorn this page.

Mica A transparent, flaky mineral (Fig. 91A) with excellent insulating and heat-resisting properties, and characterized by the formation of thin-layered sheets. It is often found in igneous and metamorphic rocks. Mica color ranges from colorless to black; it is mined in small particles called schist or larger pieces called blocks (Figs. 91B–91F), and marketed under the registered name Mica Tiles.

Fig. 91B: Mica—*Barefoot* Sparkling bits of mica flakes were attached to this page, using an ATG adhesive, which is respositionable and provides a nice straight sticky line, perfect for a line or border. Whether wet or dry adhesives are used, mica adds a versatile and natural bit of brilliance to most any scrapbook page.

Fig. 91A: Large Block Mica and Small Mica Flakes

Fig. 91C: Mica—*Aunt Mary* The smooth quality and sepia coloration of the mica tiles adds a vintage quality to old or photocopied photographs.

Fig. 91D: Mica — With a generous coating of liquid adhesive and sprinkling of mica flakes, tin or paper stars are sparkling embellishments for any scrapbook page. The colorful wire adds a touch of whimsy, movement and texture.

Fig. 91E: Mica — *Practice Makes Perfect* Mica flakes adhered onto the stars mimic the sparkle of real stars.

Fig. 91F: Mica —*Magic* The seashell background paper, shown torn and embellished with mica sparkles, is deliberately pastel in color so that it does not overpower the photo.

Micro Bead A tiny holeless bead used for color and textural effect in paper-craft techniques.

Migration The movement of chemicals such as acids, plastics, paint, or inks from one item to another. Migration can occur without direct physical contact, such as the migration of acids from one degrading paper to another material or photo.

Mitering A method of cutting paper corners for perfect frame, box, and album making applications.

Mizuhiki Cord A delicate paper and metallic cord used for embellishing, bows, borders, and cloisonné paper effects, becoming the wire between the colored pieces of paper (Fig. 92).

Mold A flat screen with wire mesh onto which the deckle is placed during handmade papermaking.

Mold Made A sheet of paper that simulates the look of hand-made paper but is actually made by a cylinder mold machine.

Fig. 92: Mizuhiki Cord—*Manitou Springs* Mizuhiki cord, cut and pieced, edges colored papers resembling miniature stained-glass windows.

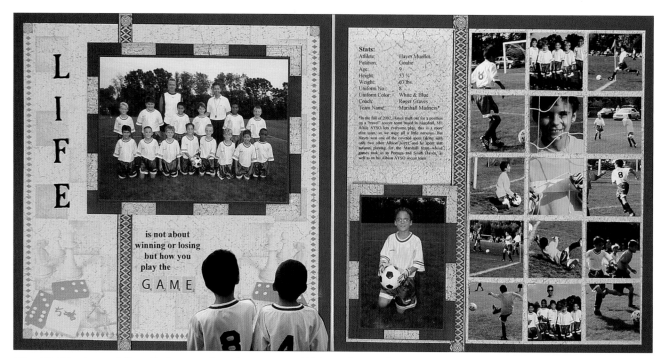

Fig. 93: Montage—*Life* Both a mosaic and a montage, *Life* is a wonderfully balanced composition with a bold linear design. The two boys silhouetted on the bottom of the first page, add a touch of whimsy, direction, and softens the angles of the photos.

Fig. 94A: Mosaic— *Potato Chips* Colorful chaos reigns in the potato chip aisle of most grocery stores. This photo mosaic depicts that chaos with a puzzle-like quality, forcing the viewer to study the page more closely than normal and encouraging them to decipher the many labels, brands, and types of chips found on store shelves.

Montage 1. A composite image made by joining together and printing portions or all of more than one negative, in order to synthesize an image not found in reality. 2. A composite art piece made by cutting or tearing multiple photos then adhering them together to produce a homogenous creation (Fig. 93).

Mosaic The paper-craft technique of taking multiple photos, cutting them into equal squares and reassembling them onto paper to create a new picture (Figs. 94A & 94B). In this process, the paper acts as the mortar.

Fig. 94B: Mosiac— *Sunset* The mosaic on this page was made by cutting a photo into squares and reassembling it around the red lines.

Motif A design that is the predominant theme or a distinctive repeated pattern, design, or shape in a work of art.

Mount or Mounting To place a photo or object onto a background paper. A double-mount has two papers, a triple-mount has three, etc., (Figs. 95A & 95B).

Mounting Square A small square of double-sided tape-like adhesive dispensed from a box.

Mylar A protective clear covering for photos and album pages. Mylar is currently regarded as the highest quality material used for this purpose. (See also Plastic.)

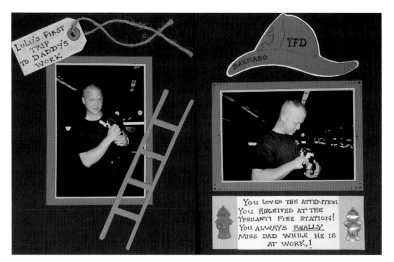

Fig. 95A: Mounts—*Daddy at Work* Double-mounts help highlight these photos. Bright-colored mounting papers help separate them from dark background papers.

Aging Photographs: Mounting Tips

- Choose mounts that complement the photo in terms of color, theme, or mood.

- Place a clean piece of paper over a photograph immediately after adhering it onto a mount.

- Rub over the surface with your hands to smooth out any air bubbles. The paper will serve to protect your photograph as you do this.

- The corners of a mount can be decorated using punches and templates.

Fig. 95B: Mounts— *At the Beach* Limiting the color palette to just three colors and double-mounting the photos on this page add a little punch to these romantic photos.

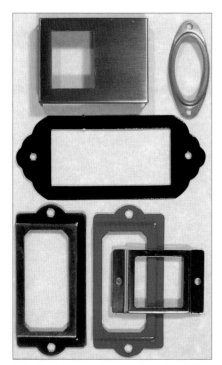

Nameplate Open-faced metal frames (Fig. 96A & 96B), often with a fastening hole on either side, once used to label pantry, apothecary, library, and hardware drawers. Scrapbookers have a variety of nameplates available for embellishing and framing captions and titles, commonly found in paper, metal, plastic, and sticker material.

National Scrapbook Day
The first Saturday in May.

Negative 1. Any image produced on a photographic emulsion by the product of exposure and development, in which tones are reversed so that highlights appear dark and shadows appear light (Fig. 97). 2. The camera film exposed that is subsequently developed to produce a negative image.

Fig. 96B: Nameplate— *Dusty & Spencer*
A nameplate is not only for names Here, it frames the famous quote about what little boys are made of. The silver accents with the monochromatic color scheme cause the captions to "pop". The nameplate looks much like a buckle and belt, anchoring the bottom of the page.

Fig. 96A: Nameplates—Metal and Paper

Fig. 97: Negatives

O

Organization Having an orderly process of keeping scrapbook materials. Taking the time to organize photos, negatives, and supplies into one space simplifies the scrapbooking process and more importantly, can actually help make someone a better scrapbooker.

Having a set space and one or two ready-made organizational storage systems (Fig. 98), allows for a certain freedom that is immensely satisfying, giving rise to a more creative time. Simply said, more scrapping, less searching!

Oozing Liquid adhesives that seep out from under the edge of an applied element, or over time when a dry adhesive begins to deteriorate. To prevent oozing, apply adhesives with a brush, smoothing down the thinnest coat possible to hold the piece in place. Lay a flat object onto the piece for even weight distribution.

Fig. 98: Carrying Organizers

Organization: Sorting Materials and Supplies

Begin sorting items into several large categories and then smaller subcategories. Examples of these categories include:

- Adhesives: dots, glues, tapes, etc.

- Art materials: chalk, colored pencils, markers, pastels, pens, watercolors, etc.

- Cutting implements

- Organizing supplies: containers, drawers, folders, labels, etc.

- Embellishments: beads, buttons, corners, eyelets, frames, paper clips, ribbons, stickers, and miscellaneous items

- Negatives

- Papers: cardstock, patterned, plain, and specialty

- Photos

- Tools: punches, scissors, templates, etc.

Chronological Order Sorting photos in chronological order makes the most sense to this author. Materials needed for this task include:

- Acid-free folders and storage boxes

- Black marker

- Index cards larger than the photos, or cut scrapbook paper

- Large pieces of scrap paper

- Page protectors for large photos

In order to carry out this task, follow these steps:

- Gather every single photo in the house and put them in one place. (This could actually be the most difficult step of all.)

- Using large numbers, write each year onto the scrap paper, beginning with the year of the oldest photo found and ending with the newest. Sort first by year, then by month.

Storage Containers and Systems There are dozens of systems available for storage. Search office supply, organizational, and box stores' storage aisles for accordion files, folders, file systems, standard notebooks, etc. Wander several stores before deciding on a particular set of drawers or containers. Make certain the containers are transparent.

Labeling Keep scrapbooking supplies clearly and concisely labeled in a prominent area. Consistency is key. Use a uniform-sized label and an easy-to-read computer typeface to print labels.

USArtQuest Art Department Organizational System

Photos All containers for photos and negatives should be acid-free and lignin-free environments. You may choose to sort them into photo boxes, sorted by year, person and event, or store them in simple sleeve-type albums in chronological order, to be viewed while waiting for their end-home in a yet-to-be-made scrapbook.

Digital Photos Digital cameras have made photography amazingly convenient and efficient; but if the photos are unfiled and unorganized, days can be spent searching for just the right photo. To organize these:

- If stored on a computer, make sure there is plenty of available hard-drive space or they will bog down the system. Delete poorly taken photos immediately.

Photo Organizer

- Store digital photos in file folders chronologically by year.

- Within the folder, keep the photos in monthly files or file names that match the boxed photograph labels, so that digital and traditional photos can be matched for an album page.

- Keep the camera's photo identification number as the file name, since there may only be 15–20 photos per month. Otherwise, photo names will be quickly used up, e.g. Joey blowing candles, Joey candles, Joey & cake, Joey with candles, etc.

- Create a text file journal, giving it the same name as the photo folder. Journaling will help remember special memories and actual remarks or observations when it is time to make an album.

- Archive. Computer crashes are nearly inevitable. Back up all digital photos and journal documents onto CDs or DVDs.

- Sort older photos by the decade and more recent photos by year, keeping the groups of photos together as well as possible, and placing them next to the year titles.

- Place and label each year into its own folder or box, depending on the size of the group. Label the front of the folder or box.

- One box at a time, sort that year by month, then person or event, sliding the labeled index cards in between each category.

- Keep all photos, good or bad. There are several charming techniques using cut-up bad photos to enhance the good ones.

Negatives Materials needed for organizing negatives include:

- Three-ring binder

- Negative pages

- Permanent marker

Organize the negatives by following these steps:

- Gather the negatives at the same time as the photos.

- As the photos are removed from the envelopes, date the paper folders by year and put them aside.

- When all of the photos are sorted, sort the negatives, arranging them by year into the protective sleeves in their complete strips.

- Use a permanent marker to write on the plastic, labeling the negatives by year, month, person, and topic.

- Store the binder away from light.

Papers When sorting the different types of paper, emember to sort the full sheets separately from the scraps. Sorting full sheets of paper into categories and sizes is a simple process. Scraps are another story. Keep in mind that stockpiling paper uses a great deal of the available scrapbooking dollars that can be used on embellishments. Also, it is best to buy paper as you plan pages or albums, rather than build up a huge quantity of theme-Patterned papers.

Cardstock and Solid-colored Papers Ideally, purchase multi-packs of colors, or only a few of any given color. Sort these by color families such as red, blue, and green; then if necessary, by value such as pastel pink, then rose, tomato, fire-engine red, and burgundy.

Patterned Papers Sort by pattern such as florals, plaids, stripes, textured designs, etc.

Specialty Papers Mesh, metallics, mulberry, and vellum can be kept in individual folders, sorted by color. Full sheets may be kept in folders, bins, or specially made totes by style, then color. Scraps are best kept in well-labeled folders or accordion folders. Using scraps is ideal for double- and triple-mounted photos.

Theme-patterned Papers

Sort by holiday or event, then by topic such as Victorian floral, congratulations, heritage, or children's papers. Scraps may be trimmed to use for embellishments on a coordinating page, such as balloons, candles, flowers, or toys

Embellishments

Organizing embellishments is simple if they are kept in their original bags and put into three-ring binders. Indexing aids in finding items quickly, but leafing through them with regularity also gives constant reminders of the available inventory.

Tackle or Specialty Boxes

them in a small box with their loose ends all pointed in the same direction, able to be pulled off and cut to length.

Pens, Markers, and Tools

There is a variety of different ways to store pens, markers, and other vertically styled tools, including pencil boxes or cups. You could also make

For punches and other horizontal tools, drawers and boxes work best.

Sort these items into categories such as:

- Colored pencils
- Leafing pens
- Permanent markers
- Pastel pencils
- Watercolor markers

Tin Rounds and Boxes

Miscellaneous Items

Paper trimmers, diecut machines, large punches, and other bulky items are best kept in one location and covered with a dust cover.

Wire drawer units also have wheels and tops that are useful. Smaller items must be kept in a container when they are in the drawer, or they may fall through the holes.

Binder, Folder Organizers, and Organizational Accessories

Tackle boxes and specialty boxes are ideal for the hardware and tiny parts. Fibers and ribbon can be easily seen and retrieved if kept in pocket folders. If they are on reels, place

your own to match any decor, using embellished potato chip tubes or decorated tins, anything that does not tip over is fair game.

Workspace

If a permanent location is not available, then rolling carts are the ideal storage units. They can be rolled right up to the kitchen table. In addition, two of them pushed apart will support a board, creating a work surface. While maybe not ideal, it is a functional solution for small spaces.

that direct light can also damage your paper and supplies. Several clamp-on, swing-away, or portable-armed daylight lamps are available and an excellent choice for good lighting.

Scrap-bag/Beverage Holder

Clamp-on organizers are perfect for keeping the table tidy of scraps, while using recycled grocery bags in the process. More importantly, the unique cup holder allows even the largest cup to be placed at hand, but inside a wire holder, preventing spills and ruining photos and pages.

Ultimate Storage of Vellum at Scrapbooking Memories

Scrap-bag/Beverage Holder

When the day is done, the board can be taken down and the carts rolled away. When it comes to the curiosity of children, keeping the bulk of the scrapbooking materials out of harms way is important. A closet or armoire is ideal for hiding those items that children enjoy, such as stickers, scissors, and paper trimmers.

Chair Select the most comfortable chair possible, choosing one that supports your back.

Lighting Select good lighting. Working in natural light is best if it's available; but keep in mind

Magazine Holder It is best to store only one year of each magazine. To begin, for ease and neatness, keep each magazine in their own labeled holder. When reading each magazine for the first time, use small, brightly colored self-adhesive papers to mark interesting items. After one year, cull through each magazine cutting out only the most interesting tips, techniques, layouts, and ideas. Put them into labeled three-ring reference binders, indexed by subject.

Shelves Several sturdy shelves store toolboxes, paper, photo boxes, folders, works in progress, and albums. In addition, space will be needed for magazines, books, and videos.

Trash Cans Believe it or not, this is an essential organizational tool. Keeping bits of paper, tape scraps, label backing, and other items on the working surface make for messy scrapbooking.

Origami The Japanese art of folding paper into familiar slightly dimensional or sculptural shapes, usually without cutting (Figs. 99A–99D). Introduced to Japanese artisans by the Chinese, origami comes from the Japanese words meaning oru, "to fold" and kami, "paper."

Fig. 99C: Origami Pattern Books and Paper

Fig. 99A: Origami—*Star Frame* Origami pieces and frames can be made in various sizes.

Fig. 99B: Origami—*Good Friends* An origami star frames the journaling on this scrapbook page.

Fig. 99D: Origami—*Daughter of Mine* Used as an alternative to photo corners, origami photo frames hold the photos securely in place, adding a decorative touch.

Out-gassing Gasses expelled from scrapbook materials (Fig. 100). For example: gaseous emissions from vinyl binders that result in a strong odor.

Overlay A transparent sheet placed over artwork (Figs. 101A–101C).

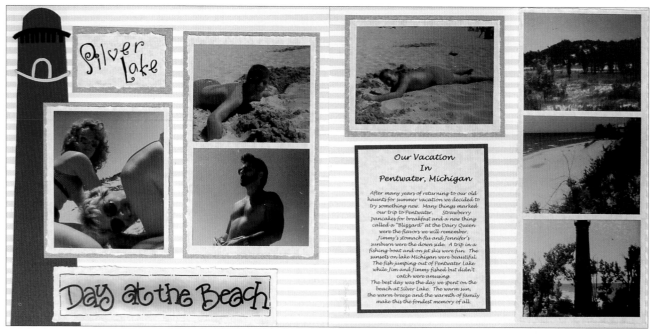

Fig. 100: Out-gassing—*Silver Lake* The out-gassing of chemicals had turned these photos yellow. To help prevent further yellowing, the photos were remounted onto an acid-free environment.

Fig. 101A: Overlay—*Playing at the Park* The subtle use of vellum, overlayed on vibrantly colored diecuts hidden underneath, keeps the pages from becoming too busy, yet gives them texture and detail.

Fig. 101B: Overlay—_Reebie_   Detail

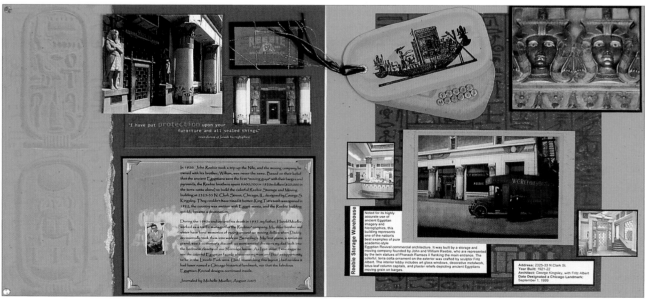

Fig. 101C: Overlay—_Reebie_   The interesting four-color scheme on this page was derived from the paper, the photo of the truck, and the building's architectural accents. The vellum overlaid onto the photo includes the journaling for the page, yet is translucent enough to allow a subtle view of the photo underneath. For further emphasis, the vellum was cut and edged with gilding, to frame the one person most important in the group shot.

P

Page Protector Photo-safe protective plastic sleeves (Fig. 102) made to slip over scrapbook and memory album pages. Sealed at the top and bottom, page protectors keep photos free of fingerprints, abrasions, accidental spills, and protect against environmental contaminants. Page protectors are available in a variety of sizes. The most common include A4, 8½"x11", or 12"x12". Page protectors can be top loading, side loading, or top and bottom loading.

Page Topper A hand-drawn, illustrated word and phrase (Fig. 103), often in bright colors, used as a title at the top of a page.

Page Protection Tips

• The best material for sheet protectors is Mylar. Mylar is more costly than polypropylene sheet protectors. Polypropylene, also a clear, flexible, chemically stable plastic is as good as archival albums need, and a lot more cost effective.

• Avoid sheet protectors made from acetate or sheet protectors containing polyvinyl acetate (PVC).

• If you can smell the plastic, it is in the process of breaking down, creating a corrosive and acidic hydrogen-chloride gas, which will then migrate to your page and damage your photos.

• Albums containing sheet protectors should be stored vertically to avoid moisture from accumulating, allowing the maximum amount of air to flow into your album, and preventing the trapped moisture, which encourages mold growth.

Fig. 102: Various-sized Page Protectors

Fig. 103: Page Toppers

Paint A pigment dispersed into a liquid, called a vehicle, that includes a binder. Paints adhere both to themselves and to the surface to which it is applied, converting it to a solid film. Paint should have qualities that both protect and decorate a surface. Types of paint suitable for scrapbooking include acrylic, gouache, specialty paints such as tempera, and watercolor (Figs. 104A–104F).

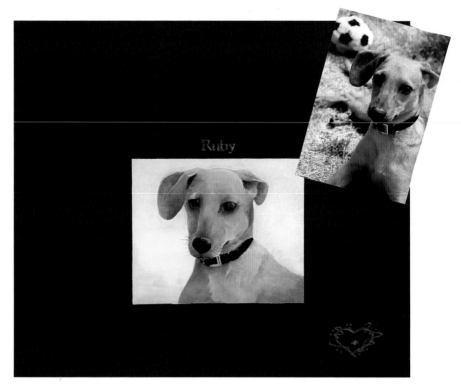

Fig. 104B: Paint—*Ruby* Reproducing photos onto album covers is a specialty of this artist. She used acrylic paint for durability and lightfastness.

Fig. 104A: Paint—*Fiesta* The brightly colored acrylic paint gives these pages punch and a real hand-painted quality.

P

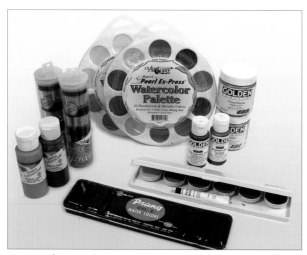

Fig. 104C: Water-based Paints

Fig. 104D: Paint— *Your Thoughtfulness Is Appreciated!* **A stamped, then watercolored pond scene makes this an easy and lovely greeting card.**

Paint Types

Acrylic Water-based paint that dries quickly. Unlike many other water-based paints, it is not water soluble once it has dried. Therefore, it can be gently wiped clean if needed. Acrylics are manufactured by adding dry pigments into a vehicle containing polymers, which when applied to a surface, forms a plastic film. They are ideal for painting pages, album covers, and page protectors.

Gouache Gouache is similar to a watercolor except that it contains a white lead pigment, which produces a characteristic brilliant, light-reflecting quality. The addition of the white pigment and a higher proportion of binder such as gum arabic, gives gouache a paint thickness. Use gouache for highlights, particularly white highlights, or in place of watercolor paints.

Specialty Paint Any paint used for scrapbooking that does not fall into another category. New paints are developed regularly and have different vehicles and different characteristics than other paints currently on the market. One such paint is a webbing spray, which is an aerosol paint splattering web-like effects when sprayed, making unusual and interesting background patterning.

Tempera A mixture of pigments and a water-soluble glutinous emulsion binder. Tempera is often found commercially in a powdered form, to be mixed with water after purchase. When mixing tempera paints for scrapbooking, use distilled water.

Watercolor Pigments dispersed into a water and gum arabic mixture, often containing amendments that aid in the smooth handling and resoluble quality of watercolor. Watercolor is usually translucent, but is also available in metallic or pearlescent palettes that are more opaque. Watercolors are the perfect paint for delicate background washes, bold colored accents or adding a touch of pearlescent glimmer.

Paper A material made of cellulose pulp, derived mainly from wood, rags, and some grasses. The fiber held in aqueous suspension is then deposited onto rollers to make flexible sheets and rolls of paper. Standard scrapbooking papers come in two main sizes 12"x12" and 8½"x11", and several subsizes, such as 12"x15", 8"x8", and 6"x6" as well as several others. Papers for scrapbooking, both solid and printed, should be acid-free and lignin-free to produce the best archival result.

Fig. 104E: Paint—*Lily Pads* Traditional watercolor techniques such as washes sprinkled with salt, as shown here, make beautiful scrapbook pages with lots of vibrantly colored texture.

Fig. 104F: Paint—*His and Mine* Watercolor accents were cut out and attached to embellish the background paper and the photo.

Paper Terminology

Background Plain, colorful, or decorated papers that are used as the surface (ground) for mounting photos and set the tone for the rest of the page. The manufacturer often designs these papers, but scrapbookers can design their own or even alter premade designs. (See also Paste Paper.) Balance is the operative word when using busy or colorful papers.

Background Papers

Coated Chemically treated paper with a glossy or matte finish used to enhance brightness.

Color-blocked Papers printed in large squares or geometric shapes of color.

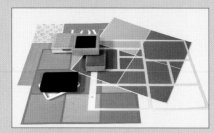

Templates and Ready-made Color-blocked Papers

Cork A paper-like material made of natural cork or a synthetic material resembling cork. Cork paper adds texture and a casual sophisticated quality to scrapbooking.

Corrugated Resembles the bumpy inside layers of a box. Corrugated paper is difficult to layer; but when used with other three-dimensional elements, it adds dimension, fun, and visual movement to a page.

Embossed Paper featuring raised, or relief, sculptural images. Embossed papers are machine-made stamped papers, often including metallic hot-foiled stamped areas. (See also Emboss.)

Embroidered Machine-made papers, specially stitched with embroidered patterns. (See also Embroidery.)

Enamel Glossy paper coating.

Finish The surface quality of paper.

Flocked Paper Paper coated with powders of wool or cotton (flock).

Foil Paper with a surface resembling metal.

Glossy Paper with a shiny finish resembling a photograph.

Background Paper —*Friend* Brightly colored textural papers, punched and then cut with fancy paper trimmers, look terrific with black-and-white photos, or would work well with other photos that have large color masses such as sky and water.

Cork—*Peace, Tranquility* There were many unique materials used on this page. The cork used as a background and the fiber cord mimics the fishermen's nets and floats.

Corrugated Paper—*Swim*
On this page, a corrugated wavy paper repeats the wave pattern in the water.

Handmade Paper made by hand that is often rough and uneven in texture. Handmade papers often have embedded flowers, leaves, grasses, and sparkling glitters.

Iridescent or Pearlescent Paper with mother-of-pearl or metallic-sheen finish.

Corrugated Paper—*Lantern Parade*   Corrugated paper borders this spread and frames the photos. Buttons and fibers also provide texture to these pages.

Glossy Paper—*Perfect Moments*   Layering complementary glossy papers can add whimsy to your page background.

Handmade Papers

Kraft Coarse, unbleached paper used for printing and industrial products such as paper bags. Kraft paper is unsuitable for scrapbooking.

Kromecoat Cover-weight paper, double-coated on one side to produce a very shiny surface. This glossy paper is ideal for stamping, giving a crisp look to stamped images.

Lace Paper with a delicate openwork design imitating fabric lace.

Laid Finish Parallel-lined paper with a handmade look.

Linen Paper that emulates the look and texture of linen cloth.

Matte Finish Coated paper finish that goes through minimal calendaring.

Metallic or Mirror Finish High-shine paper exhibiting mirror-like qualities.

Metallic Foil Papers

Mulberry Paper that has a natural organic look. Each sheet varies slightly. Mulberry paper is the same paper used in ancient cultures to record words of wisdom and scriptures on documents that still exist today.

M-weight Actual weight of 1,000 sheets of paper, regardless of size.

Newsprint Light, low-cost, ground-wood paper made especially for newspapers.

Offset Uncoated paper.

Opacity Opaqueness or ability to see through a paper.

Parchment 1. Fine paper made from the skins of goats, sheep, or cow. Parchment is an ancient technique of papermaking practiced today by skilled craftsmen, whose papers are available for calligraphers and crafts artisans. 2. Hard-finished paper that emulates animal skin; used for documents such as awards that require writing by hand.

Handmade Paper—*Let It Snow* Torn mulberry papers give these pages a frosty appearance. Die-cut circles reassembled as a top-hatted snowman repeats the snowman embellishments, keeping with the wintry theme.

Parent Sheet The name used to refer to a manufactured sheet of paper before trimming.

Patterned Paper with designs repeated on the entire page.

Rag Papers with at least a partial content of cotton fibers.

Ream 500 sheets of paper.

Satin Finish Smooth, delicately embossed, finished paper with sheen.

Theme-patterned Paper specially printed to be used for specific events or topics such as birthdays, holidays, or hobbies.

Authentic Goat and Sheepskin Parchment

Theme-patterned Paper—O *Christmas Tree* Strips of green paper and photos, layered over the top of this busy tree-themed paper unify the photos, thus causing the eye to follow the story. Photos and journaling, mounted onto green paper, give the eye a place to rest.

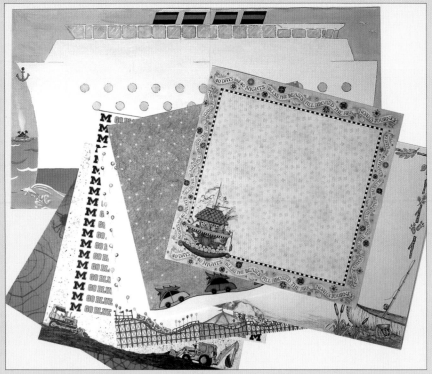

Theme-Patterned Papers

Vellum Lightweight translucent paper.

Papers often have coordinating vellums to assist you in creating pages with real harmony.

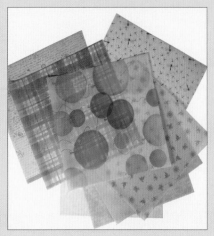

Vellum Papers

Theme-patterned Paper—*Warmth of Family*   A bold two-page title, accented with tags, tells the story about a trip to find the perfect Christmas tree. The tree-themed papers happened to work perfectly with the photos.

Velveteen Archival paper with a velvety texture.

Vivelle Archival paper with fabric-like texture similar to a terry-cloth towel

Vellum Paper—
I Pick You
These handmade vellum envelopes are so pretty, and perfect for holding and displaying this page's double-mounted photos.

Vellum Paper—*Mother's Day* Floral-printed vellum was used to create a pocket that holds a special Mother's Day greeting. Floral patterns, cut from a second piece of vellum, add to the balance of the composition.

Paper Designer: Anna Griffin

The Newlyweds

With a degree in environmental design from North Carolina State University, Anna Griffin began her career as an art director for a design firm, then worked as a marketing director for a software company and an associate for designer Vera Wang. In 1995, she made her first foray as an entrepreneur, creating custom wedding invitations. "I had always dreamed of having my own business," she says, "and it is no surprise, considering that my family is full of entrepreneurs. I was fortunate to be raised in an environment where I was encouraged and taught that anything is possible."

Her invitation business was a success; but it was her line of papers, introduced the following year, that transformed the invitation industry. "The originality of the designs and the attention to detail immediately filled a void in the wedding industry," Anna explains. "We offered a much-needed high-quality alternative to the traditional engraved invitation." Anna's papers reflected her enthusiasm for antiques, prints, and fine textiles, as well as flea-market finds from all over the world. "What motivates me in design are luxurious patterns, rich florals, and antique textile prints," she says. "Simple and elegant!"

Soon, brides were looking for invitations that they could personalize. So Anna obliged, offering local stationery stores her signature vellums and ribbons, combining them with antique engravings and botanical papers, starting a trend still popular in the industry today. From there, it was a short step to greeting cards, social stationery, and home-office items.

In 2001, Anna launched Anna Griffin Decorative Papers—a sophisticated line designed for the discriminating scrapbooker, filled with her colorful antique and botanical paper images, which coordinate with solids, stripes, and tone-on-tone patterns. The response was overwhelming, and it's still growing. Anna has been featured on DIY Scrapbooking, QVC, PBS, and The Christopher Lowell Show, as well as in magazines including *Martha Stewart Living, Southern Living,* and *Better Homes and Gardens* *Creative Home.* "I am living proof that you can have and do anything you want in life," she says. "I strive to be the very best person I can be, personally and professionally."

Baby and the Beanstalk

Always a Bridesmaid

Virginia Allan Porter— Anna Griffin's scrapbook pages show off the lucious patterns and textures that she so loves. The romantically nostalgic quality is carried through in its entirety by the complete use of multi-paper-layered pages festooned with complementary ribbons and embellishments.

Paper Designer: Kay Stanley

"The very first birthday gift I remember receiving was a ring-bound sketchbook," Kay Stanley says. "I quickly filled it with sketches, never knowing I was beginning an artistic journey that would, in many ways, shape my life."

At the University of Kansas, she focused her studies on the business side of advertising, but a few of her design professors saw her artistic talent and offered her a position on a student design team called the "Arts." After she graduated with a B.S. in journalism in 1986, her experience with advertising and design helped her land jobs art-directing catalogs for Hallmark Cards, then creating advertising and promotions for Campbell Soup, Nestle Foods, and other companies. Her work won her more than fifty awards for art direction and design.

In 1990, she met Curt Seymour, and they began to date and

work together successfully, with Kay helping Curt design gift products for his company, FSA Designs. In 1996, Kay came up with a line of sorority stickers that Curt's business partners chose not to market or invest in. Not wanting to see all that time and work wasted, she decided to manufacture the line herself, and K&Company was born.

"I remember how excited and nervous I was on the flight to Chicago for the very first K&Company trade show," Kay

recalls. "We had just spent $100,000 on an idea, and I had no idea if it would fall flat or succeed." With fingers crossed, she took two vacation days off from her full-time agency job and headed out to set up a booth in the Chicago Gift Mart. Curt joined her the next day to help with sales and see if their investment would pan out. "Within the first hour of the show, we took orders for 'Frame a Name' from gift stores and Hallmark stores," Kay

Bits and Pieces

says. "What a relief! Apparently, we were on to something here."

When Kay began work on K&Company's scrapbook line, she aimed to give her scrapbook papers a sophisticated, elegant "designer" look, something that would truly set them apart. "I approached scrapbooking much as wallpaper and fabric companies design their lines for the home market," she explains. "Coordinated collections of papers, stickers, borders, and eventually albums would come together to make it easy for the scrapbook consumer to create beautiful and elegant scrapbooks." In 1999, she introduced the first twelve K&Company paper kits, followed by bulk papers in 2000,

Button Frame

Best Wishes Card

using the elegant look she'd envisioned: antique botanical engravings, wallpapers, classic vintage fabrics. K&Company's recent honors include the Ernst & Young

Entrepreneur of the Year award and a spot on *Inc.* magazine's Inc. 500, a list of America's fastest-growing private companies.

New Zealand Wedding

Paper Craft Technique
Transforming cardstock and paper into paper-crafting works of art. (See also Paper Doll Making, Paper Piercing, Paper Tearing, Paper Tole, Paper Weaving, Pop-ups, Rubber Stamping, and Scherenschnitte.)

Paper Doll Making Die-cut images in the shape of a person (Figs. 105A & 105B), which may be dressed and posed to match a layout.

Paper-cutting Tools

Oval or Shape Cutters
Specialty paper trimmers that cut paper and photographs into ovals or other geometric shapes.

Paper Cutter Available in numerous sizes and configurations, a paper cutter has a long metal blade attached to a pivoting arm, which is then attached to a tabletop measuring board. The paper is cut by a chopping action. The most accurate paper cutters have a steel arm and blade, allowing little or no flexing when the paper is cut.

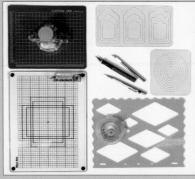
Cutters and Templates

Paper Trimmer A paper-cutting device using a razor or razor-sharp wheel set into a track in a plastic bar. The bar lifts and paper can be sliced rather than chopped.

Personal Trimmer Small portable version of a paper trimmer used for trimming or cropping photographs and paper.

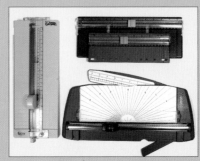
Paper Trimmers

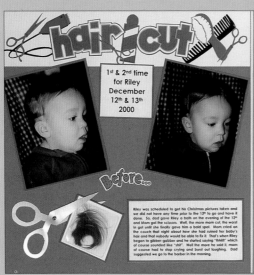

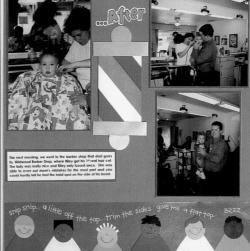

Haircut— The paper embellishments such as the barber pole and scissors on these pages were handmade using various paper-cutting tools.

Fig. 105A: Paper Doll Making—*Lachie* The paper doll on this page is handmade to resemble the tour guide Lachie, from the trip detailed on this page. Lachie's bag, reproduced and enlarged, is covered with a fur-like paper. The picture hidden inside the bag is a bit risqué, and answers the perennial question, "What does a Scotsman wear under his kilt?"

Fig. 105B: Paper Doll Making—*Silly Signs* The jester-shaped paper doll on this two-page spread propels the eye to move into the composition, while adding character to the layout. It also foretells the silliness mentioned in the road signs.

Paper Fastener A device that holds two or more pieces of paper together (Figs. 106A–106E).

While a bit confusing, the apparent overlapping of names associated with most paper fasteners is in part due to manufacturers attempting to differentiate their product from others. Primarily though, it is due to the crossover from different industries, that use different terminology. For instance, we all know a tack is commonly used to post a message on a corkboard. However, in the interiors/upholstery industry, that same product is called a nail head. In scrapbooking, a nail head is different. Whatever the name of the item, if it serves your purpose, adding both function and/or a decorative feature, feel free to use it.

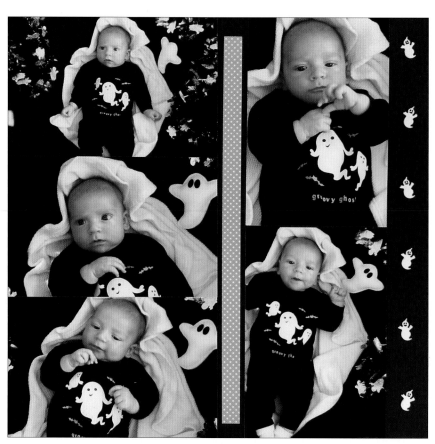

Fig: 106A: Paper Fastener—*Ghost Baby*   Keeping with the theme, charming little ghost-shaped brads seem to fly all over this page. These brads were used as decorative elements instead of paper fasteners.

Fig. 106B: Paper Fastener—*Clarissa* The title and hand-torn background papers are attached to this page with brads. Notice that the vellum is overlayed on vertically striped paper that repeats the pattern of the chair back in the photo.

Paper Fastener Types

Brad Hardware with a top portion and two posts. The posts pierce through one or more papers, then open and fold back, opposite one another, making for a very functional, yet highly decorative fastener.

Brads

Concho Rings, squares, or numerous other shapes of metal, usually open in the middle, with two or more triangular pointed ends. These ends pierce through the paper and fold or are hammered over on the back to secure it in place. A large concho can actually be used as a miniature picture frame.

Conchos

Eyelet Metal ring or other shape designed to reinforce a hole. Eyelets are the most common metal fastener used with paper or fabric.

Eyelets have come a long way from the simple utilitarian rings found in sneakers. Today eyelets are available in a variety of sizes, shapes, and colors.

Setting eyelets into paper is a simple technique that uses a hammer and hole punch.

Large and Standard Eyelets

Eyelets, Hammer, Mat, and Setter

Grommet Two-piece eyelet. In addition to a traditional eyelet, a back ring is provided to protect the back paper.

Nailhead Generally found with a decorative top, there are usually several triangular points that pierce through the paper and fold over to secure it from the back.

Nailheads

Paper Clip Metal paper fastener that slides onto the edges of paper, holding two items together. Paper clips are decorative and functional.

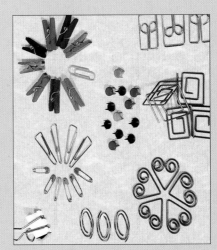

Paper Clips

Snap Paper fastener that snaps together with a post from the topside and a clasp in the back.

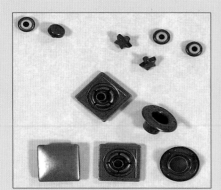

Snaps

Tack Hardware that simply pierces through the paper and has no back clasp.

Zipper Much like zippers used for clothing, a zipper in scrapbooking opens to reveal a surprise inside, usually a photo, quote, or journaling.

Fig: 106C: Paper Fastener—*The Clock* These charming heart-shaped brads give this page lots of character and color, adding texture and sparkle to the solid cardstock.

Technique 13: Paper Fasteners: Setting Eyelets

1 To simplify the process, punch a hole in thicker papers prior to setting the eyelet.

2 Place the eyelet in the hole, face down on a mat. Place the setter on the eyelet shank. Strike the eyelet setter with the hammer until the shank is flat.

Fig. 106D: Paper Fastener—*Petanque*   This double page has lots of photos and not much room for decorative titles or captioning. The paper clips add embellishing that makes sense, providing just a bit of texture and sparkle.

Fig. 106E: Paper Fastener—*Preschool*   Snaps and eyelets add a whimsical pattern to plain, torn, and color-blocked cardstock. The overlapping of photos solidifies the composition, creating a strong focal point—a good counterpoint from the random scattering of the paper fasteners holding the captions on one end, allowing them to pivot.

Paper Grade and Weight

Systems for measuring paper characteristics. Understanding these two concepts is the secret to selecting the right paper. There are five basic grades of paper. Within each grade, there are other characteristics based on brightness, opacity, and fiber content. For instance, matte, premium, and ultragloss-finish coated paper. Paper weights are measured by weighing 500 sheets of parent sheet paper.

Paper: Make and Cast

The craft of papermaking and making shapes from paper. Papermaking kits are available to make scrapbook papers and embellishments. The kits have different levels of difficulty so that there is something for everyone (Figs. 107A–107D and Technique 14). Paper casting is the art of using pulp from handmade papers, pressing into a mold and forming scrapbook embellishments.

Fig. 107A: Papermaking Kit and Materials and Handmade Papers

Standard Paper Grades:

- **Bond** Used for letterheads and business forms.

- **Coated Book** Glossy sheets that show off vivid colors at their best.

- **Cover** Used for book covers, postcards, and business cards. It is available coated or uncoated.

- **Offset or Uncoated Book** The most common sheet for printing. It has a smooth, uncoated look.

- **Text** A high-quality textured paper. Softly colored and available in a number of finishes including smooth, vellum, felt, embossed, laid, and linen.

Fig. 107B: Paper Casting—*Emma and Frank* Rubber-stamping a preprinted background paper gives this page an even more interesting texture. Paper-casted flowers make a nice border, adding texture, balance, and a creative touch. The casted-flower border blends well with the background and the ivy frame, while keeping with the overall theme.

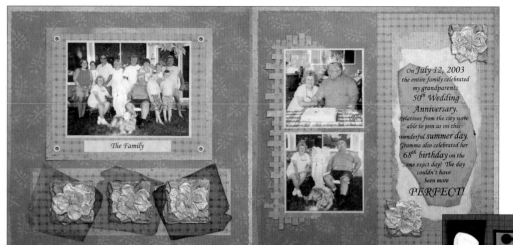

Fig. 107C: Paper Casting—*The Family* Paper-casted flowers adorn this two-page spread. Note how the flower texture repeats that of the paper and the woven-paper mount.

Fig. 107D: Paper Casting—*I Love* The paper-casted footprints on the left side of this page add texture and charm along with the buttons and eyelets.

Scrap of History: Papermaking

According to Chinese tradition, in 105 a.d., Ts'ai Lun, an official of Emperor Ho-ti, invented the process of using vegetable fibers to make paper. Reaching the Islamic world via the trade caravans, it was then introduced in Spain in the eleventh century, probably by the Moors.

Papermills were in operation in Europe at least 250 years before the invention of printing, but parchment continued to be used for handwritten and illustrative purposes long after the printing press became an established duplication process.

Prior to the mid-nineteenth century, nearly all paper was made from rags and cloth fiber, produced by hand-dipping a screen (mold) into a large vat containing pulped fiber in water suspension, called furnish.

Commercial papermaking began in the early nineteenth century, and in 1841, a technique for making paper from wood pulp was developed in Nova Scotia.

Following tradition, these four steps of papermaking remain the same:

- Prepare the fiber, converting it into a product called furnish.

- Distribute furnish, across a webbed or roller surface called a fourdrinier machine.

- Remove the water.

- Finish the paper, giving it the surface desired.

P

Papermaker: Arnold Grummer

Arnold Grummer has based his entire life on something that nearly everyone takes for granted. For more than thirty years, he has written, lectured, and taught about paper.

"Paper is amazing. It is thin and relatively fragile, yet most of the world's wealth and much of the world's fate are committed to it," Arnold says. "Consider your marriage. If you are married, people accept that fact—not because they were at your wedding and saw it occur, but because you have a piece of paper somewhere that states you are married."

"Looked at totally, everything from your personal identity to your wealth to relationships between entire nations is on, and depends upon, paper," he continues. "Your whole legal identity is not what you might say it is or claim it to be in a particular instance. Rather, it is what one or more pieces of paper in one or more places say it is. With an instant disintegration of all paper, the whole world would be violently rearranged. Princes might become paupers, and strong paupers might become princes."

With a B.A. from Iowa State Teachers' College (now the University of Northern Iowa, for which he wrote the lyrics of the school song) and an M.A. from the State University of Iowa, Arnold is today the nation's premiere papermaker to the arts-and-crafts industry. He has been a faculty member of the Institute of Paper Chemistry and curator of the Dard Hunter Paper Museum and is currently the president of Greg Markim, Inc. The author of four books and scores of articles on paper science and paper crafting, he has taught everyone from preschoolers to printers, to FBI forensic scientists about the marvels of fibers and hydrogen bonding in paper; his students include such diverse celebrities as former Wisconsin governor Patrick Lucy, author Monroe Leaf, former President Richard Nixon, and even Mr. Whipple of "Please don't squeeze the Charmin" fame.

Arnold Grummer's Papermaking Products

Arnold's credits also include television programs, Smithsonian presentations, and the first-ever Lifetime Achievement Award from the prestigious papermaking society Friends of Dard Hunter, given "For advancing the art of papermaking and sharing your infectious joy of the craft with us all."

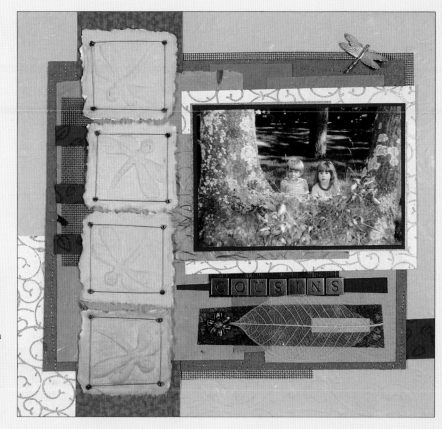

Cousins—Using several of the castings makes an effective border for this natural and organically inspired collaged scrapbook page.

Technique 14: Paper Casting

1 Tear handmade paper to size and place it onto the casting mold, centering it over the pattern. With a dampened sponge, gently press the paper into the casting motif.

2 When dry, gently lift the paper out. Drying can be encouraged by gently heating the paper with a heat tool. Note: If the paper should stick to the casting mold, dust it first with a complementary color of powdered pigment or talcum powder.

3 If desired, the finished paper casting can be painted or sprayed with glitter spray. A sparkling lavender watercolor paint is used here to color the paper. Use lots of water to keep the paint pale in color, and dry the brush a bit before application.

Paper Piecing The paper-craft technique of cutting then re-assembling the pieces to form a pattern. Ready-made patterns and kits are available for ease of use in scrapbook pages (Fig. 108).

Paper Piercing, Ornare, or Pricking The paper craft of piercing paper, using a pin and a pricking cushion (Fig. 109). While there are many patterns and stencils readily available for this technique, patterns can be easily made by drawing simple dots on paper or following the outline of a picture or coloring book.

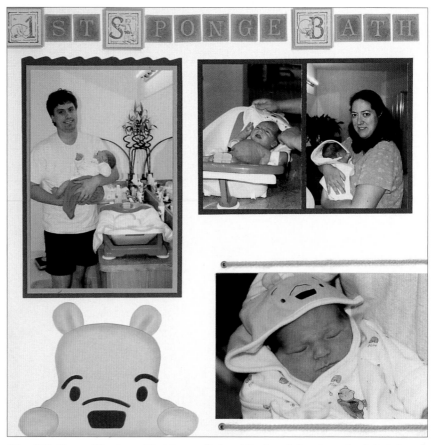

Fig. 109: Paper Piercing Templates and Tools

Fig. 108: Paper Piecing—*First Sponge Bath* The bear's head on the baby's hood inspired this paper piecing. The paper bear's head was made using the paper-piecing technique and then adhered onto the page.

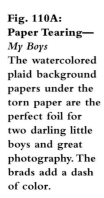

Fig. 110A: Paper Tearing— *My Boys* The watercolored plaid background papers under the torn paper are the perfect foil for two darling little boys and great photography. The brads add a dash of color.

Paper Tearing The paper-craft technique of tearing away excess paper from around a motif or image (Figs. 110A–110C).

Paper Tole A paper-craft technique in which part or all of an image is raised from the surface to give a three-dimensional effect, enhancing the natural shape of the image. For example, emphasize the curves of several flower petals by assembling them to achieve a dimensional flower. (See also Fig. 79: Layering).

Fig. 110B: Paper Tearing—
Bouncy. . . Bouncy. . .
This funny paper-torn and pieced character, resembling one of many on the child's bouncy seat, makes a great border and it is the page focal point. Notice how the character's eyes replicate the humorous look in the photo.

Fig. 110C: Paper Tearing—
Come Walk with Me
Hand-torn papers were applied to this page to mimic the look of the wave-carved sand, creating bordering, balance, and texture.

P

Paper Weaving Weaving thin paper strips to create a larger woven paper. Paper weaving is similar to weaving fibers (Figs. 111A–111D).

Fig. 111A: Paper Weaving

Use a paper trimmer to cut two or more colored papers to the size desired. Weave the 12"x12" paper, alternating the colors both horizontally and vertically. When complete, tape the back of each edge piece with acid-free tape.

Fig. 111B: Paper Weaving—*Straw Hat* **The paper-woven background looks darling against the straw hat worn by this little boy. There is lots of room left for journaling and still the background will look coordinated and dominant.**

Fig. 111C: Paper Weaving—*At the Playground* **Unlike** *Straw Hat,* **where a separate piece is added to a background paper, this entire background is woven. The rounded corners on the** photo framing contrast nicely, softening the overall geometric squared look. Here, too, room has been left open for captions and even a title.

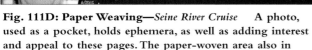

Fig. 111D: Paper Weaving—*Seine River Cruise* A photo, used as a pocket, holds ephemera, as well as adding interest and appeal to these pages. The paper-woven area also in corporates the patterning of the original papers, making for an attention-grabbing border.

Papuela The technique of weaving thin paper strips through slotted paper to create a pattern.

Parchment Craft 1. Embossing or piercing translucent paper, to create delicate lace-like patterns. 2. Using parchment paper for decorative purposes (Fig. 112A).

Fig. 112A: Parchment Craft— *Yes, Virginia* The vintage quality of this page is brought about by mixing aged-looking background papers, black-and-white photos, and real parchment. Even real parchment can be run through an inkjet printer using a font resembling calligraphy and older styles of handwriting.

P

Paste and Artist Cement

A specialty class of adhesive, traditionally made from starch or flour and prepared by heating together a mixture of starch and water and cooling the resulting product. Today, artist cements and pastes are mostly made from acrylic polymers, some of which are archival and acid-free and used where strength and durability, as well as flexibility, are required. These pastes and cements are also used for specialty techniques, such as dimensional stenciling, suede paper techniques, and impasto paper.

Paste Paper

Decorative papers whose colors and patterns are applied with a colored paste (Technique 15). Save bits and scraps from a day of making paste papers. These can be used nicely in future pages (Figs. 113A & 113B).

Technique 15: Paste Paper

1 Use any number of tools to create patterning for paste paper, including cutting plastic milk cartons with deckle-edged scissors.

2 Select any patterned or solid paper and brush on the paste paint. For this example, we used three different colors painted in stripes diagonally across painted striped paper.

3 Brush quickly so that paste remains wet, but do not over-manipulate the paste.

4 While the pasted area is still wet, drag a combing tool through the colors, making wavy lines or other patterns. After each layer dries, subsequent layers can be applied to add more colors.

5 Already beautiful papers, paper that is less than "special," or even marked or damaged paper can be altered to become exactly the right piece for scrapbook pages.

6 To finish, enlarge a photo on a copy machine, printing it onto vellum. Place vellum photo over paste paper.

Fig. 113A: Paste Paper

I'd like to hold your hand in mine
And have you walk with me,
So we could share the peace that comes
From being by the sea.

We'd hear the purling of the waves
That nibble at the shore,
And watch the lovely grey-backed gulls
That dive and wheel and soar.

We'd smell the seaweed's salty tang
And find some shells to keep
And maybe paddle for a while
In pools that aren't too deep.

We'd feel the gentle wind's caress
Come rumple up our hair;
We'd fill our souls with happiness
To be together there.

We'd watch the setting sun grow red
And sink beneath the sea,
And then we'd find the evening star,
If you were there with me.

Though time and space may come between
And keep us far apart,
Whenever I am by the sea
I'll take you in my heart.

Jeanne LeBaron Sawyer
from _the times of my life_ 1970

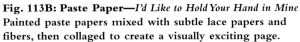

Fig. 114A: Pastels

Fig. 113B: Paste Paper—*I'd Like to Hold Your Hand in Mine*
Painted paste papers mixed with subtle lace papers and
fibers, then collaged to create a visually exciting page.

Pastel 1. Crayon-like sticks of varying hardness (Fig. 114A). Pastels are pure pigment with a small amount of gum binder holding them into shape and available in different hardnesses from very soft to very hard. Pastels are also available in a pencil-like format. When a surface is completely covered with pigment, the work is considered a pastel painting; leaving the surface more exposed produces a pastel sketch. 2. A pale color. Pastel papers can be sprayed to prevent pigments from smudging.

PAT (Photographic Activity Test) The only test that can predict harmful chemical reactions between scrapbook products and photos. This is an ISO standard method.

Surface Designer: Frankie Fioretti

Originally from beautiful upstate New York and now living on cosmopolitan Long Island, Frankie Fioretti enjoys traveling around the United States sharing her love of the paper arts, fiber arts, rubber stamping, and art materials. And when she comes home, Frankie's two sons and her husband Gary know that her passion for dreaming up and developing new and exciting art classes may keep her locked in her studio for days.

Frankie's students give her rave reviews for her highly creative classes and her extraordinary teaching style; store owners delight in her ability to generate sales beyond their expectations. She's always willing to share her marketing skills and the knowledge gained from her extensive retail experience, as well as consulting on design and layout, traffic flow, display, and product blend.

In addition to being a highly sought-after independant rubber-stamp instructor, Frankie also enjoys designing cards and beautiful papers for the Penny Black stamp company. Her work photographed on dozens of catalog covers and advertising may be anonymous to some, but those who know her work are wowed with every issue.

Early on, Frankie discovered USArtQuest as a natural fit with her interests, her style, and her diverse background as an artist, stamper, instructor, and marketing advisor. Working side by side with USArtQuest reps, pros, staff, and owner Susan Pickering Rothamel, Frankie teaches with authority on product integrity and usage and creative exploration.

Home—This complex collage incorporates many techniques, media, and compositional styles, including paste-papermaking, artist's cement leaves, and handmade background papers.

Our Own Winter Wonderland— Using several photos, this wintry scene has been cut into strips and carefully reassembled. This technique is a photo manipulation or photo montage.

Examples of Frankie Fioretti's Pages, Frames, and Handmade Paper Boxes

Pen Acid-free, photo safe, non-bleeding, and fade-resistant utensils (Fig. 115A), safe to use on scrapbook pages. Pens come in a variety of colors and styles (Figs. 115A-115F).

Fig. 115A: Gel Pens

Pen Types

Blending Pen A pen with ink that blends the drawn lines from wax-based pencils, watercolor markers, and other drawing tools and art materials.

Fountain Pen The most classic writing instrument. Fountain pens work on the free flow of wet ink through capillary action. The nib, responsible for the unique feel of the writing, is available in various sizes, metals, and complexities of design to accommodate the style of writing and preference of the writer.

Gel Pen Medium-point pens that use opaque ink. Gel pens are ideal for journaling or outlining letters and made to use on both light and dark papers.

Leafing Pen A pump-like dispensing pen, with "ink" that resembles plating. Check with manufacturer's labeling for permanent acid-free leafing products and toxicity.

Paint Pen A firm felt, brush-like tipped pen. The pressure applied to the tip controls the amount of ink, or paint, dispensed.

Roller-ball Pen Roller-ball pens use liquid ink and have a smooth fluid feel. Standard roller-ball pen refills use a wet ink system, similar to a fountain pen. Most roller-ball pens must have caps to prevent the ink from drying out.

Fig. 115B: Pen—*Hencho en Mexico* A light-colored gel pen, used to write this page's journaling, stands out from the dark paper, giving this page a vintage quality reminiscent of the black-paged albums of a bygone era.

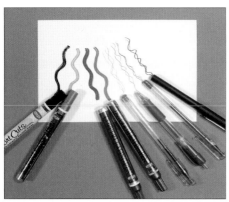

Fig. 115C: Various Pens

Fig. 115D: Pen—*Road Trip*
The short, narrative journaling on this page was written with a paint pen in light-colored ink. A road map was cleverly used to border the photo and journaling.

Fig. 115E: Pen—*Flowers Leave a Fragrance* Little dots, squiggles, and lines drawn with a fine-line pen delicately enhance ready-made stickers, as well as hand-lettering gilded with gold leaf.

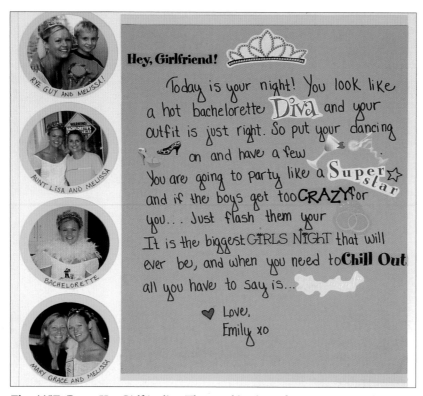

Fig. 115F: Pen—*Hey Girlfriend!* **The combination of permanent pen handwriting and stickers make this clever invitation worth saving on a special scrapbook page. Important photos, cut using a circle cutter, then framed, are used as a border. Compositionally, the photos balance the letter nicely.**

Pencil A writing utensil with an outer covering usually made of wood and an inner shaft of graphite, wax-based material, or other marking material. Pencils offer scrapbookers a diverse group of drawing, coloring, and writing tools (Fig. 116).

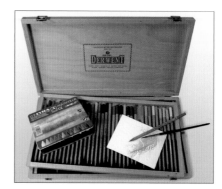

Fig. 116: Watercolor Pencils

Pencil Types

Colored Pencil A pencil often used for coloring. Colored pencils come in hundreds of colors and a variety of finishes. White or other light-colored pencils are ideal for journaling on dark-colored papers.

Mechanical Pencil A pencil that uses a continuous lead-feeding system, with various-sized leads, controlled by either a push button or twist mechanism. Popular lead sizes include .5mm and .7mm.

Metallic Pencil Similar to colored pencils, metallic pencils offer a bright metallic color. They are often used for resist techniques in watercolor or stamping.

Watercolor Crayon A crayon that blends and smooths with water and a paintbrush or sponge. Use watercolor crayons for filling in areas drawn with watercolor pencils or making broad swashes of color on a page.

Watercolor Pencil Similar to regular colored pencils, watercolor pencils may also be dipped into water or used with a damp brush for subtle blending.

Wax Pencil (Grease Pencil) Soft pencils designed for use on photographs and page protectors.

Permanence The ability of a material to resist chemical deterioration or changes in its properties. Proper storage environment plays a large part in a paper's permanence quality.

Permanent Paper The type of paper needed for absolute archival integrity, which means that it must last several hundred years (Figs. 117A & 117B.) According to the NISO (National Information Standards Organiza-tion), to be permanent, the paper must comply with Standard ANSI Z39.48–1984, and must meet the following requirements:

- Must have a pH level of 7.5 or greater.

- Must contain an alkaline buffer of calcium carbonate or another alkaline.

- Must be free of chemical impurities and, optimally, contain cotton or other rag fibers.

- Must be resistant to tears and folding.

Permanent papers are labeled with the mathematical symbol denoting infinity, set inside of a circle (Fig. 117C) and placed above the number of the international standard, indicating clearly that permanent paper has been used.

Fig. 117C: Permanent Paper Symbol

Fig. 117A: Permanent Paper—*Art Art Art* Scrapbook pages don't all have photos. This page makes a rubber-stamped, then watercolored artwork a standout.

Fig. 117B: Permanent Paper—*Sam 2002* Printing color photographs in a single color makes effective and interesting pages. Printed on permanent paper, these photos will last a long time.

pH Facts

- pH can only be measured on water-soluble materials.

- The pH scale runs from 0 to 14.0.

- 7.0 is considered neutral.

- 7.0 or below indicates increasing acidity.

- The lower the pH, the more acidic the paper.

- 7.0 or above indicates increasing alkalinity.

- The higher the pH, the more alkaline the paper.

- The pH scale is a logarithmic progression, which means that 6.0 is ten times more acidic than 7.0.

pH (Potential of Hydrogen)

A measure of acidity or alkalinity. Paper with a pH below five is considered highly acidic and should not be used in scrapbooks.

pH Neutral The center reading of 7.0 on the pH scale. It is neither acidic nor alkaline. Pure water has a pH of 7.0.

pH Testing Pen A pen containing an indicator dye that, when applied to the surface of a material, discolors in relation to the material's surface pH.

Photo Clean-up Removing dust, dirt, and other marks and stains from photos with any number of approved items (Fig. 118).

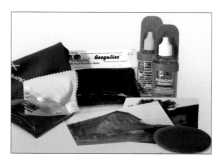

Fig. 118: Photo Clean-up Products

Fig. 119B: Photo Corner—*Easter 1998* Ribbon adds a textural softness to a scrapbook page, as seen here. The photo corners give the designer one more place that ribboning makes sense and adds just the right touch.

Photo Clean-up Tips

- Dirt and dust on photographic prints can be abrasive. Brush both off with a soft clean brush before placing them into a sleeve. Work gently, brushing from the center of the photo outward toward the edges.

- Erasers may be used on some photos to further reduce dirt. Use a plastic eraser that contains the fewest harmful chemicals.

- Some photos benefit from cleaning and flattening with water; however, a conservator should first be consulted.

- Do not attempt to clean photos with water- or solvent-based cleaners, such as window or film cleaner.

- Photos can adhere permanently to glass under high-humidity environments or direct exposure to liquids. Consult a photographic materials conservator before attempting to remove the adhered materials.

- Improper cleaning of photographic materials can cause serious and often irreversible damage such as permanent staining, abrasion, alteration, or loss of binder and image.

- Do not use pressure-sensitive adhesive tapes to repair torn photos.

- Broken, torn, or cracked photos should be placed carefully in a polyester sleeve with an archival board support.

- Most but not all photos consist of a final image material, a binder layer, and a primary support. The binder layer is a transparent substance usually made of albumen, collodion, or gelatin applied to a primary support, usually paper or plastic. Paper fibers, albumen, and gelatin binders are just some of the components in photographic materials that provide an attractive food source for insects and should be stored appropriately.

- A conservator should be consulted for problems of mold, pressure-sensitive tape, aqueous cleaning, brittle or broken mounts, remounting, strong curling, and extensive tears.

Photo Corner A small self-adhesive paper (Fig. 119A), usually triangular in shape (Figs. 119B & 119C). A photo can be safely removed from photo corners.

Fig. 119A: Photo Corners

Fig. 119C: Photo Corner—
Mother and Daughter
There is a clean simplicity to this page with decorative flower-shaped photo corners, adding nearly the only textural elements. The vellum was strategically placed, using the metal plate as the anchor and opening up into the photo as the focal point.

Fig. 120A: Photo Kaleidoscope—
Riley In this page's photo kaleidoscope, the baby's legs were the meeting point for the photos. It almost looks as though he is climbing out of the page.

Photo Documentation
The activity of photographing people, events, projects, travels, or locations, and then organizing the photos and recording data to tell a coherent visual story.

Photo Kaleidoscope The photo-paper-craft technique that uses multiple copies of the same photo in both regular and reverse formats to produce a pattern resembling a kaleidoscope (Figs. 120A & 120B).

Fig. 120B: Photo Kaleidoscope—
Puppy Love The puppy's shadow on this page provided a good place for the photos to meet to form the kaleidoscope effect.

Figs. 121A & 121B: Photo Restoration—This photo was in very bad condition and was carefully restored to nearly original condition by using a computer's photo software.

Photo Restoration The process of restoring a torn, damaged, spotted, or faded photograph (Fig. 121A) to nearly new conditions (Fig. 121B), by means of airbrush, computer, and hand-painted techniques. Skilled artisans provide the service of complete black-and-white, or color photo restoration.

P

Photo Safekeeping Tips

- Photos incur some amount of damage even through gentle handling. Dust and other common environmental factors, such as peanut butter and jelly fingers and spilled drinks, cause them to be soiled and quite possibly irreparably damaged.

- Photos should be quickly placed into boxes, then into albums.

- Once placed in albums, photos should be covered with sleeve protectors to assure longevity.

- Store photo boxes and albums in a temperate dry environment. Heat distorts photos and causes a more rapid disintegration. UV light rays harm photos, causing fading and paper disintegration. Moisture causes mold spores that can be damaging to photos.

Recommended storage conditions:

- 77°F (25°C).

- Twenty to fifty percent relative humidity.

- A dark environment.

Photo Sleeve Polypropylene or Mylar sleeve used to store and protect photos or memorabilia.

Photo Split Permanent self-adhesive tab with easy-to-remove backing paper.

Photo Tape Permanent double-sided rolls of tape with easy-to-remove backing paper.

Photo Tinting, Hand-tinting, or Tinting 1. The process of applying color tints, in the form of paint or colored pencils, to a photographic image to create or enhance the color effect (Fig. 122). 2. The process of applying color to black-and-white images by using certain computer software.

Julien, March 2002

Fig. 122: Photo Tinting—*Julien* Julien is subtly photo-tinted in this simple brag book and embellished with little tiles that add color without bulk. Photo tinting is easy and can also be a great way to save a less-than-perfectly taken black-and-white photo.

Photo Tinting Tips

- When using oil-based photo-tinting pens, matte-finished photos will accept the color more readily than glossy photos.

- When using oil-based photo-tinting pens, avoid going over the same spot on the photo too many times or the dampness of the ink will cause the photo to disintegrate.

- Colored pencils are opaque and can be used to create detail and dimension, as well as to remove blemishes or to highlight.

- Pencils can be used by themselves or in combination with photo oils.

- Pencils can cause damage to the print's surface. However, many colored pencils today have softer leads and while the point is fine, the side of the lead can be used for shading large areas safely.

Photocopier An instrument using light-sensitive photographic materials to reproduce written, printed, or graphic work.

Photography From Greek, photos (meaning light) and graphos (meaning writing), photography means to literally write or draw with light, first suggested by Sir John Herschel to William Fox Talbot in 1839 (Figs. 123A–123Q).

Fig. 123A: Various Types of Photos

Fig. 123B: Black-and-white Photos and Scrapbook Materials

Photography Types

Black-and-white Photography A photo that has an image made up of only shades of gray (Figs. 123B–123G). (See also Film.)

Close-up Photographs taken very close to a subject, or appear to be close by using a special camera lens. This technique is an effective way to capture the gleam in the eye of a child, or the delicate mound of snow on a flower.

Color Photography Color photos are made by recording images on transparent film in opposite tones within three dye layers; cyan, magenta, and yellow (negative). These tones are then reversed onto color photographic paper to re-create the image in its natural color scheme (Figs. 123H–123J).

Digital Photography Also considered color photography, the preservation issues with digital

photography are different, requiring the use of acid-free papers and ink for reproduction.

Enlargement A photo that has been blown up from the original size (Figs. 123K & 123L).

Matte or Glossy Finish The two most popular finishes for processed photos. The finish makes little difference in the life expectancy of a photo; however, it does make a considerable difference in the color. Glossy photos will exhibit brighter more intense colors. Matte photos are less shiny and tend to show less dust and fewer fingerprints and abrasion scratches.

Panorama A photo presenting a continuous view of the landscape, produced either by using a panoramic camera or from a composite of several images (Figs. 123M–123O).

P

Fig. 123C: Photography—*Ian*   The close-up black-and-white photos are nicely balanced with the shots of Ian apparently reading a literary masterpiece. The background paper offers a lot of interesting movement and texture, making it unnecessary to add much in the way of embellishments.

Fig. 123D: Photography—*Sweet Megan*   The photos here are strong by themselves and need little enhancing. This simple red-and-white motif nicely frames the black-and-white photos, without overpowering them.

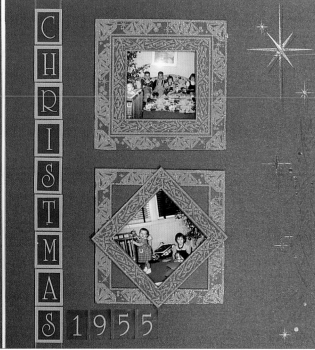

Fig. 123E: Photography—*A Jewel of a Christmas*   When there are not many photos of a particular time or place, enlarging one makes sense. Here, the family photo is enlarged and cropped nearly square. The facing page utilizes a more intimate look for the remainder of these Christmas photos.

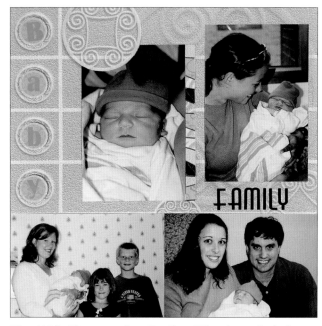

Fig. 123F: Photography—*Friends and Love*   This clean and simple black-and-white design is smashing with the addition of pink. The movement created by the strings complements the geometry and adds texture.

Fig. 123G: Photography—*Family*   What is particularly noteworthy about this page is that it wasn't necessary to have the photos in black-and-white, but it really makes a statement by doing so.

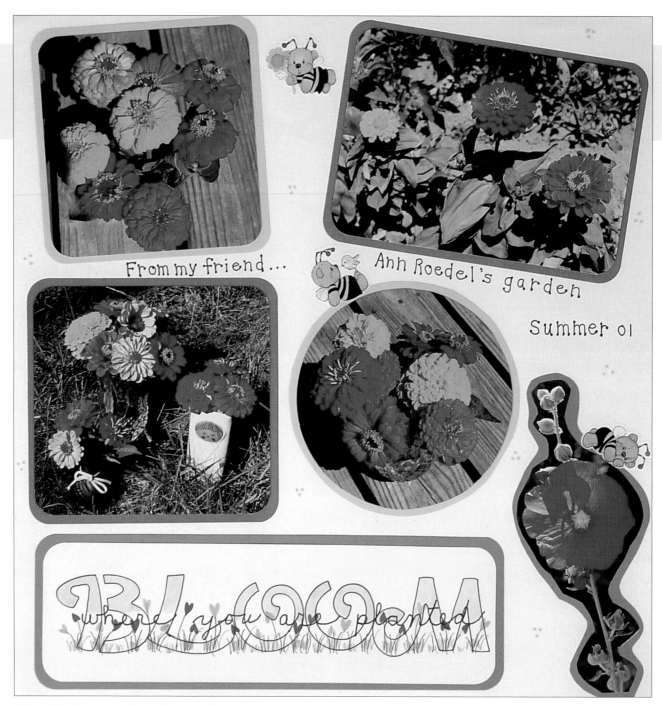

Fig. 123H: Photography—*Bloom*   This page has a colorful
story to tell as well as a bit of "colorful" advice. The
carefully placed bee stickers add a touch of whimsy and charm.

Fig. 123I: Photography—*Phanuef's Lupines*   These photos were carefully shot, revealing the wonder of color in our own gardens. The color value between the greens and purples are equal in saturation and make a bold statement. The meticulous framing accentuates the flower's vertical characteristic.

Fig. 123J: Photography—*Everyone Smiles in the Same Language*
There is a lot to see and sort on these pages. The solid black background, broken only by the red bordering, helps the eye organize and process the information. The buttons add the punctuation while actually being functional components.

Fig. 123K: Photography—*Come and Walk with Me*   Enlarge photos to make your own background papers. Here, the flowers blooming outdoors were brought in and used behind the vellum overlay.

Fig. 123L: Photo Enlargement

Fig. 123M: Photography—*Elephants* There couldn't be a much better use for a panoramic photo than the long trunk on an elephant, or a much better use of close-up photography than the anatomical details usually overlooked, such as an elephant's tail, eye, and foot.

Fig. 123N: Photography—*Organ Museum* The panoramic photography used as a border for these pages was picture perfect. Close-up photography or stock photography, ready-made and available at scrapbook stores, adds punch and emphasis to almost any page.

P

Fig. 123O: Photography—*Tastes Like Christmas*   The panoramic view of the Christmas cookies borders the bottom of the page nicely, treating viewers to a tasty scrapbook page that nearly smells as good as it looks.

Fig. 123P: Photography— *The Pumpkin Patch*   The oversized color photos are perfect for this little boy amongst the pumpkins. Corrugated paper, Mica Tiles and brads, along with rubberstamped fall leaves frame the photos, adding both smooth and rough textures as well as shine.

Fig. 123Q: Photography— *100% Athlete* This all black-and-white page is cleverly softened by the use of ribbon and buckles and a quirky use of words, phrases, and the repetitive pattern of Michaela's name, making a unique and inexpensive background paper.

Pigment An oil-based substance used to color ink, paper, and textiles. Pigments are generally more stable than dyes, but they produce a narrower color selection.

Pixel Short for picture element. When pixels (or dots) are small enough, the eye naturally merges them into a continuous tone. (See also DPI and Scanner.)

Plastic A binder combined with plasticizers, fillers, pigments, and other additives. The binder gives a plastic its main characteristics. Plastic will not rot or decay.

Plastic Terms

Mylar The proprietary name for sheet polyester, an inert material in which fragile documents are often stored. With the advent of Mylar, the need for lamination became obsolete.

Plasticizers Substances used in the production of plastics to make them more flexible and less brittle. Plasticizers are considered unsuitable for being in contact or near photographs and most materials used in archival scrapbooking.

Polyester A strong film having good resistance to moisture, solvents, oils, and many other chemicals. Polyester can be transparent or have a metallic finish.

Polyethylene A transparent plastic safe for storing photographs and other memorabilia.

Polypropylene A photo-safe clear plastic that does not contain acid-forming chemicals that may damage photos. It is used in photo-safe page protectors.

PVC (Polyvinyl Chloride) An unstable plastic that discharges a chlorine gas harmful to photos and albums.

Scrap of History: Plastic

The first important plastic celluloid was discovered (c.1869) by the American inventor John W. Hyatt; however, plastics did not come into modern industrial use until after the production (1909) of Bakelite. Since then, new uses for plastics have been continually discovered, many well-known names being Plexiglas, Lucite, and Cellophane.

P

Pocket Page A removable album page with two or more pockets used to hold photos and memorabilia.

Pop-up Dimensional paper silhouettes that "pop" up from the page surface and reveal the shape or motif. Pop-ups are a form of paper crafting that explores the dimensional and sculptural aspects of scrapbooking. There are manufacturers that specialize in pop-ups, pullouts, and other action parts. But devising your own pop-up to fit a theme can be a fun challenge and remind us all of the shoe-box dioramas we used to make in elementary school (Figs. 124A–124C).

Fig. 124A: Pop-up—*I Love NY* This page's flip card includes pop-up photos, which add dimension to an otherwise flat page.

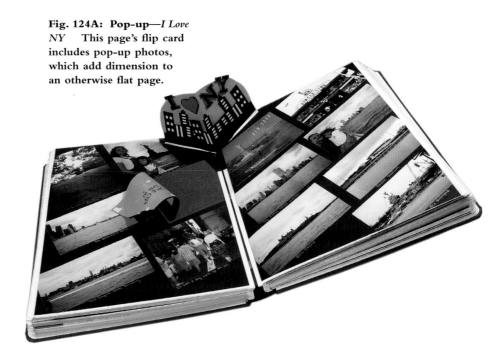

Fig. 124B: Pop-up— *Christina*

Fig. 124C: Pop-up—*Zoo-pendous Towel Creatures* This two-page spread features a three-dimensional pop-up scene, charming titles, and captions.

Portrait   The pictorial representation of an animal or person, generally considered to be more formally photographed (Figs. 125A–125D).

Portrait Sleeve A polypropylene or Mylar album page-sized sleeve, generally found with a reinforced edge, closed on three sides. Used for storing portrait-sized photos or larger documents.

Fig. 125A: Portrait— *Baby Michelle*   This portrait page, bordered with sparkling mica bits on tape, is tucked neatly into highly decorative photo corners. This mount makes the photo removable for duplication at a future date.

Fig. 125B: Portrait—_Family Traditions_   There is a serene simplicity in the color and composition, giving each photograph an individual importance and quality. The paint strip marked with captions like harmony and tranquility makes the page have a special meaning; while adding color, light, texture, and balance.

227

Fig. 125C: Portrait—*Dreaming of a White Christmas*   Paper tearing can really give a page a snowy effect, perfect for framing a portrait or any wintry photo. Placing the photo on the left corner compostionally keeps the boy's eye looking inward and upward into the page.

Fig. 125D: Portrait—*Julien* The portrait photo of Julien is simply framed with soft papers that coordinate nicely with her dress. Between Julien's serene pose and the unusual lighting, which creates strong light and shadow play, there is a sweet old-fashioned quality to this page.

Positive   Film that contains an image with the same tonal values as the original; opposite of a negative.

Power Cropping   A method of cropping photos in which all the materials and photos are gathered and stored in a single folder until ready to use.

Preservation   Using archival-quality products to prolong the life of a scrapbook. Considering all the paper, plastic, and art materials used to create scrapbooks, preservationists can only base assumptions about their potential longevity on historical evidence and current science. The rest is up to the scrapbooker.

Pressure–sensitive Adhesive An adhesive that bonds by contact and pressure. (See also Adhesives.)

P–series Paper   Paper that passes the PAT, is acid-free, lignin-free, buffered, bleed resistant, and generally fade resistant and complies with ISO 18902–2001.

Safety Methods for Preservaton

Safety methods for ensuring the preservation of scrapbooks include:

- Use only acid-free or alkaline buffered (archival) products.

- Photocopy items onto archival acid-free, lignin-free copier paper. In case of disaster, keep all originals in a safe and separate location.

- Encapsulation: Incorporate "non-photo-safe" items, such as memorabilia and documents in a clear Mylar sleeve. This prevents acid migration to photos.

- Try not to write on photos. Stay away from the image area. Write on the white border if possible, using only an archival pen or soft pencil. If you must write on the reverse of the print, use only light pressure.

- Place an acid-containing item as far from photos as possible, preferably on a facing page and in a Mylar sleeve.

- Buffered paper mats surrounding photos or memorabilia slow the progression of acids toward a photo.

- Deacidification sprays are made to neutralize the acid in papers. Check on the spray label to verify safety for the photos themselves. Different manufacturers produce different products. When preserving scrapbooks do not:

  - Write on a document or the emulsion side of a photo with magic marker or ballpoint pen.

  - Use "magnetic" albums or any polyvinyl chloride plastic sleeves.

  - Have dirt, dust, sunlight, or water in the storage environment.

P

Public Domain Works not subject to copyright. These works can be freely reproduced and reused by anyone for any purpose.

When a copyright expires, or it was not properly secured from the outset, or when the government produces a work, the material is probably in public domain. The status of such works should always be confirmed, since elements of the whole may be protected by copyright in some way.

Punch A handheld or tabletop mechanical device made to punch paper shapes (Fig. 126A & 126B). From simple geometric shapes to elaborate corner designs, punches are a staple for scrapbook aficionados. For ease of use, avoid thick cardstocks, using instead thin- to medium-weight papers, sticker papers, and vellum (Figs. 126B–126E).

Punch Types

Power Punch A tool into which a punch is placed to produce a punchie. Use the power punch's lever to apply pressure. This is a much easier way to create multiple punchies than using thumb punches.

Punchie The paper shape that results from using a punch.

Thumb Punch A small punch used to create single punchies which is operated by pressing with the thumb.

Figs. 126B & 126C: Punch—*My Bridal Shower* Punches and diecuts add a dimensional as well as colorful aspect to pages. In these designs, several different punches were used and the flowerets stacked together to form pinwheels. A small brad or eyelet makes a great centerpiece, holding the pieces together and attaching the finished design to the page.

Fig. 126A: Press Type and Thumb Press Punches and Decorative Scissors used with Corner Punches

Fig. 126B: Punch and Punchies. The positive or negative shapes used for scrapbooking embellishments.

Fig. 126C: Punched Paper Close-up

Fig. 126D: Punch— *Michaela* **Corrugated paper adds lots of texture without overpowering the photography, and torn paper makes an effective frame for this page. This page was a constructive way to use paper scraps. Punched flowers are made by layering the petals and lifting the edges to reveal the layers underneath. Paper fasteners not only make a colorful center but also keep the flower together and hold it to the page.**

Punch Usage Tips

- When punches become dull, try punching through aluminum foil.

- Sharpen all edges by punching through a very fine grade of sandpaper in both directions. Do this both upside down and right side up.

- Use an adhesive remover for sticky blades.

- Punch waxed paper to keep punches punching smoothly.

Fig. 126E: Punch — *My Little Star* **The "little star" featured on these pages is surrounded by star punchies, all held into place with star-shaped paper fasteners.**

Quilling The paper-craft art of rolling narrow strips of paper (approximately ¹⁄₁₆" wide) into coil shapes, whereby sizing, pinching, and gluing the shapes together form intricately delicate filigree-like designs (Figs. 127A & 127B).

Fig. 127A: Quilling Materials, Books, Patterns, and Adhesives

Christmas in 1956

My grandpa, my dad and two of my 3 uncles, Jim and Ed. Ed the oldest, next my dad, and Jim the youngest here (I don't think Jay was even thought about yet and grandma must have been taking the picture).
I guess it would be safe to say that they had a pretty good Christmas!

Fig. 127B: Quilling—
Christmas in 1956 Although bought as a ready-made embellishment, the Christmas tree on this page is made using the quilling technique.

Quote A unique saying, scripture verse, poem, memorable word said, and everyday axioms repeated by everyday people. Quotes have a special place in scrapbooking. Besides finding quotes in books, magazines, and Internet search engines, manufacturers have made it simple by making stickers, quote books, and tag art imprinted with famous (and not so famous) words, all ready-made for every occasion possible (Figs. 128A & 128B).

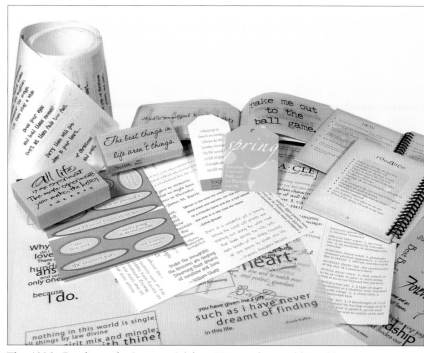

Fig. 128A: Ready-made Quotes—Stickers, Tags, and Reusable Rubber Stamps.

Fig. 128B: Quote—*Crabbing* A ready-made quote was adhered onto the top-left corner of this page. It lends itself nicely to the theme, background, and photos on the page, as well as giving insight to the page designer's personality.

R

Raffia Natural fibers used as an alternative to ribbons and bows, providing a more natural, country style.

Rag Paper or Board

A paper or board manufactured with a high content of long cotton fibers.

Ragged Edge Unjustified copy.

Recycling The act of using any paper or object that was used at least once before in a new way and thus giving it value. For scrapbookers, this includes most paper ephemera, greeting cards, fabric, plastic and wooden bits, and metal objects (Figs. 129A & 129B).

Red-eye An effect encountered when light from a flash unit travels parallel to the eye's lens axis during exposure.

Fig. 129A: Recycling—*Elvis* Recycled Elvis memorabilia was used for this page to add a touch of nostalgic musical history. Adding the keepsakes to this acid-free environment ensures that they will last.

Fig. 129B: Recycling—*Kasha* Mesh adds texture and personality to this page, and the recycled greeting card is one way to save and display cherished cards and gift tags.

Red-eye Pen A pen specially made to take red-eye out of flash photos.

Refill Page Paper and protectors (Fig. 130) made to fit, add to, and fill albums of standard sizes.

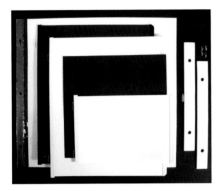

Fig. 130: Album Refill Pages

Register The arrangement of two or more images in exact alignment with each other.

Resin-coated Paper A photographic paper coated with polyethylene on both sides. All consumer color-photographic prints are now printed on this paper. Black-and-white photos can be printed on either resin-coated or fiber-based paper.

Retouching An after-treatment carried out on a negative or print, in the form of local chemical reduction, local dye, pencil additions, or air-brushing. The purpose is to remove blemishes on the negative or print.

RH (Relative Humidity) A measure of moisture content in the air. Reducing air-moisture content can significantly extend the life of photographs and scrapbook materials. The negative effects on photos and albums in a high-humidity environment include bleeding inks, items that stick or bond to one another, the reversal of adhesive bonds, and breakdown of paper fiber.

High humidity promotes the migration of acids as well as mold growth. In contrast, low humidity can cause irreversible physical deformation of photos, paper embrittlement, and adhesive inflexibility or reversal.

Ribbon 1. A fabric notion (Figs. 131A–131D) consisting of a narrow strip of fine material used for trimming, tying, and embellishing. 2. A paper notion resembling a ribbon, also known as a spring roll.

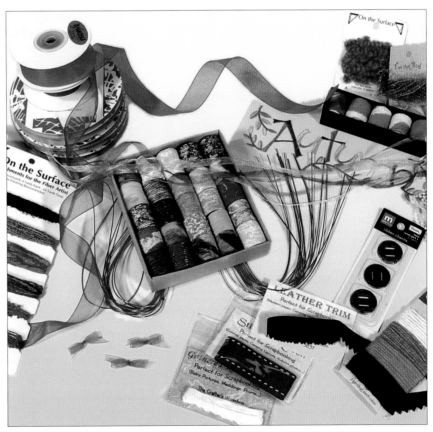

Fig. 131A: Various Ribbons, Raffia, Fibers, Cords, and Ribbon Slides.

R

Fig. 131B: Ribbon—*Grandparents* Using sheer ribbons to make a French bulletin-board scrapbook page is easy and decorative. Repeating the ribbon by framing the portrait conveys a sense of continuity and balance. The journaled notes are all handmade.

Fig. 131C: Ribbon—*Zoo Boo* Decorative ribbons and fibers add a fun and attention-grabbing texture on this collaged page, while keeping with the overall theme. The close-up photo tag unifies the different elements by touching edges with nearly every piece.

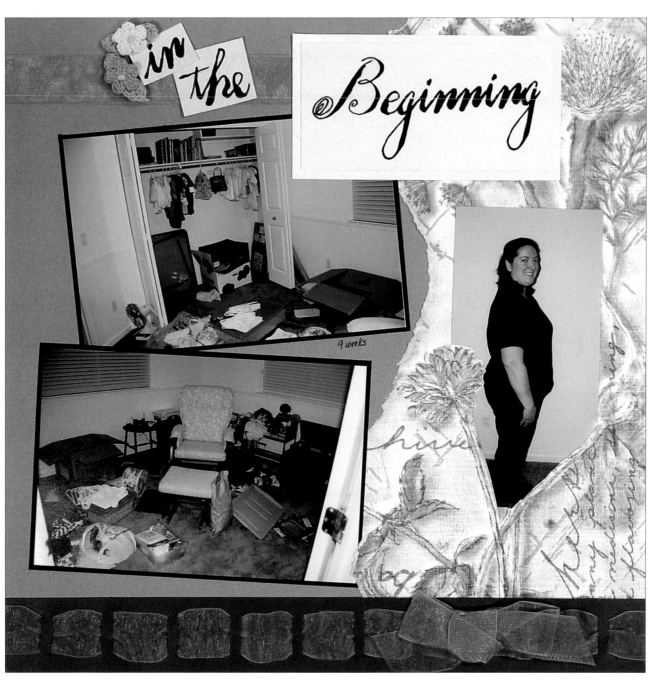

Fig. 131D: Ribbon—*In the Beginning* Ribbon weaving is easy. Use a craft knife to make the right-sized slice in the border or page and weave it through. It is effective decoratively and softens the overall look of the page.

R

Rubber Stamping A technique whereby a rubber die and ink are used to reproduce the die's design onto any surface. A rubber stamp (Figs. 132A–132J) can be used for thousands of impressions and with proper care, will last for years.

Fig. 132B: A Rubber-stamper's Dream Collection

Fig. 132A: Rubber Stamping Inks and Stamp Pads

Rubber Stamp Types

Clear Mount A die with a clear acrylic block and clear polymer. These stamps allow the artisan to "see" exactly where to stamp, for precise placements.

Foam Stamp A foam image adhered onto a foam block. These stamps are ideal for fabric stamping and stamping bolder images on textured paper.

Hand-carved Carving is an art form whereby artists use a craft knife to carve original imagery into erasers, foam blocks, or rubber sheets.

Fig. 132C: Hand-carved Stamp

Pen Score A proprietary type of foam sheet or block, heated then impressed with a raised design made of any material, causing a negative impression. The remaining positive impression, or reverse image can then be used as a rubber stamp.

Roller Stamp A stamp consisting of a single-strip die mounted on a plastic roller resembling a brayer. When rolled, it provides a continuous image on the stamping surface.

Self-inking Stamp A rubber die with an ink pad built into the handle. This type of stamp is commonly found in an office supply store, and can provide uniquely fun words and titles for scrapbook pages.

Pen Scoring Tip

Pen Score is a good material for making scrapbooking imagery from familyheirlooms, jewelry pieces, buttons, and other found objects, without damaging the object.

Rubber Stamp Types (cont'd)

UM (Unmounted Rubber) A rubber die, minus any handle. The great appeal of UMs are their size. UMs are small enough that storing hundreds in a single photo box, takes up far less space than collecting traditional rubber stamps. To use a UM, economical mounts of various types are available. Some types of mounts include magnets, Velcro, and cling vinyl.

Wood-mounted A stamp providing a rubber design or die, a layer of cushion (for "give"), and a wood block (for stability). Wood-mounted stamps also have an imprinted image on the topside of the wood, called indexing. The index indicates the exact placement of the die design mounted to the underside.

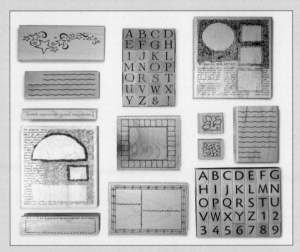

Fig. 132D: Rubber Stamps Useful in Scrapbooking

Other Rubber-stamping Terms:

Backprint This occurs when the impression of the edges of the die or foam are inadvertently stamped onto the paper. To avoid this, do not rock the stamp or trim the excess foam with a craft knife.

Fig. 132E: Rubber-stamp Backprint

Cut 'n Dry A proprietary name of a foam-backed applicator and stamping pad. Cut 'n Dry is invaluable when using inks, adhesives, and paints for stamping and other paper-craft projects.

Embossing Powder A clear or colored plastic resin that when heated, produces a shiny raised image.

Stamp Cleaner An applicator-topped cleaner that can be applied directly onto the stamp to remove ink. Use a gentle motion to clean, then pat the stamp dry on paper towels.

Stamp Pad A clear or colored ink-soaked pad used to hold ink. The ink will wet the stamp, then the paper, then hold the embossing powder in place until it can be heated.

Stamping Mat A durable foam mat used as a work surface for stamping. Mats provide a slight "give," allowing the best ink impressions. These are particularly useful for oversized stamps.

Fig. 132F: Rubber Stamping—
All the Leaves Rubber stamping is a great alternative to buying background papers. A couple of leaves and dye inks creates a background that is necessary to further embellish the page.

Fig. 132G: Rubber Stamping—
Tis the Season Here, images stamped and embossed in gold add texture and holiday designs without becoming a distraction. Overlapping the background papers unifies the many elements, and the shiny gold frame around the photo helps to identify where to look first.

Fig. 132H: Rubber Stamping—*Friendship* Special rubber-stamped verses add not only a nice saying or, in this case, a balancing element but when embossed, they add sparkle, texture, and heartfelt meaning to a page.

Fig. 132I: Rubber Stamping—*Layla* Rubber-stamping was an effective way to make the fish and the coral to embellish this page. The background paper was brayered to resemble the ocean.

Fig. 132J: Rubber Stamping—*Playtime* Rubber-stamped letters are a fun and easy way to make titles and other descriptives for a scrapbook page. The big graphic stamps add design and texture as well as balance and visual interest.

R

Rubber Stamping Product Designer: Dee Gruening

Whether she's using her graphic rubber stamps to make colorful personalized stickers, her signature line of Mrs. Grossman's stickers to embellish a page, or her personal line of Marvy markers to make luscious calligraphic letters, Dee Gruenig's scrapbooking creations are as graphically sophisticated as they are colorful and bold. Her passion and enthusiasm for the work flow from her heart right into her art—a passion that has led her to write eight books, produce eleven videos (with her husband, Warren), and teach over 30,000 students; and an enthusiasm so infectious that almost no one leaves a class without being inspired to try one of her latest tools or creative techniques.

In the early morning, you'll find Dee out for a walk on the beach near her California home. This is her private time of reflection and inspiration, a time to center herself and prepare for the day. After a healthy breakfast, a time for meditation, and an hour for her own design work, Dee leaves for work at her studio. With this careful attention to spiritual attunement and personal well-being, she keeps her energy high.

After earning a master's degree in art education from Stanford University, Dee taught art in public schools. She and Warren also spent five years teaching at an American school in Venezuela, then came home to teach in California again. Dee was still teaching in 1979 when she started her own business: a one-woman home-party operation she called Posh Presents. Then, in 1983, the Junior League of Orange County invited her to sell stamps at their annual charity fundraiser. "Stores from all over the United States were invited," Dee says. "I had never done anything like this before, but we were joyously overwhelmed!" That event, where she set a Junior League sales record that stood for ten years, was a turning point in Dee's career.

Over time, Dee opened a couple of stores and developed a line of rubber stamps called Posh Impressions; she even designed a stamp for Lady Bird Johnson after the former first lady saw Dee's booth at a Junior League show in Austin. "She wanted a stamp with the Texas state flower," Dee says, so Posh Impressions outsourced the making of a "Blue Bonnet" stamp. Today, Dee shares her passion for stamping and scrapbooking by teaching around the world, and her *Great Rubber Stamp Book* has set a record for Sterling Publishing with a half-million copies sold.

Dee also spends much of her time doing charitable work. From 1997 to 2003, she served on the Board of Directors of the Hobby Industry Association (HIA), working on the education committee to enthusiastically promote the craft industry worldwide. She has carried the message of craft as far afield as Washington, D.C., Germany, and Korea, where the morale and welfare department of the U.S. Army has sent her to promote rubber stamping and scrapbooking among military enthusiasts. It's been an adventure, to say the least. "Several years ago," Dee relates, "I went to Korea with the intention of leading the instructors in rubber stamp classes. At the same time, a North Korean stole a jet and defected to South Korea. On the brink of war, the Army got all the women and children out, but since I was not in the military, I was not informed of this." Dee ended up being the only woman left in the Demilitarized Zone on the 38th Parallel dividing the two Koreas. "When I taught the classes," she laughs, "they consisted entirely of men!"

Dee Gruenig's Rubber Stamping Materials and Sponged Background Papers

Examples of Dee Gruenig's Work from Her Great African Adventure

The Apple of My Eye—Stamped and cut-out apple shapes gleefully embellish this page, mirroring the title. Silhouetting techniques such as the beautiful little girl shown here, enlarged and perfectly placed, draw the eye in, create a focal point, and capture the imagination.

Examples of Dee Gruenig's journal pages, These journals generously stamped and graphically designed, provide extensive handwritten notations of a day's events. Even the handwriting is part of the overall textural design element.

Examples from Dee's Great African Adventure

Ruler A metal or wooden straight-edged strip used for measuring lengths (Fig. 133A – 133B).

Ruler Tips

- When used while scrapbooking, rulers are not just for measuring. Metal rulers can be used as guides for cutting with a craft knife, or for tearing a relatively straight line with paper.

- Triangular rulers, also known as scales, are helpful for those with fine-motor-skill problems, by allowing the ruler to be handled more easily.

Ruler Types

Centering Ruler A ruler used for centering an object on a page. The center of the ruler is marked with a zero and numbers increase to the right and left, both beginning with one and working toward six or more, depending on ruler length.

Deckle-edged Ruler A ruler with an edge that resembles the deckle of handmade paper. Pulling paper along the edge will produce a feathered edge. Oftentimes, deckle-edged rulers have a centering rule as well.

Metal Ruler A steel, cork-backed ruler. A metal ruler is not only a very accurate measuring device but invaluable for drawing lines with markers because the cork elevates the ruler and prohibits the ink from being pulled by capillary action under the ruler.

T-square A T-shaped ruler used for drawing straight lines and lining up page elements.

Fig. 133A: Rulers

Fig. 133B: Ruler—*Sam* Rulers, both regular and deckle-edged turn pages into colorfully balanced compositions, while giving scrapbookers a unique opportunity to use up their scraps of paper from previous projects.

S

Scanner A device (Fig. 134) used to digitize (convert to electronic format) artwork, photographs, or other items from a hard copy. A scanner works very much like a photocopy machine by placing the hard copy on the scanner bed, where it then reads the material, converting it to a data file (Technique 16).

Scannogram Creating a piece of art by placing objects, flowers, leaves, and other items directly on the scanner bed and scanning them (Figs. 135A & 135B). Each image or group of images are then loaded onto the computer and enhanced through any number of techniques from enlarging to color manipulation.

Fig. 135A: Scannogram

Fig. 134: Scanner

Fig. 135B: Scannogram— *Autumn* Saving autumn leaves can be a challenge when doing archival scrapbooking. Here a scannogram captures the texture, color, and shapes of the leaves. Using multiple leaves made a great background on this solid cardstock.

S

Technique 16: Scanning

1. Set the scanner to produce a 24-bit (16 million colors) image.

2. Set the image size.

3. If an enlarged or shrunken image is desired, set the scanner accordingly. For instance, if a smaller image is desired, set the scanner to reduce the image by fifty percent, which will make it half as large.

4. Set the resolution. Note: Resolution is the density of dots of color called a bit-mapped image. For a print—creating an image that is at least 300 dpi—change the resolution button or DPI button to 300.

5. Click the scan button. Note: The image may appear larger on the computer screen, which shows an image in 72 dpi only. Do not worry, it will print in 300 dpi.

6. Save the file in the appropriate location.

7. Print the image.

8. For the storage of many photos, use a CD-R, as high-quality photos use up a great deal of disk space.

Scherenschnitte (pronounced shair-en-shnit-teh) Scissor-cutting. Scherenschnitte paper-craft techniques used to decorate birth and marriage certificates, create Christmas decorations, and became a popular folk art in the 1800s (Fig. 136).

Fig. 136: Scherenschnitte—*Friendship*   The scherenschnitte corners on these pages embellish them nicely, adding a decorative frame. The printed vellum used on the background and the panoramic photo of the bread racks add texture and balance the scherenschnitte corners.

Scissors A hand tool used to cut paper, thin cardstock, and fabric. Scissors are among one of the most important tools a scrapbooker can have. An assortment of two or three pair is necessary for most scrapbook applications. At the minimum, scrapbookers will need one pair for general cutting and one pair for intricate detail.

Score Impressions or cuts in flat material to facilitate bending or tearing (Fig. 137).

Scrapbook A blank book in which miscellaneous items such as newspaper clippings or photos are collected and preserved.

Scrapbook Convention A local or regional gathering of manufacturers and demonstrators in the scrapbook industry. Classes and crop parties are usually offered, as well as contests and door prizes.

Sealing Wax and Seal A technique of impressing a metal die into hot melted wax or a wax substitute, yielding a disk with an image, letter, or illuminated lettering (Figs. 138A–138D).

Scissor Types

Cushioned Scissors
Scissor handles with a soft rubber material to cushion hands while cutting.

Micro-tip Scissors
Scissors with a sharpened point for precise cuts.

Nonstick Scissors
Scissors that have a Teflon coating on the blades that allows tape and glue to wipe off easily.

Razor-edged Scissors
Very sharp scissors made for fabric and coarse papers.

Self-opening Scissors
Spring-action scissors that automatically open after each cut. These scissors are particularly good for scrapbookers with hand-problems or arthritis.

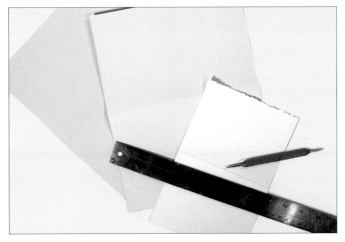

Fig. 137: Scoring Tools

Fig. 138A: Sealing Wax and Seals

S

Fig. 138B: Seals—*Love*
Traditionally made sealing waxes make interesting embellishments and also to spell out the title. These waxes were further enhanced by rubbing on dry pigment color.

Fig. 138C: Seals and Wax—Seals come in hundreds of styles and the wax in many colors, perfect for scrapbook embellishing.

Fig. 138D: Seals—*Thanksgiving*
Handmade wax seals adorn these pages as embellishments. The seals used on the page closely resemble the buttons on the tags.

Self-healing Cutting Mat-
A plastic mat imprinted with a precalculated grid pattern. The surface is suitable for cutting with rotary blades and craft knives and once cut on, appears to mend itself, allowing for more cutting.

Sepia Print A print with a reddish-brown color, with the appearance of dark lines on a lighter background. Oftentimes sepia prints are made on a semi-transparent paper so that the reproductions can be made (Fig. 139).

Sequin A small shiny disk used to reflect light and add interest to a garment. Sequins add interest when

Fig. 139: Sepia Prints

used in scrapbooks as well. Sequins are often made with a Mylar or polyethylene coating, allowing them to be suitable for scrapbooking. Vintage sequins should be used with caution. Encapsulation techniques should be considered when using them.

Sewing To fasten by stitching with a needle and thread or sewing

machine (Fig. 140A). Sewing is becoming very popular with paper enthusiasts, sewing on paper can include machine or hand-sewing, embroidery, thread-painting, and appliqué work, using many of the same techniques one would use with fabric (Figs. 140B–140F).

Fig. 140A: Paper Sewing Machine and Sewn Papers

Fig. 140B: Sewing—_211_ String was threaded through eyelets on this spread, giving the viewer the illusion that it is holding the top and bottom of the white paper together, while adding a decidedly nautical touch.

S

Fig. 140C: Sewing—
You Keep Us in Stitches
Door-frame climbing may never become an Olympic sporting event, but stitching this torn paper sure makes this page fun and worth the design effort.

Fig. 140D: Sewing—
Frilled Lizard
Stitched corners and edging actually make this sewn page functionally designed, as well as adding significantly more interest than having used double-sided tape.

Fig. 140E: Sewing—
Pumpkin Carving   The sewn fibers here actually join the upper and lower portions of this page, which allows the eye to move up and down without stopping. The composition, divided into thirds, is very effective.

Fig. 140F: Sewing—
Detroit   Sewing doesn't always have to use threads. Sometimes using wire and a few beads can add a whole new textural flavor to what would have been a simple layout.

S

Shadow Box Scrapbooking

Frames especially designed to cover and protect photos and collected memorabilia (Fig. 141A). Items are arranged into a pleasing layout then framed and hung for viewing (Figs. 141B & 141C). Ready-made shadow-box frames are available for 12"x12" scrapbook pages. When hanging shadow-box scrapbooks, avoid areas of high humidity and direct sunlight. Consider using UV protecting glass, also known as E-glass, to aid in preserving the items from harmful light rays.

Fig. 141B: Shadow Box—*Ft. Myers Beach* Here, the corner pieces are colorful beach glass and the fibers visually mat the photos. Notice how the palm tree is stratigicly placed to draw the eye into the artwork.

Fig. 141A: Ready-made Shadow Box

Fig. 141C: Shadow Box—*Dad*
This shadow-box page has charming and dimensional lettering that might be too lumpy for a traditional scrapbook. The placement of the leaves was carefully considered, balancing the page and enticing the eye to view the double-mounted photos. Notice that the beads are scattered to separate each of the page's elements.

Shaker Box A shallow-windowed box containing small items, such as confetti, beads, sequins, sand, shells, etc., that when shaken, provides kinetic action. Shaker boxes are available already made for paper crafters or they can be made by using die-cuts for shape (Fig. 142), acid-free acetate for the window, and adhesive or tape for attachment.

Shrink Plastic A craft plastic originating in 1973 by the Shrinky Dink Company. Shrink plastic was designed to be unique in that when decorated and heated, it shrinks, producing a significantly smaller product nearly identical to the original, except for size. A colored design will shrink to approximately one-third its original size and become nine times thicker (Fig. 143). Colors will intensify.

Fig. 143: Shrink Plastic—*Lemon Fresh*   **Lemons made from shrink plastic adorn this scrapbook page. The fiber underneath the lemons resembles a vine running up the page while grouping the photos and providing a visual boundary. Lemons from the backgound paper were cut with a craft knife and placed over the photos on the right side of the page to complete the theme.**

Fig. 142: Shaker Box—*Bean Lover* **You can almost smell the roasted coffee beans when the page turns in this album. In fact, the shaker-box coffee cup actually contains ground coffee, adding a touch of reality and dimension to the page.**

S

Technique 17: Silhouette

Enlarge a photo, make several copies, and trim around the people or objects you wish to silhouette. Reassemble them as necessary. This photo was enlarged 225% before each figure was cut and reassembled.

Silhouette   1. The shadow of an object. 2. The paper-cutting technique of removing the background from a photo, leaving only a person, place, or thing (Fig. 144 and Technique 17).

Fig. 144: Silhouette— *World War II*   This photo was enlarged, then cut apart and reassembled so that the men formed a dimensional border along the bottom of the page. The men's names were listed on the back of the original photo, which allowed the artist to make individual name tags for each man, making this page become historically accurate as well as personally special.

Simple Scrapbooking

A method of scrapbooking using clean simple lines for the paper cutting, mounting, or gluing techniques, without the addition of intricate design or patterns. Prepackaged kits that contain all of the paper, stickers, and embellishments needed to complete two or more pages. Many manufacturers encourage scrapbooking by using kits that include all the papers, stickers, and embellishments needed to complete two or more pages (Figs. 145A–145E). There are also kits that offer nothing but the embellishments. Whichever kit is selected, simple scrapbooking is a fast and satisfying way to scrapbook.

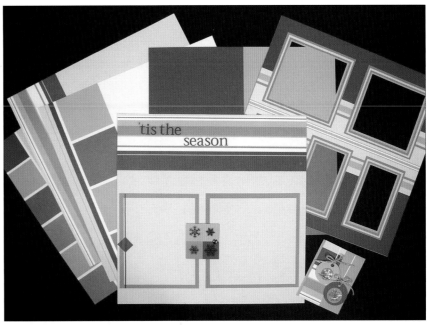

Fig. 145B: Simple Scrapbooking Kits

Fig. 145A: Simple Scrapbooking Kits

Fig. 145C: Simple Scrapbooking—*Sisters* The background paper included in this scrapbook kit dictated the color scheme, but not the design. The simplicity of the dragonfly, leaving fairy trails made of fine gold wire (about 20–24 gauge), adds a sweet touch to the photo of the two girls.

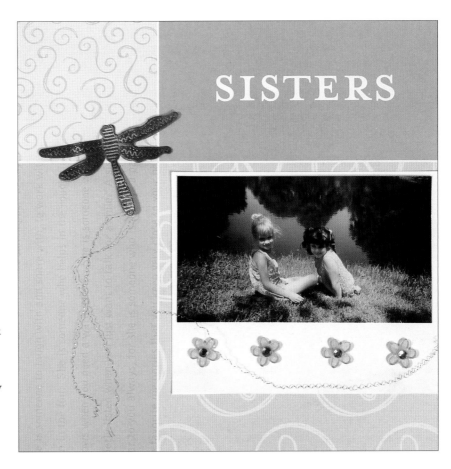

Fig. 145D: Simple Scrapbooking—*Life's a Beach*
The beach-themed kit used to make these pages was a great choice for remembering this trip. All papers and embellishments were included, making quick but appealing pages.

Fig. 145E: Simple Scrapbooking—*Moments*
Eyelets with fibers threaded through them add lots of texture to this page but so do the glass cabachons. Smooth texture is just as important as coarse texture. Repetition also plays a strong part in balancing the composition.

Slide   A transparency of film or glass, mounted in a cardboard sleeve so that it can be viewed through a projector.

Slide Mount   Cardboard, plastic, and multicolored paper frame-like shapes used for embellishing scrapbooks (Figs. 146A & 146B). Innovative ways to use slide mounts include: photo frames, quote frames, hanging them "clothesline" style using eyelets and ribbon, suspending dimensional items in their frame, and gilding them. Once only available in paper, slide mounts are made from metal and translucent plastic, which makes them perfect for use as a photo frame or dimensional scrapbook page element.

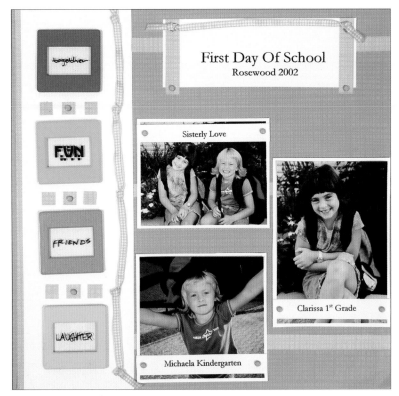

Fig. 146B: Slide Mount—*First Day of School*   Slide mounts have become a hot scrapbooking embellishment. Here, brightly colored plastic mounts are used for captioning.

Fig. 146A: Slide Mount—*Pedal Cars*   Metal slide mounts work as photo frames; they also frame journaling captions.

Snapshot A term used to describe a photo taken with the preset (instantaneous) setting on cameras. The term originally came from rifle shooting, when little or no time is allowed for aiming.

Soft Focus A diffused image. This can be achieved at the camera or enlarging stage.

Souvenir An item of rememberance. Meaning literally, the act of remembering, the French word "souvenir": to remember. Also, from Latin "sub venire" :to come up, come to mind, something that serves as a reminder.

Spacer Flexible cardboard or foam strips (Fig. 147) placed in between scrapbook pages to allow added space for lumpy or assemblage pages.

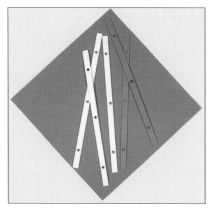

Fig. 147: Spacers

Spacer Usage Tip

Spacers are available for sale, but can be easily made by cutting strips of sheet foam purchased from toy or office supply stores. However, when adhering strictly to archival methods, only acid-free cardboard spacers should be utilized.

Spine A decorative removable piece of reinforced book cloth that is inserted into a closed-back album to cover the edges of the pages.

Sponge Types

Compressed Sponge A synthetic sponge. These sponges are custom-made using a proprietary process. Compressed sponges are particularly useful with quick-drying water-based dyes on glossy paper for bright graphic effects and paste-paper effects.

Cosmetic Wedge Sponge A synthetic sponge used to apply paint to stamps by loading the paint or ink onto the flat edge of the sponge, then onto the surface of a stamp. Wedge sponges can also be useful as a tool to sponge color onto a variety of surfaces such as paper, fabric, and wood, producing a smooth finish.

Foam Applicator A foam sponge available in a variety of sizes and styles, from tiny cosmetic sponge applicators to foam brushes. Foam applicators are useful for stenciling, chalking, detail painting, and various wet techniques.

Sea Sponge Natural sponges used for stenciling, texturing, and faux finishing.

Sponge Stylus A foam-tipped stylus used for controlled stenciling, brushing, or color blending on paper.

Texture Sponge A sponge made of synthetic materials. Texture sponges are useful for applying pigments, dyes, and paints to paper, creating textured background effects.

Sponge The porous skeleton of a living organism harvested from the sea. Sponges are also made synthethically to resemble the real thing (Fig. 148). Sponges have a multitude of different uses, one being the application of chalk. Sponges are valuable tools, giving paper crafters affordable and interesting ways to accomplish various techniques, from applying paint and adhesives to removing them, and from patterning paper to removing its layers.

Fig. 148: Sponges

Stenciling Repeating patterns, using a cut-out image or motif, and applying color or dimensional material to the exposed parts with a brush, sponge, or other applicator (Fig. 149).

Stenciling Terms

Dimensional Stenciling
Creating an image or motif by applying a dimensional material such as artist's cement, within a cut-out pattern called a stencil. See also Technique 8: Wet Relief Embossing.

Negative Stenciling
Creating an image or a motif on a surface, often in a repeated pattern, by applying a form or design and then painting around it. The shape of the image remains on the painted surface after the form is removed.

Positive Stenciling Creating an image or a motif on a surface, often in a repeated pattern, by painting within the cut-out pattern.

Fig. 149: Dimensional Stenciling Materials and Stencil

Sticker An acid-free adhesive-backed decorative accent made from paper or plastic (Figs. 150A–150I). Usually die-cut and printed on acid-free paper with acid-free inks, stickers are used as embellishment accents for pages and photographs, and used in cardmaking and other paper craft projects.

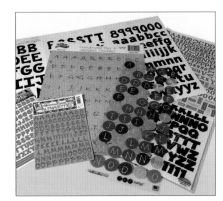

Fig. 150B: Letter Stickers

Fig. 150A: Sticker Rolls and Border Stickers

Sticker Types

Clear Printed clear plastic or acetate depicting various designs, clear stickers give an appearance of a painted design.

Dimensional Dimensional stickers are prelayered paper designs that often include metal, wood, and fabric.

Gum Gum stickers must be moistened to activate the adhesive and are generally reserved for photo corners and older styles of stickers.

Paper Printed stickers of various patterns, paper stickers may be printed with bled edges or have a white border.

Rub-on As the name suggests, rub-on stickers work by burnishing the surface and applying the motif to the paper surface. These are most often available as letters and numbers.

S

Fig. 150C: Stickers

Fig. 150D: Stickers

Fig. 150E: Sticker— *Kindergarten* Take note of the clever graduation cap sticker used here to help the viewer find the one child amongst many. Sometimes one sticker is more effective than using many. The busy colored squares on the background paper is nicely offset with the large title letters and the plainer black-and-white class photos.

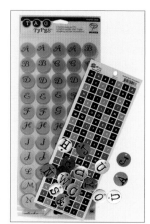

Fig. 150F: Stickers

Fig. 150G: Sticker Maker

Sticker Usage Tips

- Frame photography.
- Add dimensional texture using premade or hand-made layered stickers.
- Accent journaled areas.
- Hide mistakes.
- Create borders.
- Make your own with label sheet stock and computer graphics.

Fig. 150H: Sticker—*My Baptism Day*   This sticker looks like a delicate lace antimacassar, an appropriate detail for a photo taken in this era.

Fig. 150I: Stickers—*Aloha*   Here the colorful translucent stickers, matching the stripe of the paper, are a softer color choice than opaque white paper stickers would be.

Sticker Artist: Andrea Grossman

Twenty-five years ago, there was no such thing as a decorative sticker—until Andrea Grossman came along. As Barbara Marino, community and public relations manager for Mrs. Grossman's Paper Company, explains, it all started in 1979 when Andrea was working as a freelance graphic artist, designing stationery and paper goods. When a local retail store asked her for a small red heart sticker, Andrea couldn't find anything available commercially, so she designed the sticker herself and had it printed. To her surprise, the stickers were delivered not on a sheet, as she'd expected, but on a roll—and just like that, Mrs. Grossman's got rolling, too.

Today, the company is America's largest sticker designer and manufacturer, producing 15,000 miles of stickers each year; but it still remembers that first roll of hearts: outside the factory entrance flies a large white flag with a red heart.

Andrea knew that if she could be the first gift sticker designer on the market, she'd be onto something big. With Calvin, a friend and business consultant, and her then-husband John, she set to work preparing a display for a Long Beach gift show. "We rushed to produce a whole line of stickers," she says. "Ducks, teddy bears, lips, clouds, suns, stars, clouds, men in the moon, lightning, rainbows, and—of course—vulnerable hearts."

Calvin came up with a "providential packaging" concept that turned out to be a stroke of marketing genius. For every six rolls of stickers purchased, store owners received a free Lucite rack they could display attractively on the counter, along with

a yardstick and a pair of scissors. "Our 'Stickers by the Yard' were the hit of the show," Andrea says. "A month later, we headed to New York, where we found the same enthusiastic response."

The sticker roll, with its unique point-of-sale appeal, soon made Mrs. Grossman's stickers one of the hottest products around. As the sticker craze swept the country, children and adults alike collected, catalogued, and traded them, stickering everything from lockers, mirrors, books, and albums to the walls of their rooms. Eventually, interest in stickers waned, but the company hung on, looking for other outlets and opportunities—such as

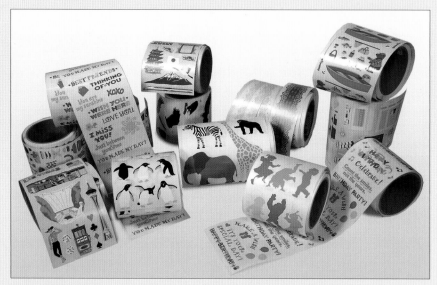

A Plethora of Charming Mrs. Grossman's "Stickers by the Yard"

**Designing Pages Using Decorative and Letter Stickers by
Mrs. Grossman's Paper Company**

scrapbooking. Even in the 1980s, with "memory making" still in its infancy, Andrea had the foresight to recognize that stickers and scrapbooks made a natural pair.

At the time, no other sticker company in the country had its own printing facility. But Andrea's son Jason, who saw what a luxury it would be to control all aspects of the printing process, brought printing in house with state-of-the-art technology. Today, Jason is the company's vice president, overseeing production, while Andrea continues to serve as president and oversee the art department.

"I've always felt that being in business and being successful means that we owe something back to the community, that we want to share what we've been given," Andrea says. To that end, she's started Mrs. Grossman's Helping Hands program, a powerful force for change in San Francisco's inner-city Hunters Point neighborhood. Helping Hands works closely with the community's children, helping them build job skills, then helping them put those skills to use as they package sticker "seconds"—millions of them—to send to physically or developmentally challenged or at-risk youth in pediatric hospitals and other institutions around the world.

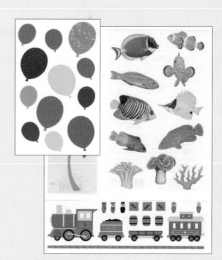

Stickers

The Palace of
Fine Arts
April 1998

The Palace of Fine Arts—Thin-lined metallic border stickers, from Mrs. Grossman's sticker line, were used to border this page as well as the photo mounts.

Jacob and Logan—
Vellum letter, polka-dot, and
border stickers adorn this page.

WE HAD A
MAGICAL TIME
IN FLORIDA!

Dawson David and **Lazy Summer—
Days** Bright background papers and
border, letters, and themed stickers
jazz up these pages.

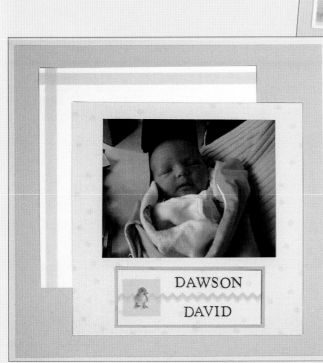

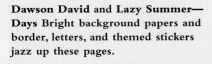

DAWSON

DAVID

OCT 21
2003

Stippling Using a large round brush and paint, ink, or chalk, tapping it onto the paper surface, producing a diffused cloudy effect. This is a particularly effective technique for forming a vignette look around photos.

Stock Photography Ready-made photographic elements (Figs. 151A–151C) for use in scrapbooking. Stock photography does not mean copyright free, unless noted. Stock photography still belongs to the artist/photographer; however, they have made the copies available for use.

Fig. 151A: Stock Photography

Fig. 151B: Stock Photography *Pumpkins* **The pumpkin border on this page is the perfect piece of stock photography. It matches the theme of the page and gives a close-up** view of the pumpkin's texture, as well as providing compositional balance and weight.

Fig. 151C: Stock Photography—*Smart Car* "Tire track" stock photography nearly matches the real-life-sized tires on this European mini-car. It also adds compositional balance and character.

Storage and Shelving The storage requirements of scrapbooks and albums vary, depending on their size and condition. (See also Conservation, Organization, and Preservation.)

Stylus or Burnisher A small hand tool with blunt rounded ends used to emboss or deboss paper.

Swivel Blade A small curved-blade knife, used for intricate cutting, containing a blade that turns with the motion of your wrist. A swivel blade is particularly useful when working with templates, as they often have a track for the blade to follow.

Album Storage Tips

- Store small and medium-sized volumes upright on open shelves next to volumes of similar size, to discourage warping.

- Scrapbooks may be integrated with archival materials in document boxes or folders, keeping them separated from contact with unprotected materials.

- Scrapbooks exhibiting a weak cover, or those attached with strings and ribbons sewn through the pages, should be retied with unbleached linen or cotton tape.

- Slipcases may cause abrasion every time the album is slipped in and out of the case.

- Position the bow or knot on the spine to prevent interference while shelving, or indentations on the cover caused by pressure.

- Wrapping scrapbooks with acid-free paper and storing them in a protective box provides additional archival protection.

- Oversized scrapbooks should be stored flat and fully supported on open shelves; otherwise, warping or distortion may occur if they extend beyond the edge of the shelf.

- Scrapbooks stored in boxes should be placed spine down.

T

Tag Any tag-shaped item used in a scrapbook or on its own (Figs. 152A–152J). Tags are especially popular because they are useful for labeling and adding texture, dimensional character, and may also add a kinetic quality to a page.

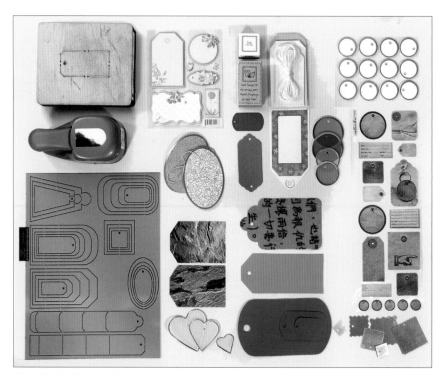

Fig. 152A: Various Tags

Fig. 152B: Tag—*A Dad for Our Kids* The tags used on these pages display the title. Notice the leaves under "Dad." All of the tags are attached with brads.

Fig. 152D: Tag—*Picnic Tag* This tag stands on its own and can be used for a variety of things such as a bookmark or just a decorative element. The red-and-white checkered background paper is the perfect background for these ants to crawl across.

Fig. 152C: Tag—*Skeleton Leaf Tag* When making a scrapbook page, or when there is a plethora of paper scraps and ephemera around, make tags. Tags add zest to any plain scrapbook page and they are especially entertaining to make when children are not quite old enough to help you make the pages.

Fig. 152E: Tag—*Express Yourself* To create this page, photos were taken from yearbooks and pictured alongside an e-mail letter from a counselor. The award appears authentic at first glance because of the traditional looking vellum framing. The pages are held together with fibers fancifully decorated with hand-embossed metal tags.

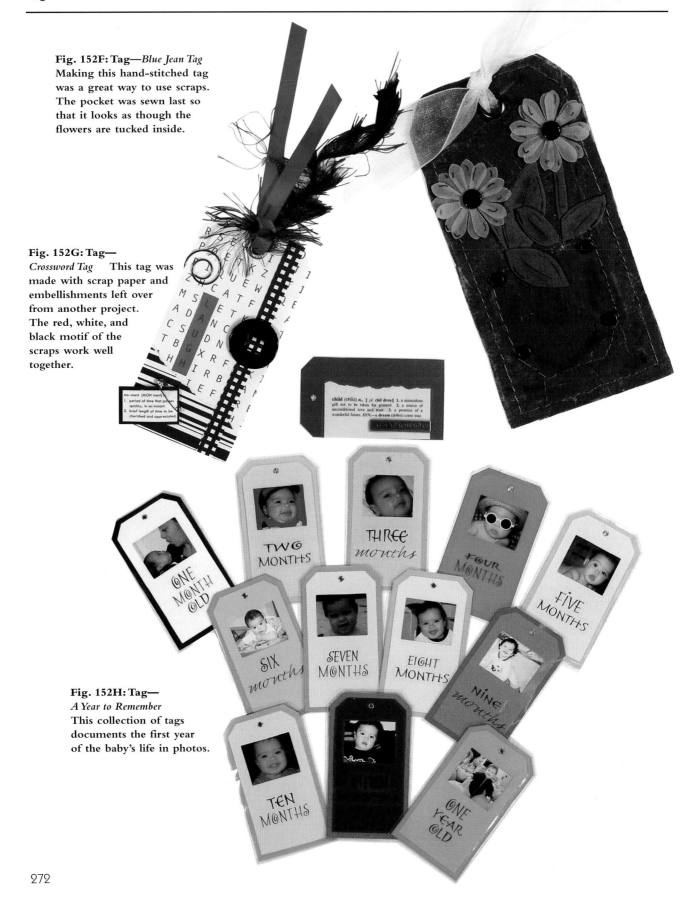

Fig. 152F: Tag—*Blue Jean Tag*
Making this hand-stitched tag
was a great way to use scraps.
The pocket was sewn last so
that it looks as though the
flowers are tucked inside.

Fig. 152G: Tag—
Crossword Tag This tag was
made with scrap paper and
embellishments left over
from another project.
The red, white, and
black motif of the
scraps work well
together.

Fig. 152H: Tag—
A Year to Remember
This collection of tags
documents the first year
of the baby's life in photos.

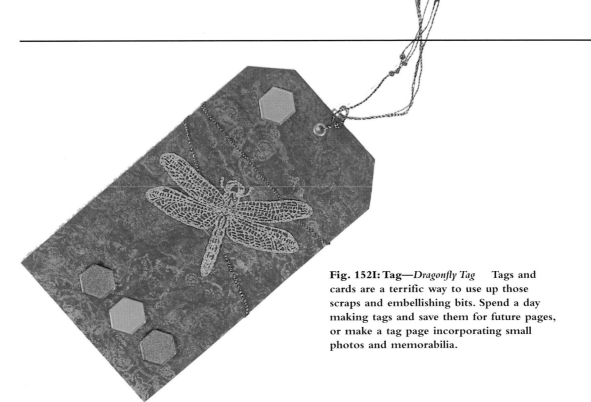

Fig. 152I: Tag—*Dragonfly Tag*   Tags and cards are a terrific way to use up those scraps and embellishing bits. Spend a day making tags and save them for future pages, or make a tag page incorporating small photos and memorabilia.

Fig. 152J: Tag—*An Armful of Dogs*   The puppy-paw background paper was ideal for this page featuring the armful of puppies. The decorative tags were a great choice to display the journaling.

273

Tag Designer: Sarah Lugg

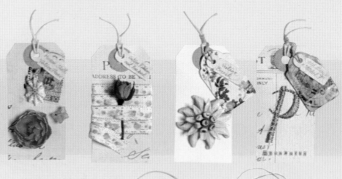

Inspired by the delicate, organic forms of nature and fired by a passion for discovering and creating beauty, artist Sarah Lugg creates mixed-media collages that are rooted in the physical world, yet often transcend it.

Sarah discovered early in life that the natural world—its textures, colors, shapes, and sensory elements—offered her both spiritual peace and endless inspiration to create. A native of Great Britain, she spent countless childhood hours combing the beaches of the Isle of Wight and wandering the countryside around her home in the south of England. In those years, she came to appreciate the exquisite detail inherent in organic forms: the grace of seashells, the range of colors in a hedgerow, the poetry of a delicately twisted seed pod. Through her art, she strives to emulate (and often incorporates) these natural treasures.

Sarah's lifelong love of collecting, her talent as a painter, and her attention to the smallest detail combine to create artwork that is

deeply intuitive and intimate, warmly expressive, and uniquely her own. By taking natural and found objects out of their everyday context and casting them in a fresh light through her painting and composition, she imbues these fragments with new resonance. Her collages offer glimpses of a world that passes by most people unobserved—a world with which, she fears, we are fast losing touch.

Sarah holds a degree in graphic design from Kingston University; in her early twenties, she worked as a designer for Sir Terence Conran. Her art has gained broad exposure through highly successful gallery shows, three book collections of her work, and extensive lines of stationery, gift, and home decor products. In 1999, she spent a year as Artist in Residence at *Victoria* magazine; in 2002 and 2003, she was the featured artist at the Marshall Fields department store, which made her designs the focal point of its Christmas and Valentine's Day displays.

Sarah Lugg's tag designs are a collage of natural objects such as dried flowers and shells, and found objects such as vintage ribbon, paper, and buttons. Sarah carefully chooses background papers to help portray the mood she is trying to create in each tag design.

Sarah's distinctive style has led to many prestigious commissions and exhibitions. The United Kingdom Mission to the United Nations in New York has commissioned her to do sixty collages; the British High Commission in Trinidad has commissioned thirty. Many interior design companies, art galleries, and private collectors worldwide have commissioned her originals as well. She has been a longtime exhibitor at Accent on Design in New York, where her shows are always sold out.

Tape   Paper, plastic, or foam with adhesive on one or both sides (Fig. 153A – 153C). Many tapes are available for general use, but tapes for scrapbooking must be acid-free (See also Adhesives.)

Fig. 153B: Foam Tape and Dots

Fig. 153A: Various Types of Tape

Fig. 153C: ATG Adhesive transfer tape, rolled into ropes, laid into patterns on paper, then coated with mica flakes and embossing powder create intresting lace effect frames.

Tape Usage Tip

Never use traditional cellophane tapes or masking tape for mounting. The adhesive is corrosive, nonreversible, and leaves a residue of adhesive upon removal. In addition, cellophane tape loses the adhesive quality and turns a yellow or brown color in a very short time. Use only tapes labeled acid-free and photo-safe for scrapbooking.

Tape Types

Cellophane Tape   An all-purpose light-duty transparent tape that can hardly be seen when applied to papers. Currently a few acid-free photo-safe cellophane tapes exist for use in scrapbooking. Read the labels carefully.

Double-sided Tape   A shaped piece or length of cellophane or plastic coated on both sides with various-strength bonding adhesives ranging from repositionable to heavy-duty. Dots are a no-mess alternative to glue for light-duty attaching and mounting tasks, and come in both permanent and removable varieties.

Foam Tape   A double-sided adhesive foam available in assorted shapes such as dots, squares, and tape rolls. Items secured with foam tape have an added dimensional lift of up to 1" from the page surface. Foam tape is available in several different strengths as well as removable and permanent varieties.

Masking Tape   A highly acid and lignin-loaded paper tape for holding items temporarily. Uses for masking tape include holding stencils in place and enlarging stencils for easier use.

Photo Squares, Photo Splits, or Tape Runners   Small squares of double-sided tape with top and bottom disposable paper or plastic liners. Often found in hand-held dispensers.

T

Tea-bag Folding The paper-craft technique of cutting and folding the sachet enclosure of tea bags into equal-sized squares and joining them to form the effect of a kaleidoscope or other repetitive patterns (Figs. 154B–154E). Since the technique sometimes involves 12–15 pieces of the same pattern, paper companies have specially designed and printed papers ready-made for this technique (Fig. 154A) (See also Accordion Folding, Iris Folding, Origami.)

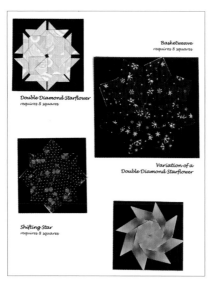
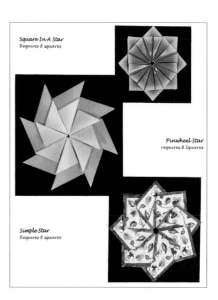

Fig. 154B: Tea-bag Folding Examples

Fig. 154A: Tea-bag Folding Books and Papers

Fig. 154C: Tea-bag Folding—*A Mother's Love* Tea-bag folding for scrapbooks and cards shows the creatively expressive side of scrapbook page designing. The stitched paper and bold frame completely make for balanced composition.

276

ONE FLAG, ONE LAND.
ONE HEART, ONE HAND.
ONE NATION EVER MORE.

-Oliver Wendell Holmes

Fig. 154D: Tea-bag Folding—
One Flag, One Land   Here the flag-print-
ed paper replicates the flag in the photo
and frames the photos. With such boldly
ornate corner elements, strong blocks of
color are necessary as a counterpoint.

Fig. 154E: Tea-bag Folding—
Elizabeth   The right combination of
papers, carefully selected to coordinate with Elizabeth's dress, adds a
sweet personal touch, handmade by
the scrapper, as well as cheerful page-
filling patterning. Handmade elements not only add to a page, but
reveal the maker's creativity.

Elizabeth - Baptismal Day
July 6, 1998

Template A thin metal or plastic plate with a cut outline used as a guide in making something repeatedly and accurately that establishes or serves as a pattern. Templates are available for nearly every conceivable pattern, design, or shape (Figs.155A–155D).

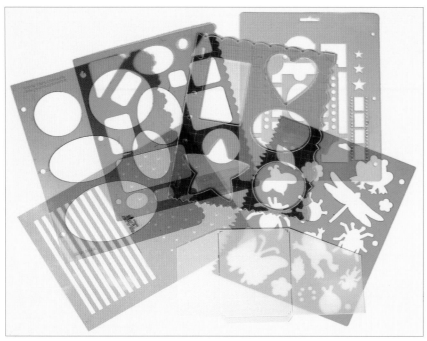

Fig. 155A: Shape Templates

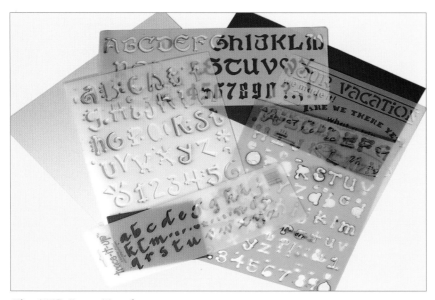

Fig. 155B: Letter Templates

Template Types

Geometric Templates
These templates can be used to make shapes for paper or of the photos themselves. For instance, cutting paper into two sizes and the photo into a third smaller size, and then stacking the three, provides a frame for the photo that matches the color scheme of that layout.

Journaling Templates
Templates providing lines for writing captions and making borders, to assist in aligning handwritten journal material.

Letter Templates
Templates that provide alphabetic and numeric shapes in nearly every typeface imaginable. Use a sharp pencil to outline the shape and detail scissors for cutting.

Fig. 155C: Template—*Megan and Celine Bee-Having* Using a honeycomb-shaped template to cut the photos and also in mounting them, means this page literally buzzes with excitement and charm. Filling in with favorite coordinating greeting cards makes the page more personal.

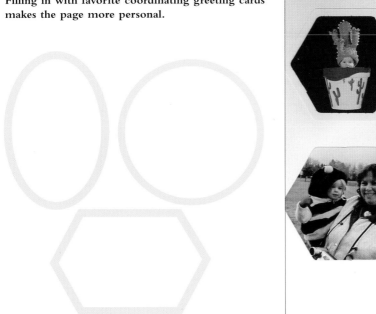

Fig. 155D: Template—*Ray and Heidi Scheffield* This is a nice double-page spread featuring the bride and groom as the focal point on the left, balanced by the compositional grouping on the right. Several geometric template shapes were used to cut photos, showcasing many other special moments worth remembering.

Texture The surface characteristics of a page (Figs. 156A & 156B), that when viewed, look as if or actually has a textural appearance.

Fig. 156A: Texture— *Love* There were a multitude of textural elements chosen by this artist. Red mesh underlays the hearts, which are tied on by string, adding more texture. The treasure chest of hearts was enameled and the black-and-white heart-patterned background paper gives the illusion of even more texture.

Fig. 156B: Texture—*In the Dog House* Details such as bone buttons, puppy prints, and hand-cut doghouses are charming textural embellishments on these pages. Great journaling, strong composition, and sophisticated color choices add to the layout. Every detail is crisp and well planned.

Texture Plates A tool for use in adding texture to paper, metal, and clay because the design is molded right to the plate. Generally, plates are flexible, durable, made of rubber or plastic, and easy to use, adding overall patterns quickly to nearly any design. Simply place paper over the plate design and rub the paper with a crayon or pencil, or use the plate to stamp into clay, or ink the plate and use it as an allover rubber-stamped background.

Theme The overall emphasis of a page or scrapbook. A variety of themed papers (Fig. 157A), stickers (Fig. 157C), and embellishments are available for purchase. All of these elements are helpful in assembling a themed scrapbook page or album (Figs. 157A—157P).

Fig. 157B: Scrapbook Theme Kits and Materials

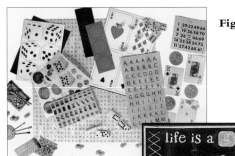

Fig. 157C: Themed Stickers

Fig. 157A: Sports-themed Papers and Embellishments

Fig. 157D: Theme— *Bingo* Games are definitely the theme on this page. If the bingo card, chessboard background paper, and definition of "competition" aren't enough, surely the photos provide the final clues. The cleverly phrased title fits the page well.

Figs. 157E–157J: Theme—
U.S. Attack   From the patriotic album cover and through each page, the attack on 9/11 and the subsequent events facing the United States were meticulously documented in this extraordinary scrapbook. Using photos from magazines, newspapers, and online photographers (with permission of course), this scrapbooker created a memorable album that focused on the anguish and heartache, as well as the heroism and patriotism of U.S. firefighters, police, military, and ordinary citizens, all of whom experienced that devastating event, and how it affected their lives.

Fig. 157E: Theme— *Operation Enduring Freedom*

Fig. 157F: Theme— *God Bless FDNY and NYPD*

Fig. 157G: Theme— *Flag Album Cover*

Fig. 157H: Theme— *Our Nation Grieves*

Fig. 157I: Theme— *FDNY*

Fig. 157J: Theme— *The Attack*

T

Figs. 157K–157O: Theme—

Christmas Ornaments Many years from now, and at each tree-trimming party, this family will enjoy leafing through this album. Each ornament is carefully catalogued and photographed, with journaling describing how and when each was acquired.

Fig. 157K: Album Cover

Fig. 157L: Theme— *Santa Stops Here*

Fig. 157M: Theme— *USMC*

Fig. 157N: Theme— *First Christmas Together*

Fig. 157O: Theme— *Christmas Lights*

Fig. 157P: Theme— *Snuggle in Wine Country* These pages tell the story of Snuggle's trip to wine country. Wine- and vineyard-themed charms, paper, and diecuts help to tell the story.

Thematic Designer: Michelle Mueller

An interior designer by training, Michelle Mueller left the commercial design field after twenty-five years of practice to become, she jokes, a "professional do-gooder" in the nonprofit sector. She didn't miss her former creative outlet, or so she thought—until the day, three years ago, when she put together her first scrapbook layout and found that it was just like creating a client's project board, filled with pictures of furniture and lighting and swatches of color and texture. She stuck with it, and scrapbooking became a stress-free way to satisfy her creative drive, made easy by the design education that taught her the basics of space, balance, repetition, and color theory (as well as her years of experience in pattern mixing, photography, and writing). She's renowned in her scrapbooking community for her generosity in sharing her work and her ideas, and her lighthearted spirit is positively contagious.

"Cutting-edge creativity was never my forte, even when I was an interior designer," Michelle explains. Now, as then, she considers herself a great re-creator. An avid researcher, she pores over idea books and online layout galleries to gather the best, most appropriate design solutions and put them together in a technically sophisticated, aesthetically pleasing way.

Perhaps because she once designed themed restaurants, Michelle now specializes in themed albums. Her natural inclination is to tell an entire story, making sure all the elements—the album's shape and size, colors, motifs, paper selections, and embellishments such as souvenirs, photos, and journaling—re-create as faithfully as possible the atmosphere of an event, a place, or a time in a person's life.

"I find scrapbooking satisfying for several reasons," Michelle says. "First, I am creating pages about my son or a great trip we took together. When we look through an album together, I get to relive those experiences. Second, after

Honor

286

my mother died, I became the recipient of my family's photos and our genealogical information. With each box of photos I archive into scrapbooks, I get a sense of satisfaction that I am preserving them in such a way that future generations can better learn and enjoy their heritage.

"And, of course, there is that creative outlet part," she laughs. "I really didn't know I missed it until I took up scrapbooking, which is a perfect match to my creative style. I thrive on the instant gratification of creating a layout. I also love that we're such a generous bunch, sharing our work and encouraging 'scraplifting,' yet having new products and techniques come to market that keep pushing the envelope."

Michelle lives in Albion, Michigan, with her husband Bill, who cheerfully helps her pack her car to head out on scrapbooking jaunts, and her dynamite eleven-year-old son, Hayes, who happily looks at all her albums (though he jokes that he doesn't look forward to having to move them around with him for the rest of his life).

Toast—Michelle's albums were beautifully designed and assembled predominately to tell stories about events or places. All of the pages in her gallery shot portray her life as an interior designer. From her college days, awards received, finished projects, and business letters praising her talents, this scrapbook shows her lifetime of achievements. It is worth noting Michelle's various encapsulation and attaching mechanisms as well as her skilled, intricately balanced compositions.

Michelle Mueller's Work

Three-dimensional Effects

Use foam risers or foam double-stick tape to add dimension to your projects. You can also use paper "risers" to raise a piece of paper when a card or book is opened.

Tintype or Ferrotype A positive image made directly on an iron plate varnished with a thin sensitized film.

Title The words that indicate the subject of the page. Manufacturers provide dozens of styles of titles for every conceivable subject or event (Figs. 158A–158D). Ready-made titles come in a variety of materials. Titles can also be handmade. Die-cut, punch, trace, or free-form designed photo titles, using blurry or duplicate pictures that coordinate with the photos on your scrapbook pages. Sky and water photos can often be used with nearly any page, even those unrelated to the die-cut letters. Another option is to simply write or print a title onto the background paper or cardstock on a page containing a simple layout.

Fig. 158B: Title—*Ram-a-Lam-a-Ding Dong*   **This is an amusing and appropriate title for these pages, which repeat the memory of the bell people. Stringing the bells across the pages added texture and gave the illusion of ringing bells.**

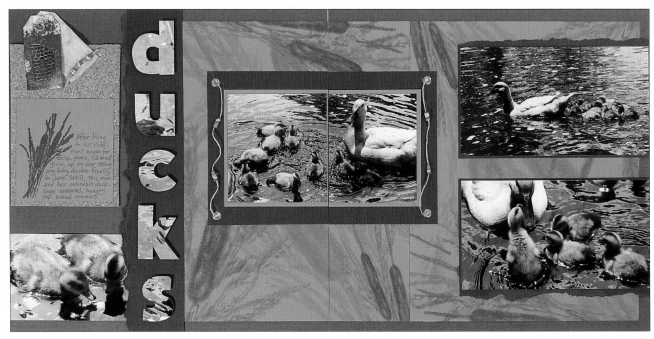

Fig. 158A: Title—*Ducks*   **To make the title of this spread, photos are die-cut to form letters and adhered onto the page with foam dots, creating dimension.**

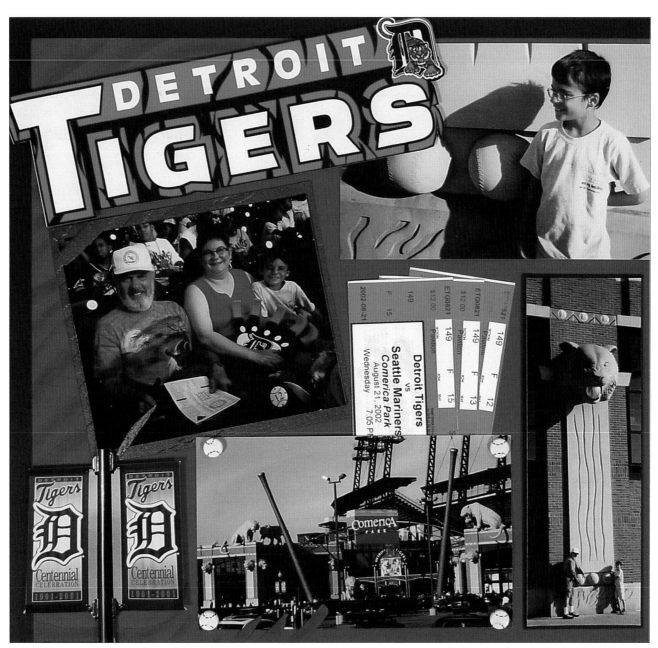

Fig. 158C: Title—*Detroit Tigers*   Saving all the printed material from a special event can give a page an authentic quality, different than ordinary store-bought embellishments are able to do. The tickets, programs, and photos tell the story of this day at the ballpark.

Fig. 158D: Title—*Thursday's Child* **Even though the composition of this page is quite simple, it has a peacefully restful quality that works so well with the photo. Charming travel stickers fit the theme and add bits of color.**

Tools Various tools are used in making art, paper crafts, and scrapbooks. Shown are some of the many tools used regularly in this author's studio (Fig. 159).

Transparency or Slide Image An image on a transparent base material, such as film or glass, that is viewed by transmitted light. Photos can be easily made from a slide.

Travel Journal A journal specifically used to document and photograph a travel experience.

Typeface The style of typed letters used for the body text. (See also Font.)

Fig. 159: Tools

U V

UV (Ultraviolet Light) A type of invisible light, just beyond the violet in the visible spectrum. Its wavelength is shorter than that of visible light, and longer than X-rays. Ultraviolet light is the primary cause of degradation in pigments, photos, papers, plastics, adhesives, fabrics, and colorants.

Vanishing Point The point at which parallel lines, appear to converge in the distance.

Vellum 1. A term commonly used for translucent paper (Fig. 160). 2. A slightly irregular paper finish. 3. Formal use: social and personal stationery. (See also Paper.)

Scrap of History: Vellum

True vellum is thin, specially treated, untanned "leather" derived from calf, goat, or sheepskin.

Also known as parchment, only the highest quality parchment is called vellum. Vellum was used for documents and for bookbindings in many early books of the sixteenth and seventeenth centuries.

Most medieval manuscripts were on vellum, sometimes beautifully illuminated with pigment and gilt. In later centuries, vellum has more commonly been used like leather, i.e. as covering for board sides. It is remarkably durable, but unable to be heated and tends to warp or cockle in dry air.

Vignette A photo or illustration in which the edge-tones fade away, blending gradually into the background or surface they are printed on.

U

V

Fig. 160: The Ultimate Vellum Collection

Vellum Paper Designer: Jill Meyer

She has a degree in art from the University of California, Los Angeles, and a master's in education from the University of Southern California—but Jill Meyer launched her career as an artist years earlier, in a different kind of classroom. "As soon as I could hold a crayon, I began making art," she says. "I remember sitting on the floor in kindergarten and coloring in blissful contentment. I wanted the coloring to go on forever. I have always thought that the real basis for my making art is that I never seemed to be able to get enough drawing, coloring, cutting, and pasting in kindergarten!"

Today, Jill is a nationally recognized paper-craft artist, working with a variety of media including rubber stamps, stencils, paper sculpture, calligraphy, watercolor, and trompe l'oeil. Her scrapbook paper and vellum designs use a broad range of images, with themes from travel, romance, fine art impressions, and vintage portraits of women to floral and Asian motifs. "I started designing scrapbook paper simply because I was asked to do it!" she says. "I thought it would be a new adventure, and I would have an opportunity to work in an area that interested me. I knew that I would want and need this look when making my own scrapbooks."

Keeping an open mind to new media and new ideas, Jill can follow her art in any direction. "Several years ago, when rubber stamping was still a new art form, it caught my attention," she says. "My husband Dave insisted that I take my interest in it as far as it would lead. It led to designing a line of rubber stamps, called Tapestry by Jill Meyer, produced by Hampton Art Stamps. Dave has always given me his unwavering encouragement and support."

With such broad creative interests, how does Jill arrange her working environment? "My studio has everything that I need to work successfully, except space," she admits. "I have recently come to realize that if I had more space, I would just fill it up by hunting and gathering and acquiring more 'stuff' with which to make art. So I have made my peace with my small studio. I have resolved to continue to eliminate that which is not necessary and jettison those things which will not be used.

"I am grateful for all the opportunities I have had," she goes on, "and eagerly anticipate what is waiting for me right around the corner. I am just going to let the art lead me where it will. It always seems to find a new and exciting, challenging and interesting direction. I can hardly wait!"

Letter-printed Vellum

Vellum Stickers

Pages Utilizing Jill's Vellum and Stickers—Printed vellums overlay solid papers, offering subtle and sophisticated backgrounds for almost any page. Because Jill has coordinated her papers and stickers, carefully mixing patterns and colors, scrapbookers can have a multitude of page-making combinations, each complementing the next. Nostalgic-themed stickers are especially designed with a distressed look, making them ideal for heritage page making.

My Child

Confirmation Memories

W

Water Soluble A material that dissolves in water.

Watermark A translucent identifying mark imbedded into a sheet of paper during its manufacture by variations in pulp thickness, seen only when the paper is dry. The mark may be a symbol, a monogram, or company logo formed in wire on the papermaker's mold. Watermarks are usually read from the image side of the paper.

Fig. 161A: Wire Shapes Suitable for Use as Paper Fasteners

Waterproof or Water Resistant A materials ability to resist change when in direct contact with water. This includes, but is not limited to, softening, migration, swelling, bleeding, or dissolving.

Wet Adhesive An adhesive that is applied while still in liquid form and dries to solid in order to achieve its full bond strength with another material. (See also Adhesives.)

Fig. 161B: Wire—*Fall Blessings* **Craft wire used on this page ropes the colorful leaves across the top and seems to tie the tag onto the page.**

Fig. 161C: Wire Cutters, Wire Phrases, and Embellishments Using Wire Accents

Wire A metal strand that comes in many shapes and colors (Figs. 161A–161E). Beautiful copper-colored epoxy-coated wire, ranging in gauges as small as 24 and as large as 16, is readily available. In scrapbooking, wire is the ideal product to attach heavy-duty found objects and dress up embellishments with a sparkle of sophisticated color.

Fig. 161D: Wire—*Festival Lights*   The wire phrase used here picks up and reflects the sparkle of the lights both in and outside the photos.

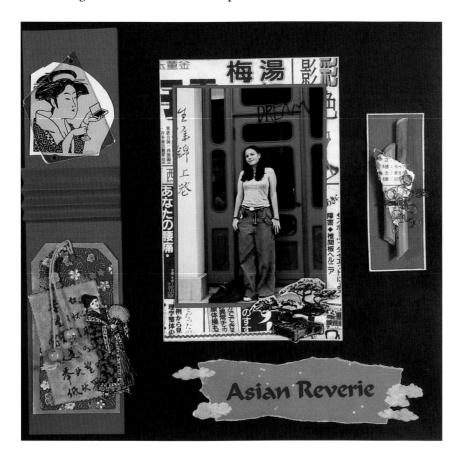

Fig. 161E: Wire—*Asia Revisited* The wire on this page is curled and attaches the embellishments to the page with a decorative flourish.

Wood-pulp Paper   A paper manufactured with wood pulp. Wood-pulp papers have various levels of stability due to the variety of lignin contents. Purified wood-pulp papers appear to be as stable as cotton-pulp papers when used for preservation purposes, and are less expensive.

Woven Paper   A smooth paper made on finely textured wire that gives the paper a gentle patterned finish, made using a mold with a fine wire mesh.

Acknowledgments

The production of this book simply could not have happened without the tremendous energy of very important people. I am a blessed woman having them in my life, and I wish to thank them all, with all of my heart.

Thank-you Shawn Hall, USArtQuest's amazingly talented graphic artist, photographer and all-around marketing guy. Your enormous effort in photographing nearly every picture in this book, while maintaining your regular schedule was "above and beyond" the call of duty. Not surprisingly, my oft-used thesaurus defines "Shawn" as synonymous with the words reliable, amazing, and unwavering.

Thanks, too, to Will Keathley for your support in assisting Shawn in every way. Your sense of humor kept us laughing and the graphics work applied to every single photo will make every scrapbooker in this book feel proud.

My sincere thanks must go to Julia Davenport. I simply could not do what I do, without you. Keeping track of every artist and every product used was a singularly heroic deed. You are the best.

Many thanks, Dawn Carley. Every manufacturer mentioned in this book was personally contacted by you. Accomplishing this feat took perseverance and a commitment to detail that I have come so much to depend upon and the readers will most certainly enjoy.

To the entire USAQ staff for holding down the fort while the above-mentioned team worked long hours on "THE BOOK!", as it came to be known.

Genuinely appreciative thanks must go to all of the biographical artists who make this book infinitely more interesting, most especially Susannah Tucker, who allowed us to use her informative and scholarly Time Line.

Many thanks go to all of the participating scrapbookers. Thank-you for allowing us to rummage through your scrapbooks to photograph your work. Special thanks to Frankie Fioretti for your support, your beautiful work, and your big push to meet the deadline, as well as Robin Jones, Tami Henry, and Christy Anderson for all the days dedicated to making pages, before that. A gigantic thanks goes to Michelle Mueller. Getting to know you quickly became one of the most pleasant parts of writing this book.

Shawn Hall

Julia Davenport

Christy Anderson

Tami Henry

Robin Jones

Thank-you to the most comprehensive scrapbook store ever seen by this author, Scrapbook Memories in Chelsea, Michigan, and owner Patti Pietryka, for giving us Kris Braun, the store manger, who in turn gave this book her staff and free reign of the store. Without that utter trust, we simply could not have produced this book in the time frame we did. Thank-you all for allowing us to come into your store, beleaguer you, and rummage through every product, package, and piece of paper. Your generosity of time and sharing of scrapbooking products made all this possible.

SCRAPBOOK Memories
Chelsea, MI • scrapbookmemories.net

Scrapbook Memories Staff and Customers

Scrapbook Memories Staff

Metric Equivalency Charts

inches to millimeters and centimeters

inches	mm	cm	inches	cm	inches	cm
⅛	3	0.3	9	22.9	30	76.2
¼	6	0.6	10	25.4	31	78.7
½	13	1.3	12	30.5	33	83.8
⅝	16	1.6	13	33.0	34	86.4
¾	19	1.9	14	35.6	35	88.9
⅞	22	2.2	15	38.1	36	91.4
1	25	2.5	16	40.6	37	94.0
1¼	32	3.2	17	43.2	38	96.5
1½	38	3.8	18	45.7	39	99.1
1¾	44	4.4	19	48.3	40	101.6
2	51	5.1	20	50.8	41	104.1
2½	64	6.4	21	53.3	42	106.7
3	76	7.6	22	55.9	43	109.2
3½	89	8.9	23	58.4	44	111.8
4	102	10.2	24	61.0	45	114.3
4½	114	11.4	25	63.5	46	116.8
5	127	12.7	26	66.0	47	119.4
6	152	15.2	27	68.6	48	121.9
7	178	17.8	28	71.1	49	124.5
8	203	20.3	29	73.7	50	127.0

yards to meters

yards	meters	yards	meters	yards	meters	yards	meters	yards	meters
⅛	0.11	2⅛	1.94	4⅛	3.77	6⅛	5.60	8⅛	7.43
¼	0.23	2¼	2.06	4¼	3.89	6¼	5.72	8¼	7.54
⅜	0.34	2⅜	2.17	4⅜	4.00	6⅜	5.83	8⅜	7.66
⅝	0.46	2½	2.29	4½	4.11	6½	5.94	8½	7.77
⅝	0.57	2⅝	2.40	4⅝	4.23	6⅝	6.06	8⅝	7.89
¾	0.69	2¾	2.51	4¾	4.34	6¾	6.17	8¾	8.00
⅞	0.80	2⅞	2.63	4⅞	4.46	6⅞	6.29	8⅞	8.12
1	0.91	3	2.74	5	4.57	7	6.40	9	8.23
1¼	1.03	3¼	2.86	5⅛	4.69	7¼	6.52	9⅛	8.34
1¼	1.14	3¼	2.97	5¼	4.80	7¼	6.63	9¼	8.46
1⅜	1.26	3⅜	3.09	5⅜	4.91	7⅜	6.74	9⅜	8.57
1½	1.37	3½	3.20	5½	5.03	7½	6.86	9½	8.69
1⅝	1.49	3⅝	3.31	5⅝	5.14	7⅝	6.97	9⅝	8.80
1¾	1.60	3¾	3.43	5¾	5.26	7¾	7.09	9¾	8.92
1⅞	1.71	3⅞	3.54	5⅞	5.37	7⅞	7.20	9⅞	9.03
2	1.83	4	3.66	6	5.49	8	7.32	10	9.14

Acknowledgments

Materials and information from the following companies were used in putting this book together.

3L Consumer Products
(847) 808-1140
www.scrapbook-adhesives.com

3M
www.3m.com

7 Gypsies
(800) 588-6707
www.sevengypsies.com

ANW Crestwood
www.anwcrestwood.com

Accent Design Craft Supplies
(541) 485-1406
www.salesatpeterson-arne.com

Accu Cut System
(800) 288-1670
www.accucut.com

All My Memories
(801) 619-8808
www.allmymemories.com

All Night Media
(800) 842-4197
www.plaidonline.com

American Crafts
(801) 226-0747
www.americancrafts.com

American Tag Company
(800) 223-3956
www.americantag.net

American Traditional Designs
www.americantraditional.com

Andromedan Design
(888) 488-8400
www.googlies.com

Arnold Grummer
(800) 453-1485
www.arnoldgrummer.com

Art Accentz
www.softflexcompany.com/
art_accentz.htm

Art Institute Glitter, Inc.
(877) 909-0805
www.artglitter.com

Artistic Wire
(630) 530-7567
www.artisticwire.com

Artograph
(888) 975-9555
www.artograph.com

As You Wish
(801) 553-7095
www.asyouwish-products.com

Autumn Leaves/7 Gypsies
(800) 588-6707
www.autumnleaves.com

Bazzil Basics Paper
www.bazzillbasics.com

Beacon Adhesives
(800) 865-7238
www.beaconcreates.com

Boxer Scrapbook Productions, LLC
www.boxerscrapbooks.com

C-Thru
www.cthruruler.com

Cardinal Brands
www.Generationsnow.com

Carl Mfg. Co.
www.carl-products.com

Chatterbox, Inc.
(888) 416-6260
www.chatterboxinc.com

Chartpak, Inc.
www.chartpak.com

Circle Journey
www.circlejourney.com

Clearsnap
www.Clearsnap.com

C-Line Products
(888) 860-9120
www.c-line.com

Cloud 9 Design
(763) 493-0990
www.cloud9design.biz

Club Scrap
(888) 634-9100
www.clubscrap.com

Colorbok
www.colorbok.com

ColorCutter Division of
Gizmo Enterprises, Inc.
(954) 587-6777
www.colorcutter.com

Coluzzle
www.provocraft.com

Crafts Etc.
www.craftsetc.com

Craft-T Products, Inc.
www.craf-tproducts.com

Creative Imaginations
www.cigift.com

Creek Bank Creations
www.creekbankcreations.com

Crop In Style
(888) 700-2202
www.cropinstyle.com

Cropaholic
www.janlynn.com

Cropper Hopper by Advantus Corp.
www.cropperhopper.com

Cross-My-Heart
www.crossmyheart.com

Darice
www.darice.com

Deluxe Designs
www.deluxedesigns.com

DeNami Design
(253) 437-1626
www.denamidesign.com

Destination Stickers and Stamps, Inc.
(866) 806-7826
www.destinationstickers.com

Die Cuts With a View
www.diecutswithaview.com

DMD, Inc.
www.dmdind.com

Doodlebug Design
(801) 966-9952

Dreamweaver Stencils
www.dreamweaverstencils.com

298

Dress It Up
(610) 435-7899
www.dressitup.com

Duncan Ent.
www.duncancrafts.com

EFG, Inc. scrapbookstorytelling
www.scrapbookstorytelling.com

EK Success
www.eksuccess.com

Emagination Crafts, Inc.
(866) 238-9770
www.emaginationcrafts.com

Excel Hobby Blades
www.excelhobbyblades.com

Expression Magazine
www.expressionartmagazine.com

EZ Laser Designs
www.ezlaserdesigns.com

Far and Away
(509) 340-0124
www.farandawayscrapbooks.com

Filexec
(888) FILEXEC (345-3932)

Fiskars Brand, Inc.
www.fiskars.com

FoofaLa
(402) 330-3208
www.foofala.com

Francis Meyer, Inc.
www.chartpak.com

Freckle Press
(877) 437-3255

Gagne, Inc.
(607) 729-3366
www.gagneinc.com

Generation Next Design
contact your local retailer

Generations
www.Generationsnow.com

Glue Dots International
www.gluedots.com

Granny's Bitty Bows
(425) 985-5261

Henzo Photoalbums BV
contact your local retailer

Hermafix
contact your local retailer

Highsmith, Inc.
(800) 554-4661
www.highsmith.com/corruboard

HyGlo/American Pin
www.HyGlocrafts.com

Inkadinkado
(781) 938-6100
www.inkadinkado.com

It Takes Two, Inc.
(800) 331-9843
www.ittakestwo.com

Jesse James Button and Trim
(610) 435-7899
www.dressitup.com

Jotters
(877) 568-8371
www.jotters.net

Junkitz
www.junkitz.com

K&Company
(816) 389-4150
www.kandcompany.com

Karen Foster Designs
(801) 451-9779 wholesale only
www.karenfosterdesign.com

Katee Kut-Ups
contact your local retailer

KI Memories
www.kimemories.com

Kokuyo Co., Ltd
(877) 465-6589

Lake City Craft Co.
(417) 725-8444
www.quilling.com

Lasting Impressions for Paper, Inc.
www.lastingImpressions.com

Leeco Industries
see cropper hopper

Li'l Davis Designs
(949) 838-0344
www.lildavisdesigns.com

Lineco, Inc.
www.lineco.com

Little Extras
www.littleextrasdiecuts.com

Magenta
www.magentarubberstamps.com

Magic Mesh
www.magicmesh.com

Magic Scraps
(972) 238-1838
www.magicscraps.com

Making Memories
www.makingmemories.com

Maude Asbury
www.maudeasbury.com

McGill Paper Punches
www.mcgillinc.com

Me and My Big Ideas
www.meandmybigideas.com

Memories Complete LLC
(866) 966-6365
www.memoriescomplete.com

Memory Mates
(610) 435-7899
www.dressitup.com

Meri Meri, Inc.
www.merimeri.com

Midori
contact your local retailer

Morning Star Rubber Stamps
contact your local retailer

Mrs. Grossman's Paper Co.
www.mrsgrossmans.com

My Mind's Eye, Inc.
www.mymindseyeinc.com

My Sentiment's Exactly
(719) 260-6001
www.sentiments.com

National Cardstock
contact your local retailer

Nicole Classic
contact your local retailer

NRN
info@nrndesigns.com

Offray
www.offray.com

On the Surface
www.onsurface.com

Outdoors & More
(801) 390-6919
www.outdoorsandmore.com

Paper Bliss
www.westrimcrafts.com

Paper Garden
(435) 867-6398
www.mypapergarden.com

Paper House Productions
(845) 679-7316
www.paperhouseproductions.com

Paper Jems
see Leeco

Paper Reflections
see DMD

PaperWhite, Inc.
contact your local retailer

Pazzels
(866) 729-9537
www.pazzles.com

Pioneer Photo Albums, Inc.
(800) 366-3686
www.pioneerphotoalbums.com

Plaid
(800) 842-4197
www.plaidonline.com

Polyform Products
www.sculpey.com

Posh Impressions
www.poshimpressions.com

Preservation Technologies, LP
(724) 779-2111
www.ptlp.com

Private Label Products
(800) 815-1239
www.myfact@aol.com

Provo Craft
(800) 937-7686
www.provocraft.com

Pulsar Paper
(216) 861-8800
www.pulsarpaper.com

Punch Bunch
(254) 791-4209
www.thepunch.com

Robin's Nest
(435) 789-5387

Rollabind Scrapbooking System
www.rollabind.com
Sailor Corp. of America
(800) 248-4583

Sandylion Sticker Designs
(800) 387-4215
www.sandylion.com

Sanook
(415) 775-0971
www.sanookpaper.com

ScrapArts
(503) 631-4893
www.scraparts.com

Scrapbook 101/Photogenix
(877) 526-6954
www.scrapbook101.com

Scrapbook Interiors
see Chatterbox

Scrapbook Memories
(734) 433-1478
Main Street, Chelsea, MI

Scrapbook Storytelling
www.scrapbookstorytelling.com

Scrapbook Times
wholesale only
www.scrapbooktimes.com

Scrapworks
www.scrapworks.com

SEI
(435) 752-4142
www.shopsei.com

Spellbinders
www.spellbinders.us

Stampabilities
(800) 888-0321
www.stampabilities.com

Stampin Funaddict
contact your local retailer

Stamping Station
www.stamping-station.com

Stanislaus Imprints, Inc.
www.stanislausimprints.com

State of Mine
see Destination Stickers

Stewart Superior Corp
(520) 572-4694 (wholesale only)
www.stewardsuperior.com

Suze Weinberg
www.schmoozewithsuze.com

Tapestry in Time
www.tapestryintime.com

The Paperloft
(866) 254-1961
www.paperloft.com

The Stamp Doctor
(866) 782-6737
www.stampdoctor.com

Therm O Web
(800) 323-0799
www.thermoweb.com

Tidy Crafts
(800) 245-6752
www.tidycrafts.com

Tombow
(800) 835-3232
www.tombowusa.com

Tsukineko, Inc.
(800) 769-6633
www.tsukineko.com

Uchida of America, Corp.
(800) 541-5877
www.uchida.com

Un-du Products
www.un-du.com

USArtQuest, Inc
(800) 200-7848
www.usartquest.com

We R Memory Keepers
(877) PICK-WER (toll free)
www.weronthenet.com

Westrim Crafts
(800) 727-2727
www.westrimcrafts.com

What's New Ltd.
(480) 830-4581

Wish in the Wind
www.wishinthewind.com

Wordsworth
(719) 282-3495
www.wordsworthstamps.com

Wubie Prints
(888) 256-0107
www.wubieprints.com

Xyron
(800) 793-3523
www.xyron.com

Z-Barten Productions
(800)-CONFETTI (266-3388)
www.confetti.com

Zig Memory System
see EK Success

Additional Acknowledgments

Ecstasy Crafts
www.ecstasycrafts.com

Australia
Stamp It
08-9470-5422
www.stampit.com.au

Canada
Peachtree Marketing
905-420-8283

Western Educational Activities
780-413-7055
www.westerneducational.com

Scrapbooker's Paradise LTD
403-229-0500
www.scrapbookersparadise.com

France
Ocito
33-153-198570
www.ocito.fr

PW International
33-247-946060
www.pwinternational.fr

Germany
Hobby Art Crafts
http://www.bitverlag.de/bitverlag/
hobbyart/index.asp?br=e&sc=8&z=
hobbyart

Netherlands
Accent Creative Concepts
011-31-411-625-020

Avec
31-416-567171
www.avec-creative.nl

Creatief met foto's Magazine
31-412-454387
www.scrapbookwinkel.nl

Incire
http://www.incire.com

Kars
31-344-342864
www.kars.nl

Scrapbookmate
31-20-3207370
www.scrapbookmate.com

Nobody 13
http://members.lycos.nl/nobody13/
newpage10.html

Papuela
www.papuela.com

TMS International
31-180-633400
www.tms-international.nl

New Zealand
Zig Zag Polymer
64-33-59-2989
http://www.zigzag.co.nz/

South Africa
Great Impressions
044-874-4190
avarrie@mweb.com.za

UK
FW Bramwell & Co
44-1282-860388
www.bramwellcrafts.co.uk

Crafts Beautiful Magazine
http://www.craftsbeautiful.com

Craft Stamper Magazine
www.traplet.com

Personal Impressions
01787-375241
www.richstamp.co.uk

The Scrapbookhouse
0870-7707717
www.thescrapbookhous.com

Woodware Toys and Gifts Distributors
011-44-175670024

Publications and Magazines

Bella Press
denamidesign.com/bellapress/home.html

Chapelle, Ltd. Publishing (books)
www.chapelleltd.com

Crafts Beautiful (UK magazine)
www.crafts-beautiful.com

Creative Scrapbooking (UK magazine)
020-7700-8500

Creating Keepsakes Scrapbook Magazine
www.creatingkeepsakes.com

Design Originals (How-to Books)
www.d-originals.com

Expressions (magazine)
www.expressionartmagazine.com

Hot Off the Press (How-to Books)
www.craftpizazz.com

Ivy Cottage Creations (magazine)
www.ivycottagecreations.com

Memory Makers (books, magazines)
www.memorymakers.com

PaperKuts (magazine)
www.paperkuts.com

Pine Cone Press (books)
www.pineconepress.com

Pixie Press (magazines)
www.pixiepress.com

Scrap n' Stamp (magazine)
www.scottpublications.com

Scrapbook Creations (Australian Publication)
www.scrapbookingmemories.com.au/

Scrapbook Premier (trade publication)
www.scrapbookpremier.com

Scrapbook Retailer (trade publication)
www.scrapbookretailermagazine.com

Scrapbooking Memories (UK magazine)
www.ukscrappers.co.uk

Scrapbooks, Etc. (magazine)
www.bhg.com

Simple Scrapbooks Magazine
www.creatingkeepsakes.com

Stamp It (Australian magazine)
www.stampit.com.au

Sterling Publications (books)
www.sterlingpub.com

Your Creative Spirit (online magazine)
www.yourcreativespirit

Project Index

Effort was made to find the name of manufacturers for every product used on every page; however, all were not available. Nevertheless, we have included the available information and suggest that you may be able to find other items at any scrapbook or craft store.

Summer 1963

Fall 2003

A new baby is like the beginning of all things - wonder, hope, and a dream of possibilities.

- Eda J. Le Shan

Index